AMERISTRALIA

PEACE through STRENGTH for HUMANITY

The proposed Union of Australia, Canada, Greenland, Iceland, New Zealand, United Kingdom, and the United States into one nation.

From the perspective of an American writer

Jim Ingram

Library of Congress Cataloging-in-Publishing Data

Jim Ingram
Ameristralia: Peace Through Strength for Humanity
Library of Congress Cataloging-in Publishing
Data Has Been Applied For

Print Edition ISBN 979-8-9871867-0-1

New Yorker Cartoon (pg. 239) is licensed with permission from CartoonStock.com
Photos of Theodore Roosevelt and Franklin Delano Roosevelt used with permission of Library of Congress
Photos of Winston Churchill and Margaret Thatcher obtained from Alamy
Maps of Canada, Greenland, Iceland, New Zealand, and United Kingdom obtained from www.maps.com
Map of Australia obtained from www.mapresources.com
Map Comparison of Austrailia and USA obtained from https://www.reddit.com/r/MapPorn/
Map of Canada obtained from Canada Dept of Natural Resources

Printed in the United States of America

"There is no greater power on earth than an idea whose time has come."[1]

— Martin Luther King, Jr.

CONTENTS

FOREWORD

I have always had a fondness for our Canadian neighbors. They speak English, (except the French speaking population in and around Quebec), so communication is not a barrier. Throughout the year, and particularly in the winter, many Canadians venture south, headed for warmer climates in the States. Their vehicles are indistinguishable from American cars because almost all are manufactured at plants in both Canada and the United States, leaving the only difference the name of the province on the license plate.

Because of my wife's German heritage, we have taken numerous trips to visit her family in Germany with whom she's still close. As a matter of routine, we carried our passports with us whenever we traveled overseas. In 2017, on a business trip to Ontario, Canada, my wife and I left without taking our passports. It was commonplace prior to the 9/11 attacks that most anyone could pass between the two borders with just a driver's license. Such was also the case traveling into Mexico on our youthful journey from Padre Island on spring break. A day trip into Matamoros, Mexico was part of the fun. But in 2017 we were an hour down the road on our trip to Canada when we realized the mistake: we didn't think of Canada as a foreign country and we forgot our Passport.

I drafted my first book on *Ameristralia* in the late 1970s while I was on active duty in the Army at Fort Leonard Wood,

Missouri. Yes, I had the name even back then. Ameristralia is the combination of Ameri (the first five letters of America, the country or the northern continent, your choice) and stralia (the last seven letters in Australia). Ameri...stralia, Ameristralia. At times, I may refer to it as the Union of Ameristralia, the Union, or Ameristralia. However, any name may be eventually selected, including but not limited to: United States of Earth, United Provinces of Earth, Valhalla, Atlantis, or any other agreed to name. Throughout this book, I will use the words America, United States, or US interchangeably and also use the United Kingdom, UK, Great Britain, Britain, British, Mother Britain and simply as Mother in the same vein. I will also use the terminology of sibling for our fellow British colonies—Australia, Canada, and New Zealand.

In starting my current endeavor in 2018, I did a search of the internet for Ameristralia and was surprised to find a hit on https://www.reddit.com, which is an Australian site that had a section promoting the union of America and Australia. The community at r/Ameristralia at that time had over 19,000 members supporting the union of Australia and the United States. In May of 2013, during the Obama administration, an official White House website generated a little over 6,000 signatures for the same cause, with a stated goal of 100,000 signatures.[2] Nothing materialized, but it demonstrates that others are intrigued by the idea.

My original thoughts were that Australia, Canada, New Zealand, and the United States should merge into one nation. Language and heritage, as well as our alliances in the First World War and the Second World War were the impetus. Besides, these countries are all siblings of Mother Britain. At that time, I had not thought to include Greenland, Iceland, or the United Kingdom itself.

In 2019, President Trump suggested the United States purchase Greenland from Denmark. The purchase seemed a strange and archaic way of accomplishing the result he was looking for, that Greenland become part of the US. However, in researching this book, I discovered that in 1946, President Truman made the same attempt. Many in Greenland also speak English, and the American

Thule Air Base is on their island. Although the official language is West Greenlandic, (derived from the Inuit language) most people speak Danish and English.

Iceland played a major role with the United States in the Second World War. Their official language is Icelandic, but English is their second language, and most Icelanders speak it fluently. Although both Iceland and Greenland are former colonies of Denmark, they are historically and culturally similar to Canada and the United States. Much like the Pilgrims and other European ancestors, they migrated from other countries, typically Norway or Denmark, looking for a better life and more independence and freedom. Similar to the American Dream, they also sought a better life, liberty, and the pursuit of happiness.

In early 2020, Andrew Roberts, a British author of history, said, "The prospects for a much closer English-speaking peoples has been brought forward by Boris's victory," (referring to Boris Johnson victory to "get Brexit done," which removed Britain from the European Union). Referring to Britain and her former colonies, Roberts also stated the obvious: "There's so much more that unites than divides us." Roberts also acknowledges that America is the key player to bringing this Union to fruition and that not only would it be good for the English-speaking countries, "but good for the world in general."[3]

I have divided this book into two parts. Book One goes through the justification for the Union, which includes a discussion of the advantages, possible government structure, a little about the other proposed countries, a discussion of basic unifying core values, and lastly, what an implementation plan might look like.

The joining of the proposed countries to form a new country would first require a new, agreed-upon constitution. Therefore, a Constitutional Convention would need to be held for all participants using the US Constitution as the starting point.

Book Two provides a template for a new constitution and explains the reason for the proposed adjustments in the current United States Constitution. Adjustments are necessary to bring it into the twenty-first century, solving many long-standing issues that have not been addressed, as well as accommodate the Union with the other countries.

Someone from the United States will need to step up and take a leadership role and start the discussion about this proposed Union. Unlike the White House in 2013, which posted an idea on their Website of Ideas, (a concept from Reddit Readers) but didn't expend any effort to move it forward, this book is my way of starting the discussion again and hoping that a major political figure will take on this challenge and champion the cause.

While this Union is a political act, it will also need the support of the citizens and business leaders for success. The champion of this cause will have to start at the top of the political ladder, the President of the United States. As a result, the champion will probably have to be the sitting President or someone running for President in the next election. I don't think anyone in Congress would have the ability to initiate and lead the effort let alone a private citizen such as myself. Until this happens, I'd like to be the first person to invite the people of Australia, Canada, Greenland, Iceland, New Zealand, and the United Kingdom, or any other English-speaking country, to join the United States in this Union to form a new and stronger nation. By way of example, other English-speaking nations that could be included are: Antigua and Barbuda, The Bahamas, Barbados, Belize, Dominica, Fiji, Grenada, Guyana, India, Ireland, Jamaica, Malta, St. Kitts and Nevis, St. Lucia, St. Vincent and the Grenadines, and Trinidad and Tobago, to mention a few.

The Union will create an Eternal Bond of common humanity. The French-speaking residents of Quebec and Spanish-speaking people of Puerto Rico will not be forced into this Union. Both Quebec and Puerto Rico have language anomalies that will be discussed in some detail later. The commonality of language also needs acceptance from any other country wishing to join in this Union. I want to emphasize the premise of coming together around a common language, shared heritage, and common values regardless of skin color, ethnic background, religion, or gender.

While this book is written from the perspective of an American, I would encourage you to keep reading and try and catch the vision of the kind of nation this Union would create. Individuals from other countries will have to envision how this Union would affect them and their country. It's a grand strategy for the future of humanity through a common-sense and natural political evolution where the current international organizational structures have failed us and are not the solution.

Alfred Deakin, on the Federation of Australia said, "Its actual accomplishment must always appear to have been secured by a series of miracles."[4] This process will be no different.

BOOK ONE

CHAPTER

1

Introduction

Historic institutions were formed with the leadership of the United States after each of the World Wars. After the First World War (also known as World War I, WWI, or the Great War) it was the League of Nations; and after the Second World War (also known as World War II or WWII) it was the United Nations. Both have failed the world in trying to keep rogue nations in line and preventing conflict and wars. The organizers of these institutions did not consider that major nations such as Russia and China, with veto power, are not particularly interested in peace. Instead, they gain political power and prestige by opposing (acting as the negative force) the United States and other countries at every turn. Also, many of the member nations are not democracies, and whether they are run by dictators, a single party, communists, or theocracies, their primary goal is to stay in power at the cost of its citizens and world peace. Global humanity, peace, and prosperity are on the bottom of their list of priorities. The United States and other countries need to evolve to a higher political plane so that liberty, peace, and prosperity may be maintained for all citizens making up Ameristralia and be a model for other countries.

The problem isn't that the United States is getting weaker, but rather China with its population of 1.4 billion people has suddenly awakened economically and now wants to exert its newfound strength into places outside of China. Their economic growth coupled with a seemingly behind the scenes partnership with Russia on political issues seriously complicates the peaceful future of the world.

In a speech to the House of Commons Winston Churchill said, "The English-speaking countries of the world saved Europe and our planet from the fascist powers in WWII."[5] I am suggesting that the English-speaking countries of the world unite, but not like the European Union (EU), which is primarily an economic confederation. Instead, unite into one nation; one that can more easily muster the moral, economic, and military power to help keep the planet safe and peaceful, for the sake of all humanity. I am suggesting the Union of Australia, Canada, Greenland, Iceland, New Zealand, the United Kingdom, and the United States form one nation, referred to here as Ameristralia. Other former British colonies may also have an interest. I would be pleasantly surprised if all the countries I've suggested here were to join this Union at the outset of this endeavor. Any coming together of nations is possible and I am recommending the concepts put forth in this book be used as a road map, or template. Greenland and Iceland were primarily added because of their strategic geographic position in the Northern Hemisphere. Their participation may be overly optimistic, but one very much worth considering. As was the case in the formation of Australia, where some of the states held back their acceptance of the union until others committed, the same will be true here. The United States needs to commit first and then I believe one-by-one others will join.

In sharing my ideas with others prior to publishing this book, British historian and author Andrew Roberts shared with me "CANZUK," which is the proposed unification of Australia, Canada, and New Zealand with the United Kingdom. CANZUK can be found on Wikipedia and looks like it may have been popularized in 2015. Britain may realize it needs other long-term, permanent partners since Brexit (Britain leaving the EU) on 12/31/2020. Think of this Union in terms of a family. As with any family unit, the relationship between Mother Britain and her former colonial siblings evolves over time. In life, and this proposal, the Mother (or Father) sometimes must geographically, and economically, move in with their siblings as equal partners as Mother and her siblings help each other out. The sharing of space can be justified because of a divorce, illness, death, or economic hardship within the family or just helping each other out, creating *economies of scale* for those involved.

As a family comes together, there are usually discussions between the participants about roles and responsibilities. Sometime these discussions may be casual conversations in the dating process or more formal and put into a prenuptial agreement. In this case, combining several family's members (nations) under one tent, responsibilities should be spelled out and discussed prior to all coming together. Boundaries and expectations must be established up front, a *framework* for accomplishing the desired result established, and then a written foundation must be set in the form of a new constitution.

I believe that a Constitutional Convention will provide the necessary *framework* for this new nation to come into being. The new constitution will define the boundaries, expectations, and limit the power of the national government while still leaving room for individual Provates to maintain some uniqueness and cultural identity. The word "Provate" is the combination of Prov (for the first four letters of Province, as is used in Canada) and ate (the last three letters of state). Like Ameristralia, Provate is a neutral name selected for this book and does not preclude the use of any agreed upon label such as state, province, district, etc. Also, the word state is sometime used to identify a country.

So why does this Union make sense?

The Union

I'll be using the analogy that the United States has a really large tent that covers and protects our family of 50 "individuals." Clearly there are several territories or protectorates under US control, but for illustrative purposes, they're not enumerated here in the count. They include places such as Washington D.C., Guam, Midway, the Solomon Islands, the US Virgin Islands, and Puerto Rico, among others. Australia also has a tent for its family of six "individuals" (including ten territories), Canada has a tent for its family of 10 (including three territories), New Zealand a tent for themselves (including four territories), and the United Kingdom has a tent for its family of four "individuals" (including 14 territories: the Falkland Islands, Gibraltar, two bases in Cyprus, Anguilla, Bermuda, British Virgin Islands, Cayman Islands are the major ones, with six smaller territories). Greenland and Iceland remain as two individuals in a tent by themselves. All combined, this creates a total of seven individual family tents. Once the Union of Ameristralia is established, all of the seven families previously mentioned will be united under one very large family tent with 73 "individuals" who will help and protect each other while we all prosper and promote individual freedom.

In the twentieth century, like the First World War or the Second World War, the individual "family tents" on the planet collaborated with each other to some degree to find a common approach to the problem at hand. First, the process would be that leaders of various tents would go and talk with the decision makers in their individual tents. Then they would come to a consensus about what they wanted to do and then they'd get back with the leaders of the other tents, and hopefully, they'd come to an agreed-upon solution. In the case of the Second World War, America, Britain, and Russia took leadership roles while the tents of Australia, Canada, New Zealand, and India played major supportive roles and made major sacrifices in the effort. All the other tents were mostly passive and hoped the hostilities would pass them by, except those already overrun by the Axis powers.

Perhaps a better solution would have been to have all 73 individuals in 7 different tents join under one Ameristralian tent. One joined in an eternal bond for the good of humanity, deciding together from the outset what the best course of action is for a given threat. Instead of thinking and acting as individual concerns, under this scenario, everyone in the giant Ameristralian tent would know that everyone else in the tent has their back and will protect them from any outside threats, no questions asked because now we are one. The Union also means there are no Free Riders in the group of seventy-three. A Free Rider is a country that—as in the First and Second World War—passively sits on the sideline and hopes everything passes them by without expending the resources and sacrifices needed for the greater good. To be fair, the United States also tried to play the role of being a Free Rider—a neutral country. But the United States found out that a neutral stance was not possible. In the tent of Ameristralia, everyone participates equally in any cause. Then, as necessity dictates, Ameristralia may go out and find allies in other tents on the planet to join in a particular cause.

In 1867, Canada's four provinces came together to form their first confederation. With the geographical distance and exhaustive travel time during these early and formative years, the confederation worked to everyone's advantage at that time.

In 1889, the British decided the six colonies of Australia along with New Zealand and Fiji should come together as one country because it was the easiest way to defend their Pacific possessions from Dutch, French, German, and Russian interference in the region. New Zealand and Fiji had the opportunity to join Australia in its formation but opted not to participate.[6]

Now with advances in technology and transportation bringing everyone closer together, it seems natural to take the next common-sense evolution of governments one step further by Mother and Siblings coming together under one tent in a Union of equals.

The proposed Union of Ameristralia would consist of the following:

Country	Land Mass (sq. miles)	Population	GDP (in 000,000s)	per Capita
Australia	2,969,024	25,502.800	1,365,000	51,885
Canada	3,855,520	37,602,103	1,820,000	52,144
Greenland	836,330	55,877	1,800	37,000
Iceland	39,682	360,000	19,000	56,066
New Zealand	103,483	4,981,780	199,000	41,072
United Kingdom	93,410	66,876,964	2,936,000	46,827
United States	3,535,948	327,167,434	20,494,000	63,051
Total	11,433,397	462,546,958	26,834,800	

Under the proposed scenario, the total land mass of Ameristralia would be about 11,433,397 square miles, or 6.3% of the global total 197 million square miles. For our purposes here, we'll round to six percent.

The Ameristralian population would be about 462,546,958 out of a global population of about 7.8 billion, which also equates to about 6% of the global total.

The Ameristralian Gross Domestic Product (GDP) would be $26,835 trillion out of a global GDP of about $88 trillion which equates to about 27% of the global total.

Basically, Ameristralia would have 27% of the global GDP, with 6% of the land mass and 6% of the population, numbers providing a confirmation that countries in the proposed Ameristralia currently have better governmental systems and economic systems than the rest of the world. Coupled with a common culture derived from Mother Britain, which believes in the continuity of government by the people, with guaranteed rights and individual freedoms, making unification a beneficial and strategic combination.

Conversely, as of June, 2021, Russia has a huge land mass of 16.6 million square miles and a population of 147 million, but only has a GDP of $1.7 trillion, which equates to $11,654 per capita, for a ranking of 64th in the world. Russia's GDP is less than that of South Korea or Canada, confirming that Russia's system of government and economy are not designed for success or the benefit of their citizens.

China has a land mass of 3.7 million square miles and a population of 1.4 billion; it is the most populated country in the world. The per capita income is $11,819 and is ranked 61st with a GDP of $14.9 trillion. The 61st ranking for China is a little better than Russia's 64th ranking. China is currently the major threat to world peace because it has the economic strength to exert itself on others now and even more in the future. The joint collusion between Russia and China represents a coordinated confrontation to the democratic nations.

Country	Land Mass (sq Mi)	Population	GDP in 000,000s	per Capita
Russia	16,600,000	147,000,000	1,700	11,654
China	3,700,000	1,400,000,000	14,900	11,819

The Russian and Chinese systems are designed to benefit those in power—the government, the ruling class, the oligarchs—and not to the benefit of their citizens.

The resulting country of Ameristralia would result in a nation with a greater chance of maintaining peace through strength while continuing to provide the moral leadership necessary for long-term survival of humanity. Over time, I would encourage other English countries, or non-English speaking nations willing to change their language to English, to join the Union and gain from the security, peace, and prosperity that Ameristralia will provide for its citizens and for humanity.

AMERISTRALIA

CHAPTER

2

Advantages

1) Standardization: Creating Economies of Scale

What follows are several examples of where standardization over the course of time has helped government and the people it serves to be safer and more prosperous. Standardization allows for economies of scale to kick in.

TRUTH:
There are economies of scale
in life, business, and government.

Life

The first and most important economy of scale is in life where a family has two parents participating in raising their children. The sharing of duties and resources allows for more work getting done and the ability to be more financially secure. When one spouse is tired or otherwise committed, the other can jump in and provide the needed support. Numerous studies have shown that single parent families are much more likely to slip into poverty.

Business

One of the earliest business examples of standardization is the British measurement system (feet, yards, gallons, pounds, tons), which is called the Imperial System.[6] Mother Britain wanted all of her colonies to use her standards because this made for trade normalization. If each colony had a different measurement system, it would prevent the fluid movement of goods within the British Empire. The United States based its system of measurement on the Imperial System, because it was Mother's system.

In 1963, the Weights and Measurements Act redefined the basic measures of the "yard" and the "pound" in terms of the "meter" and the "kilogram," which was adopted by the Commonwealth in 1965 with full adoption in place by 1975. According to the UK Metric Association, it is a proper system in which units are inter-related; it is easy to learn and to use because it is mainly decimal; it is adaptable to all situations; the same units can be used in both cooking and scientific research.[7] For this reason, I am recommending that the United States adopt the metric system as a part of this process for increased economies of scale.

Government

In 1904, a fire ravaged Baltimore, Maryland, and stands as an example of how bad things can happen when there is no government standardization. Engine companies from New York, Philadelphia, Annapolis, Wilmington, and Harrisburg sped to Baltimore to help only to find out they couldn't because their hoses wouldn't connect to the Baltimore fire hydrants. Because there wasn't a national standard, they all watched as 1,562 buildings burned.[8] If the fire hydrant connections had been standardized, it could have saved lives and prevented a tremendous amount of property damage.

In the 1920s, Herbert Hoover, as Secretary of Commerce and later the 31st President from 1929 to 1933, became a major proponent of standardization. Hoover thought standardization was the key to prosperity and safety, but he wanted it to be on a voluntary basis as much as possible. One example of Hoover's policy was when he met with the brick makers and within a few hours got them to reduce the varieties of paving bricks from 66 to 11, and eventually down to five varieties.[9] The upside was that a city would not be stuck using a single brick vendor to pave the brick streets which were in use at that time. Now they were able to get bids from multiple sources. The brick maker with a unique size brick no longer had single source control over the customer. Without standardization, the brick maker would simply lowball the first bid price to any city needing their streets paved because, in government procurement, the low price usually wins. Then, on subsequent orders, the brick maker could raise the price because the city was stuck with using the unique-sized bricks from this one provider. Having five standard brick sizes allowed other companies to bid for the work, keeping the cost to the city lower than it would have been otherwise. Competition is better for everyone and standardization helps make that happen. Standardization also allows companies to reduce the number of product lines and economies of scale are also achieved in production, allowing the cost of production to fall and subsequently the prices. All good things.

President Theodore Roosevelt refused to put the "u" in honor as the British did because the "u" was silent. As an extreme example, in Roosevelt's time there were 1,690 variants of the noun diarrhea. So in the summer of 1906, Theodore Roosevelt's administration issued a presidential edict (Circular number 6) that Columbia's Simplified Spelling Board usage was now compulsory in all administration documents, again government was trying to standardize to make things simpler.[10] Members of Congress and the Supreme Court announced their unwillingness to go along.[11] The standardized American English language has prevailed and today in America there is no "u" in honor or labor, unlike the British English. Consistency in language and spelling increases everyone's understanding. The proposed Union of Ameristralia will need to come to an agreement on whether the American or British Standard Language will be used based on uniform ease of use.

Lack of standardization plagued the armies in the First World War.[12] Allied Armies used different caliber weapons, which greatly complicated resupply of the armies. However, in the Second World War, the United States basically supplied all armies (Australian, British, Canadian, Indian, New Zealand, and to a much lesser extent,

Russia). Standardization of arms supplies allowed the Allied forces to greatly reduce logistical issues during the war.

Traffic lights were finally standardized in 1927.[13] Think of drivers' confusion while driving between different cities, the dangers and accidents that could result, if not standardized.

With the massive wildfires in Australia in 2019, it became apparent to me that if Ameristralia was already in place, resources could have been rotated by the government from different hemispheres based on the need, especially when one hemisphere is hot and dry and the other is cold and wet. Consequently, standardized equipment and one government to manage the resources between continents and hemispheres is needed.

The federal government's role is to create a level playing field for all businesses, so it needs to set consistent rules in all Provates, therefore rules for Occupational Safety and Health Administration (OSHA) and the Environmental Protection Agency (EPA), among others, are the same for all Provates. Individual Provates would not need to establish their own EPA or OSHA guidelines as it would be a duplication of effort, a waste of money, and very confusing for businesses. Giving the Provates the power to non-standardize protocols gives them special rights and would not be beneficial as well as counterproductive.

For economy of scale, instead of having seven different embassies, the number of countries in the proposed Union of Ameristralia, represented in most major countries on the globe, there would now be just one. Hundreds of embassies could be closed, resulting in hundreds of billions of dollars saved. As an example, globally the US currently has over 160 embassies.

Duplication of border crossings like those between the United States and Canada can be eliminated; just as now between the 50 states in the US, thus saving vast amounts of time and money.

2) Military Strength

TRUTH:
There is strength in numbers.

Benjamin Franklin said, "In the cruel world of nations, safety often resided in numbers."[14]

Theodore Roosevelt said, "It is the availability of raw power, not the use of it, that makes for effective diplomacy."[15]

Common sense suggests that if a group of 73 confronts another group of 20, 30, or 40, the lesser group will think long and hard prior to initiating any conflict or violence. In other words, one very large fleet with one purpose and common goal, versus several smaller fleets with divided goals, is more efficient and formidable. Just as we tell our kids to stick together because there is safety in numbers. As of 2021, China has 350 ships as compared to the 290 ships that the United States has in service, not accounting for our ships outclassing the Chinese vessels.[16] While our ships do outclass those of China, the differences in number is problematic. Combining forces puts Ameristralia ahead.

The United States was the first, publicly, to announce a Space Force. The other countries in the proposed Union do not have the ability to protect themselves from threats in space. By joining together in this Union, protection will now be possible for all who are under the big tent of Ameristralia.

3) Access to Technology

Whether it is space exploration through NASA or private enterprise, military research and development, or vaccine development, as the sharing and participation in technology grows and the exchange of technical information is shared, the Union of Ameristralia will flourish for all under the new family tent.

TRUTH:
There would be enhanced access to technology.

The new Union of Ameristralia can now contribute more towards space exploration and the resulting technologies. The same would be true for the technology used in defense systems and weapons. In the current environment, if Australia, Canada, Greenland, Iceland, New Zealand, or the United Kingdom wanted to have citizens explore space, or businesses wanted access to newer technologies that result from space exploration, they are currently reliant on the United States, China, or Russia. However, Japan, India, France, and Germany are all building up their space programs. The Union of Ameristralia will have an advantage in technological advancements and exploration through the pooling of resources, creating increased economies of scale.

Development of vaccines has historically been dominated by four large multinational corporations based in the United States, the United Kingdom, and the European Union (EU).[17] Similar to space exploration, smaller nations not in alliance/union with a country that produces vaccines, will most likely be left out and probably won't have access to the vaccines until the US, UK, or the EU have taken care of their citizens first. In the summer of 2020, the United States bought up virtually all the supplies of Remdesivir, leaving none for the United Kingdom, the EU, or most of the rest of the world. Remdesivir was one of the first therapy drugs proven to work against Covid-19. Again, you take care of your own tent first, then you worry about everyone else. If the tent is bigger, more can be cared for in the event of a pandemic or other global disasters.

The economic strength of the US and its allies in the Second World War translated into military strength, combined with a culture and society that encourages technological innovation, allowed the western alliance to defeat tyranny. During the Second World War, new inventions such as sonar, radar, and code-breaking machines such as Ultra, LST (Landing Ship Tank for transporting troops and vehicles to the beach), Mulberries (artificial mobile harbors used at the Normandy beaches for larger ships after the beach was secure), and the atomic bomb are all great examples of technology that led to victory in the Second World War.

Democracies are better suited for technological leaps than autocratic forms of government because, in a democracy, people are allowed to think and explore new and varying ideas to further innovation. However, autocratic governments can move faster and with more efficiency for specifically focused goals. Hitler's build-up of the German military in the lead up to the Second World War is a great example. In the current environment of the early twenty-first century, China is building artificial islands in the South China Sea and then using them as military bases or unsinkable aircraft carriers.

4) Ease of Movement

For businesses, the labor pool, the access to huge new markets, plus reduced and simplified regulations would allow for enormous possibilities. For example, if a business in Sydney, South Wales, needed a programmer and they were having a hard time filling the position in Sydney or the rest of the Australian continent, employers could then, under the proposed Union, advertise for the job under the entire family tent of 73 Provates, all of Ameristralia. All citizens of the same Union, the same language, no passport needed, no work visa needed, all that would be needed would be an individual willing to move for a better job, better paycheck, and a plane ticket. A better job also helps the individual build a better resumé for the next job, and also allows the individual the opportunity to get out of a company or position where there is no opportunity for advancement. Individuals could keep growing, rather than remain stuck. Labor becomes more mobile and goes where it can be most productive, for themselves and for society.

A business in Toronto, Ontario, having issues of getting into the United States market will no longer face those issues and have the opportunity to grow their business. Customs, duties, or tariffs will no longer be problematic. Under the proposed Union of Ameristralia, all the regulatory hurdles are the same wherever the business is located or doing business. The removal of barriers allows the company with the best product to be able to present their product or service to all customers representing 27% of the global GDP. The Freer movement and services allows customers to get better products at lower prices; therefore, better-run companies have greater success and growth. Poorly run companies fail and their employees go to work for those better-run companies. More competition makes it better for everyone in the long run.

For citizens of Ameristralia, tourism and travel just got a lot easier for everyone. The necessity for a passport, struggling through the customs or visa check points to reach 6% of the land mass (as well as all of the oceans and beaches in between) or 6% of the global population no longer exists.

CHAPTER

3

Evolution of Mankind and Government

TRUTH:
Businesses don't like competition.

Businesses don't like competition and try to prevent it whenever possible. Publicly elected officials eager to please (and accept donations) help many businesses find ways to reduce competition against the betterment of society and humanity. Some of the simple ways this is done is by creating licensing requirements for businesses or regulatory hurdles for a business to offer its product in a given Provate. The Union of Ameristralia, however, and the proposed constitution will help increase the amount of competition among businesses because those individual Provate licensing and regulatory hurdles will be eliminated and only the home Provate's requirements need to be met.

While on vacation in Germany, my wife and I met the owner of two bookstores. He told us that in Germany, bookstore retailers must sell books at the price the publisher dictates, there is no price competition for the consumer. Because there is no competition on price, the publisher, distributor, and retailer all have guaranteed profit margins if a book sells. Good for business, but not the consumer. A similar model was also true in US brick and mortar bookstores. However, Amazon has created a model that allows independent publishers and authors to set their own prices.

In Austria, my wife and I toured a vineyard and the guide told us they could only produce a given number of bottles of wine each year. We were told that the government was the one controlling the output. So if the vineyard had a bumper crop of grapes coming, the buds on the grape vines were then trimmed so that only the right number of grapes were allowed to ripen to meet the quota. These restrictions level out production each year, which I'm sure keeps prices up for the wine and the quality consistent from year-to-year. Again, good for business because it reduces competition (the amount of supply) in the market. On the flip side, if the vineyard could produce and bottle as much wine as they could make then this would push prices down because of the larger supply and be less exclusive.

In France, my wife and I toured another vineyard where cartels control the volume and ways the vineyards grow their grapes. For example, the vineyards in the local cartel were not allowed to irrigate or fertilize the grape fields. We were told it was the more "green" way to grow the grapes. The "green" way was also a way to keep their costs down especially if everyone in the local cartel was operating the same way. Again, good for business because it kept the costs of production down with less overheads to drive the price up. On the flip side, if the vineyard could irrigate and fertilize their grapes, they could greatly increase their wine production, which again would have the effect of pushing prices down.

But Cartels don't work in the long run. For example, oil futures in the United States plunged below $0 for the first time in April of 2020 as Russia and Saudi Arabia fought over quota levels and control of the cartel, OPEC (Organization of Petroleum Exporting Countries).[18]

In Canada they had three Wheat Pools (cartel/co-ops) from 1923-1929. But during the Great Depression, they fell into ruin after the price of wheat dropped. The Wheat Pools only survived because the government provided secret subsidies to keep them alive.[19]

Furthermore, businesses that are in a cartel get lazy because they don't have to compete or innovate and then at some point life passes them by.

TRUTH:
Individuals like competition in the marketplace.

Another role of government is to provide a level playing field for every individual to compete fairly for the same job. We all want to live in a society based on merit where you are judged by the content of your character and the quality of your work. The ultimate goal is that people should not be hired or promoted because of their ethnic background, skin color, gender, or religion.

For competition in schools, Federal and Provate governments will still be responsible for setting curriculum and standards, but residents will be empowered and encouraged to demand better teachers, accessibility to technology, and school choice, including charter and private schools without retribution or backlash. Regardless of where someone lives, all children deserve the opportunity to have a quality education to improve themselves and contribute as educated citizens. Education is a major driver in determining financial success later in life. In order for a country to see steady economic growth, education must be a priority. For every year of education, a person's average earnings increase by 10 percent.[20]

We also understand that accomplishments do not necessarily happen in a vacuum, and it often requires seeking out educators and mentors who consider the success of others an investment or worthwhile cause. Parents and relatives often fit into this category as a resource as well.

TRUTH:
We often do what we are incentivized to do.

I have a grandchild who during one school year regularly received candy from the teacher when she performed well in school—positive reinforcement. Kids get Christmas presents if they are on Santa's "good" list, not Santa's "naughty" list. *Incentives* are seen as rewards for specific behavior, and if given for misguided reasons, may reinforce unwanted behavior.

Misguided government incentives may lead to unintended behavior. The Congressional Budget Office calculated that "roughly five of six recipients," or 80%, were getting more from unemployment payments during the Covid-19 pandemic than they would earn from working. Many workers could receive twice as much income for staying unemployed.[21]

As a specific example, a Honda plant in Ohio could not find workers when an average worker had made $17 per hour ($680 a week) but was then able to collect $940 each week with the federal unemployment boost.[22]

On July 3rd, 2020, I was at Safelite Autoglass in Kansas City getting a windshield replaced. The acting manager was talking to one of his team members just behind the front counter and questioning whether it was smart for him, the acting manager, to return to work (a large number of employees at Safelite were laid off from lack of work) rather than take the unemployment with the extra $600 per week that the Federal government was giving out at that time. The acting manager had a good moral compass, and I applaud his work ethic. I felt badly that the government provided *incentives* that had tempted him and many others to not work. As a citizen who pays taxes, I don't want my tax dollars to go to someone who decides not to work and support themselves. The person unwilling to work is undeserving of help and needs some Tough Love.

Granted, the pandemic caused unintended consequences, such as parents having to be educators in their homes, which may have impacted their employment. Conversely, it has also given us the opportunity to rethink the workplace. If more people are able to work from home, there is less demand on the infrastructure, fewer vehicles on the road, less electricity to keep office buildings chilled or heated, and less dependence on daycare.

Unemployment insurance is supposed to help those deserving folks in need until they can find new work or, as in 2020 and 2021, when their employer reopened their doors after the Covid-19 restrictions were lifted. The implementation of the Long-Term Individual Security Accounts (LISAs, Article 5, Section 3, later in Book Two) will provide the correct incentives because the unemployment benefits will be coming out of the individual's own accounts, not government accounts collected from other people.

TRUTH:
People like freedom of movement.

In Ameristralia, a citizen can live in the northern hemisphere if they want their winters in January-March or southern hemisphere in July-September. A citizen can also decide whether they want to live on the continent of Europe, North America, Oceania (Australia and surrounding islands) or any number of islands in the Atlantic (Greenland or Iceland) or Pacific (Hawaii, Guam, Midway) or the Caribbean (US Virgin Islands, Puerto Rico).

Freedom of movement assumes a rough parity in the cost of living. For example, in the US today, if someone living in Tulsa, Oklahoma, wants to take a job in San Francisco, California, the pay and opportunity would not allow for them to maintain the same standard of living in San Francisco for the same pay as they receive in Tulsa. San Francisco's cost of living is more than twice that of Tulsa. For businesses to attract people from other parts of the country, higher salaries may be required in order to encourage their acceptance of a new job, or it may encourage a San Francisco business to move to Tulsa.

In my own career, I have moved for better jobs. When I moved from Kansas City, Missouri, to St Louis, Missouri, I received a promotion and a 30% pay increase. A few years later, I moved from St. Louis to Richmond, Virginia, also for a promotion and with a 30% increase. Individuals with skills, a good work ethic, and who are willing to move can greatly accelerate their advancement through promotions and better pay, which then gives individuals and their families a higher standard of living. You just need a skill, a good work ethic, and be willing to move.

With that being said, in St Louis, Missouri, in the 1980s there was a gentlemen's agreement among the banks to not recruit from the other banks in town because less competition for talent meant salaries stayed lower. My boss at the time jumped to another bank in town, causing an uproar between the banks. The explanation used by the bank that hired my boss was that they had not recruited my boss away, but rather, my boss approached them. Consequently, the banks put a new gentlemen's agreement in place. Again, businesses don't like competition and try to avoid it whenever possible. Individuals like competition because it provides opportunities for promotion with more money, without having to move to another city.

Before the establishment of the interstate highway system in the mid-twentieth century, businesses knew that most individuals didn't like moving and assumed that people were "trapped" for work. Large companies, like large governments are slow to change and have operated under this assumption well into the twenty-first century. Workers today have more options, including remote working and relocating with relative ease. Rather than working in the same career for decades, the possibilities exist for having two or even three careers.

Where companies put their operations are largely based on the availability of workers, regulatory overhead, infrastructure, cost of living, and the tax code. Workers want fair pay, a community that has a positive quality of life, and a manageable cost of living. Traditionally, the rural labor market has been seen as having a stronger work ethic. A strong work ethic and the assumption that the labor force is unlikely to move has been a major advantage for a business to place a facility in rural areas.

I've talked to many people in my travels. In the last couple of years I met two young individuals, one being from Topeka, Kansas and the other from Albuquerque, New Mexico. Neither one had ever been out of the county in which they lived. As a result, I would assume they have a very narrow vision of people, society, and the world. Their employers didn't need to worry about them moving to a different town for a better paying job. As another example, we had a friend of a friend in Nebraska who had an offer of a better job in Columbus, a larger town 20 miles away. However, his wife refused to move those 20 miles because her parents and family were in the smaller town where they currently lived. He accepted the job in Columbus, Nebraska, then moved the 20 miles, and divorced his wife. Moving even 20 miles is not an option for some people.

A trend among city dwellers is looking for a better quality of life. Some are moving to rural, quieter areas, maybe to start an organic farm, craft brewery, or simply working from home in a new environment. As history shows, Americans (and Australians, Canadians, Greenlanders, Icelanders, and New Zealanders) have a pioneering spirit and are willing to "pack their wagons" and chase opportunity. Ameristralia, allows for countless opportunities beyond previously defined borders.

TRUTH:
There will always be good and evil in the world.

Democratic countries rarely initiate aggressive behavior against their neighbors, but that does not mean that a Democratic country can't turn autocratic overnight, as Germany did in the 1930s. The existing autocratic countries, Russia, China, North Korea, etc, will always be a threat. The threat can be via military action, such as, when Russia invaded Georgia in 2008 or its smaller invasions into the Ukraine in 2014 (neither Georgia or Ukraine are members of NATO).[23] In February of 2022, Russia moved over 150,000 troops next to the Ukrainian border for training exercises and then started a full-scale invasion. The final outcome, as I complete this book is not known. In 1950, China annexed Tibet and invaded the island of Hainan.[24] In 1979, China also temporarily invaded Vietnam. The threats may also come through a cyber-attack or through disinformation campaigns designed to destroy the fabric of our nation.

The United States now has laws in place stating that we cannot overthrow the governments of the countries we don't like. The US used to overthrow governments as in the case of the Shah of Iran where the CIA's coup was a flop.[25] But our enemies are not similarly constrained. The political scientists Alexander Downes and Lindsey O'Rourke have counted over 100 instances since 1816 in which one country tried to impose regime change on another. [26]

According to a Wall Street Journal article in January of 2021, Sweden had increased its number of troops and Sweden's latest defense plan boosts annual military spending by more than $3 billion, a 40% hike, in the five years following 2021. "Their stated strategy," said Kenneth Howery, the US ambassador in Stockholm, "is to hold out as long as possible and hope help arrives."[27] Any strategy that relies on help coming from other countries is fraught with danger. Just ask Austria (1938) and Czechoslovakia (1939) prior to the start of the Second World War. How did that work out for them? It didn't. To be fair, a good portion of the population in Austria welcomed Germany into their country.

Not until Hitler invaded Poland in 1939 did other countries finally step in to defend those countries and themselves. And in Sweden's case, they didn't jump up to defend their Norwegian and Finnish neighbors in the Second World War.

TRUTH:
You can't trust treaties to save you.

The Locarno Pact, which Germany signed in 1925 prior to the Second World War, stipulated that any disputes Germany had with Poland or Czechoslovakia would be settled by an arbitration tribunal.[28] Hitler also signed a non-aggression pact with Russia in 1939. Both pacts didn't last long, and Hitler invaded all three countries in the 1938-1941 timeframe. On the flip side, the US government made numerous treaties with Native American tribes, but it never paid off for the Native Americans. Treaties don't work.

Britain's Neville Chamberlain chose to appease Hitler prior to the Second World War in the hope of avoiding war.[29] He failed to act in the face of repeated violations of treaties and international law. The leaders of the world's democracies allowed the international order to break down. Politicians, like many people, often look for the easy way out of a problem rather than take the harder route of doing the right thing.

According to a January 21, 2021, *Wall Street Journal* article, China has launched one of the greatest military buildups in the history of the world, seeking to create the conditions for a successful invasion of Taiwan, much like it did in 1950 when China invaded the island of Hainan. China is closer to the goal of taking over Taiwan than it was just twenty years ago. The military balance has shifted as China's buildup accelerates. The gradual decline of America's ability to forestall an invasion of Taiwan is well understood by governments around the Pacific. [30]

The fall of Taiwan would be bad news not only for Taiwan's democracy-loving and independence-minded residents, but it would also be a strategic catastrophe for Japan, leaving Beijing in control of the sea routes Japan needs for survival. A Chinese takeover would be such a conclusive demonstration of US weakness that no country, from India to Vietnam, would risk its security on US ties alone. Given that Taiwan also hosts the world's most advanced semiconductor industry, controlling Taiwan would put China on the road to world technological and economic supremacy, becoming the arbiter of Asia.[31]

No country can rely on a treaty or a confederation of countries to protect their sovereignty. Only by joining in a Union of like-minded countries can a democracy be guaranteed that others will be there to fight and defend their freedoms. Knowing this is one of the reasons why the United States refuses to surrender its sovereignty to the United Nations on any number of topics. We cannot allow lawmaking by foreign governments and international bodies, or bureaucrats, that have scant regard for the interests and values of our fellow citizens.[32] The problem becomes clear when actual democracies try to live by the agreements they've signed and believe they are enforceable in courts while other regimes, such as Russia and China, don't have an actual rule of law and control their courts. In the US, the legislative branch should not delegate its rule-making responsibilities to the executive branch. There are times when our administrative agencies not only make rules but enforce and adjudicate them with nary a check, thus carrying out the functions of all three branches of government.[33] Then the US Supreme Court, historically, has deferred to the administrative agency's interpretation of regulations in court rulings such as *Chevron, Skidmore, Auer* and *Seminole Rock* as precedents.[34]

In a recent survey, only 34% of Germans, 25% of Greeks and Italians, 36% of Czechs, 33% of Hungarians, and 41% of the French believe their country should fulfill their treaty obligation if one of their members is attacked by Russia. But at the same time, Europeans still trust the United States to save them against a Russian attack: 75% of Italians, 63% of Germans and 57% of French.[35] They are not sure they want to help their neighbors but expect the United States to be there if they are attacked.

Until 2021, Europeans may not have been willing to help their neighbors, but when Russia invaded Ukraine in 2022, and brought war back to their doorstep, there was a change of heart. Europeans took in millions of refugees who fled the fighting but did not provide any combat troops, only equipment, food, and supplies. As of this writing, Ukraine is still not a member of NATO, so there is no legal obligation to provide troops for Ukraine, only a moral obligation to provide assistance.

Drafting our young people to serve in the military is unpopular, unless as with the Second World War it was entirely necessary. From the expanded population base of Ameristralia, it would be much easier to keep a sufficient military force in place without the draft.

4

The Growth of Countries

The United States' westward expansion created territories that would eventually lead to statehood with equal standing instead of creating colonies for a central government to master. Canada had a less defined process for adding Provinces but had the same goal. If Britain would have created the colonies with the aim of incorporating them into Mother Britain as an extension of herself, today's world would be a totally different place. Benjamin Franklin originally considered himself a British Imperialist. He fought for America to join Mother Britain as equals for years prior to the War of Independence in 1776.[36] But that was not the mind set of Mother Britain or the other ruling European powers. The mercantile class of the 16th and early 17th centuries looked upon its siblings first and foremost as a source of income and military strength.[37] The Europeans were also colonizing foreign lands with indigenous people (non-Europeans), which they were loath to assimilate into their society. For Britain, the colonies were also a dumping ground for convicts and other nefarious individuals.

Ultimately, Mother Britain did see the moral imperative of its mission. As Churchill said in the summer of 1897 about Britain, "Our mission of bringing peace, civili(z)ation, and good government to the uttermost ends of the earth."[38]

Theodore (Teddy) Roosevelt

President Theodore Roosevelt said, "During the past three centuries the spread of the English-speaking peoples over the world's waste space has been not only the most striking feature in the world's history, but also the event of all other most far-reaching in its importance."

What else but destiny can explain the remorseless advance of Anglo-Saxon civilization and cultural values? A destiny that is yet to be fully realized but advanced through our evolution into the Union of Ameristralia.

Many immigrants have come to America from countries where the state interferes with people's lives under a pretense to help. What most people really want is for the government to step aside and let each individual carve out his or her own destiny. Except for enslaved people, pursuing a destiny, or dream, was the major reason most immigrants came and continue to come to America (and Australia, Canada, Greenland, Iceland and New Zealand). Pursuing a dream is the primordial truth to which almost every immigrant subscribes. Assimilation was encouraged through much of the twentieth century. For example, Eastern Europeans coming through Ellis Island and settling in New York City were given the opportunity to learn English through the Industrial Removal Office, live in given neighborhoods, and realize greater financial opportunity and mobility. [39]

Franklin Delano Roosevelt (FDR)

The Second World War was the foremost event in the twentieth century. The war required, "All hands on deck" in order to achieve victory. President Franklin Delano Roosevelt (FDR) navigated America to victory. One of the most important acts of his presidency was to sign Executive Order 8802 which established the temporary Fair Employment Practices Commission in 1941.[40] As a result, women were allowed to work in jobs they had never held before. Although segregated in some cases, African-Americans were entrusted with jobs they'd never had before and were allowed to serve overseas in military positions they had never had before, such as fighter pilot. Everyone did their part and worked as a great team. Additionally, in Australia in 1942 Prime Minister John Curtin established the Women's Employment Board. Women started earning men's wages—effectively doubling their pay.[41] Cataclysmic changes to society occurred across the planet as a result, all for the good of humanity.

Over several centuries, Great Britain invaded more countries than any other. Great Britain used these incursions to increase her colonies and create a global empire. Having jurisdictional control over more countries gave increased economic and military strength to whomever controlled a colony. In 1940, prior to the Second World War, nearly one in three individuals on the planet was colonized. By 1965 the number was down to one in fifty.[42]

Also, prior to the Second World War, bigotry, racism, and sexism was a normal part of humanity's fabric. For example, in the 1924, President Coolidge signed a ban on non-Northern European immigration. Australia also had a ban on non-European immigration policy until 1967.[43] After the Second World War, colonization, racism, religious and sexual discrimination started to be seen as a detriment within many evolving democratic nations. By the 1960s and 1970s, citizens became more vocal about the type of society in which they wanted to live. Still, as all things in life, there are those people who will never learn the appropriate and moral way to treat other people—their fellow citizens. Often, prejudice arises because those within a community are conforming to what is regarded as normal in the social groups to which they belong.[44]

A person cannot change their skin tone or ethnic background. One's religion or gender faces challenges as well. Human beings have language, which gives us the opportunity to win a detractor over if we can communicate with them. Understanding also comes from education; learning about people and the differences we have culturally is necessary to a unified people. Hate and misunderstanding of someone's culture is difficult to counter if you can't talk to another person because they speak a different language. In both science and business, English is recognized as the universal language. English is also one of the most studied languages across the world, if not the primary language, most countries teach it as a secondary language. A common language is the best way to combat prejudice and discrimination.[45]

In order to determine who the good and bad people are in society, you have to be able to communicate with them in a common language (i.e. English) in order to make that determination. Gaining understanding is why we need to speak the same language. If you can't talk to someone, you are lost, which makes it difficult to garner trust.

By default, the United States became the indispensable country in the aftermath of the Second World War and the guiding force on the planet for commerce, politics, military strength, and diplomacy. The United States' prowess made it the leader of the free world.

Ronald Reagan loved referring to the United States as "A shining city on a hill," (which he coopted from a John Winthrop speech of 1630) and although America's gilded reputation has at times been tarnished, it is still the most admired place in the world. Most people are familiar with the second verse of the poem on the Statue of Liberty, but it is actually the first verse that best expresses America's place in the world:

> Not like the brazen giant of Greek fame,
> With conquering limbs astride from land to land;
> Here at our sea-washed, sunset gates shall stand
> A mighty woman with a torch, whose flame
> Is the imprisoned lightning, and her name,
> Mother of Exiles. From her beacon-hand,
> Glows world-wide welcome; her mild eyes command
> The air-bridged harbor that twin cities frame.

In Emma Lazarus' poem *A New Colossus* she is telling us that our power comes not from conquering others, but from offering a place to flourish. To flourish means embracing what it means to be American, equal opportunity for those willing to assimilate with us, not stand apart from us. Ameristralia continues the American Dream, Australian Dream, Canadian Dream, Greenlander Dream, Icelandic Dream, and the New Zealander Dream. Hopefully, the people of Mother Britain will want the same dream.

5

Different Government Structures

W hen considering the idea of Ameristralia and the combination of several governments there are some different
organizational approaches to consider.

Federation/Confederation vs Union

In a letter dated July 1, 1706 from Queen Anne to the Scottish
Parliament, she summarizes the importance of the Union then
forming between England and Scotland, which merited further
attention, including, "An entire and perfect Union will be the solid
foundation of lasting peace: It will secure your religion, liberty,
and property; remove the animosities amongst yourselves, and
the jealousies and differences between our two kingdoms. It must
increase your strength, riches, and trade; and by this Union the whole
island, being joined in affection and free from all apprehensions of
different interest, will be enabled to resist all its enemies;" and then,
"We most earnestly recommend to you calmness and unanimity
in this great and weighty affair, that the Union may be brought
to a happy conclusion, being the only effectual way to secure
our present and future happiness, and disappoint the designs of
our and your enemies, who will doubtless, on this occasion, use
their utmost endeavors to prevent or delay this Union."[46] The

same positive effects would apply here to Ameristralia. Also, the possibility of others creating distractions or throwing obstacles into this proposed Union in order to prevent or delay, also apply to this endeavor of Ameristralia.

There is a difference between a federation and a union. The United Nations is a Federation of countries. Individual nations can do as they please, either cooperate for the common good or be selfish and do what is right for their own country/government/leaders. Today, there are only about 30 countries that can be considered wealthy, consolidated democracies.[47] With the exception of Australia and New Zealand, all the consolidated democracies are in the northern hemisphere of East Asia, Europe, or North America.[48] But the membership of United Nations consists of 193 countries. Therefore, almost 80% of that body has a much different view of the world than wealthy consolidated democracies, such as the United States, and cannot be trusted with our future security or our best interests.

The Act of Union of 1840 was passed by the British Parliament and created the Province of Canada.[49] Canada also started off as a federation of four provinces that consisted of one million French-Canadians and two and a quarter million British-Canadians. Canadians hoped that prosperity would dissolve any differences in ethnic background, language, and religion.[50] Unfortunately, Canadians didn't get to make their own decisions. The British were involved in the process and gave the French-speaking Catholics special recognition and privileges rather than treating all citizens alike and letting assimilation over time solve the problem. Between 1864 and 1867, the terms of the Canadian Confederation were formulated and debated. The "deal" that was struck anticipated the expansion of the Dominion into the Northwest and they dared to dream of a nation from "sea to sea."[51]

The idea of unification is not new. In the 1860s, Charles Hursthouse who was an Englishborn settler in New Zealand, proposed a federation (an Australasian republic) between New Zealand and Australia.[52] However in 1900, when formally asked to join Australia, New Zealand opted not to join because they thought they were superior to Australia since they had not been a penal colony.[53] Also, the Prime Minister of New Zealand at that time, R. J. Seddon, preferred to be on an equal footing with the Prime Minister of Australia, not a subordinate.[54] Political egos prevailed over common sense. In 2010, a New Zealand poll revealed that a quarter of the people favored another look at becoming an Australian state, while 41% said that the idea was worth discussing.[55]

Several Canadians and several Americans over the course of time have contemplated the union between the two countries. Multiple examples are given in the section that talks specifically about Canada later in this book.

How a Union is formed, and the expectations of the various member states needs to be agreed upon before any ink is put to paper. A framework must be put in place. Ameristralia will be more than an economic confederation as has been attempted by the European Union. An alliance that does not have a shared military commitment, diplomatic service, and foreign policy is not a true Union. The European Union (EU) has no armed forces of its own. The EU's diplomatic service has limited authority. Germany, France, and Italy, the union's most powerful member states, often speak movingly about the need for a common European Union foreign policy, but they usually remain committed to their own views and national interests.[56]

The organization of the European Union (EU) is partly a problem of structure and process. The EU is not configured for quick action and the EU isn't designed to be a geopolitical actor. On important foreign-policy issues, where any one of the 27 member states can block action with a veto, getting to a consensus requires so much compromise that the ultimate policy often loses all coherence and any real chance of success. So much time is needed to reach an effective policy decision that by the time the EU reaches a decision, the situation has changed.[57] As Frederick the Great once said, "Diplomacy without arms is like music without instruments."[58] The EU without a military has no political strength.

A Union is better than a Federation/Confederation.

Socialism/Communism vs Capitalism

TRUTH:
There will always be workers, managers, and the people with the money or power to make things happen.

In socialist/communist governments, officials and their bureaucrats who write the regulations and distribute the tax dollars have no incentive or motivation to make people happy, or make better and less costly products. Their primary goal and motivation is to remain in power and keep their jobs. Too often, some government bureaucrats get wealthy through graft and corruption, and their only incentive is to hold on to their authoritarian powers. Then, as in the Soviet Union/Russia's case, the whole system breaks down and falls apart.

Comparatively, the primary goal of capitalism is to serve a need in the market, or identify new and emerging needs, such as technology. Being financially successful by identifying and serving a need is not only an economic prerogative, fulfilling the needs of society is also a part of the democratic process (the people decide what is best for themselves) as it encourages those with the best ideas and deepest hunger (passion) to pursue their interest. The inner hunger motivates us to put food on the table, find love, start a family, have financial success, find the money to start a business, grow a business, provide employment opportunities, and hopefully, fulfill more societal needs. The profit motive provides the necessary incentives to make better and less expensive products to make consumers happy, and for the advancement of employees who make the products and provide the customer service when there are issues.

Monetarists and supply-side economists' research have found that a sense of life's meaningfulness is tightly tied to positive views of capitalism and entrepreneurship. People want more than safe and comfortable lives; they want their struggles to matter. The more Americans believe they can achieve a life of meaning, the more they will push for economic freedom and be inspired by the entrepreneurial spirit, which has helped our nation flourish.[59] What is valuable in life must be earned.

In an October 11, 2020 Wall Street Journal opinion piece, Andy Kessler contends, "No, profits aren't greedy. They are a critical price signal—a measure of how well a company is deploying capital and creating value for society. The stock market sums all expected future profits, funding companies with great profit prospects and starving unworthy ones."[60]

How would a government bureaucrat know which companies are doing well on a real time basis and which ones need additional funding? An example would be the Soviet Union in the 1980s when domestic car production satisfied only 45% of the domestic demand and there was a 10-year waiting list for a car; nevertheless, cars were not allowed to be imported.[61] The Soviet Union then invades Afghanistan in December 1979, the Chernobyl nuclear reactor melts down on April 28, 1986, withdrawing from Afghanistan in defeat in 1989, and then Soviet Union collapsed as a country in 1991. The Soviet Union's government was not interested in fulfilling the needs of its people or making its citizens happy. Russian President Gorbachev's later admission that the Russian controlled economy and its economic development was lagging "ten to fifteen years behind the capitalist countries"[62] confirms this conclusion.

In 1903, when some wanted to nationalize the railroads, Theodore Roosevelt said that he knew, better than anyone else, how "inefficient and undependable" federal employees were. It would be "a disaster" to have them in charge of free enterprises.[63]

A recent example to confirm Theodore Roosevelt's thoughts could be a report from Amtrak's Office of Inspector General on the Moynihan project concerning a new train station in New York, New York. The Inspector General's report found that a series of management and budgeting mistakes in the first two years of the Moynihan project, including failing to account for basic construction costs, added $72.8 million to budgeted costs. Among the errors, Amtrak initially lacked controls to prevent employees from unilaterally committing to cover some construction expenses. The report said that the lack of daily oversight led to expensive redesigns during construction. Ultimately, the station's opening date was thrown into doubt because signage for passengers might not comply with the Americans with Disabilities Act.[64] Government employees have no business trying to run a business. The incentive to do the right things for a business and its customers is the profit motive.

Furthermore, Adam Andrzejewski, CEO and founder of OpenTheBook.com tells us that in Los Angeles being a government lifeguard can be pretty lucrative. They found 82 county lifeguards making at least $200,000, including benefits. Seven individuals were making between $330,000 and $392,000. Thirty-one lifeguards made between $50,000 and $131,000 in overtime.[65] From an outside perspective, it's easy to make the judgment that local government employees have no problems mismanaging government funds.

A government run economy is called socialism or communism. By the end of the Cold War in the 1980s, with the communist collapse in the Soviet Union/Russia, the battle between Socialism/Communism and Capitalism was presumably over. Socialism, both moderate and dead-end command socialism of the communist countries were vanquished.[66] But there are still several countries living in denial like Cuba, North Korea, and Venezuela.

Branko Milanovic notes that never before has a single mode of production, capitalism, become universal. Today, there are two choices in capitalism: a liberal merit-based society and one led by advancing democracies (which dominates), or the state-lead political autocratic capitalism one headed by the likes of Russia and China, which limits individual political and civil rights. The biggest advantage of liberal capitalism is democracy and the rule of law. The political autocratic capitalist must try to limit corruption, which is inherent in the system and results in an ever-growing inequality of the classes.[67]

Embracing capitalism to ensure a higher standard of living and freedoms does come with a trade-off, primarily some loss of stability, tradition, and community. Capitalism moves money and resources around freely, and quick changes can occur both in technology and society. Technology usually changes faster than society, and sometimes the lag time can be seen as a deterrent or misinterpreted as the unfairness/inequity of the capitalist system. However, there are even worse inequities in the political autocratic capitalist system of Russia and China. So do we reward the hard-working individuals who have made their own fortunes (Byron Allen, Jeff Bezos, Sara Blakely, Garth Brooks, Warren Buffet, Andrew Carnegie, Thomas Edison, Henry Ford, Bill Gates, Jay-Z, Steve Jobs, George Lucas, Tyler Perry, Kendra Scott, Robert F. Smith, and Oprah Winfrey, to name a few) or do we give our allegiance to individuals such as Russia's Putin and his oligarchs in political power? Graft in government is nothing new; "it may be the second-oldest profession."[68] Political autocratic capitalism also has a greater tendency to generate bad policies and bad social outcomes that are difficult to reverse because those in power do not have an incentive to change course.[69]

One of the key factors of liberal capitalism versus political capitalism, as found in Russia and China, is that liberal capitalism does a more seamless job of moving capital and labor towards the most productive uses. People want to be respected, appreciated, and paid what they are worth, and they want to be able to follow their dreams. A society based on merit means that life is an open competition in which the most deserving succeed.[70] Socialists and communists want you to hate the likes of Amazon, Apple, Facebook, Google, and Microsoft. Although there are downsides, these corporations have done great things for humanity in the modern digital wonders they have produced. These companies have greatly improved our lives. To begrudge the financial success of their founders who started their companies from scratch would be a great disservice. These innovators deserve the riches that are derived from their vision, risk taking, perseverance, and many long hours. We should not be jealous, disparage or discredit their success (The Tall Poppy Syndrome), but celebrate their success. Historian Henry Adams noted that politics is about the systematic organization of hatreds.[71] All anyone has to do is watch the political ads in any election to find this to be true.

As a side note, many statistics have been published on new businesses failing. Failures have ranged from 80-85% failing between the second and fifth year, depending on the source. Therefore, the individuals who have successfully gone through this gauntlet of fire are to be admired. Successful entrepreneurs create new jobs and provide better products or services for society.

The Republic/Democracy vs the Autocrat

Thomas Jefferson said: "The republican is the only form of government which is not eternally at open or secret war with the rights of mankind."[72] An autocrat or dictator doesn't care about the right of its citizens.

As Margaret Thatcher said, "Democracy, I contended, required the limitation of the powers of government, a market economy, private property—and the sense of personal responsibility without which no such system could be sustained."[73]

Autocrats can move faster to given goals they might have from a military standpoint, or specific economic goals, and this gives them an edge in moving a tremendous amount of resources for a defined project. For example, Hitler was able to move decisively to rebuild his military capabilities and then later invade several countries prior to the Allies finally realizing that a negotiated peace was not in the cards. As a result, the Allies then lacked the military preparation to counter Hitler's moves. The autocrat doesn't have to convince a legislative body of the need to go to war, they just do it. Hitler was able to move faster than his European counterparts to invade the Rhineland in March of 1936. The Sudetenland (the German part of Czechoslovakia) was given to Germany in appeasement in October of 1938. Hitler then invaded Austria in March of 1938 and the remainder of Czechoslovakia in March of 1939. The invasion of Poland followed in September of 1939. Similarly, Japan could move against its Asian neighbors faster than the world could react in the 1930s. China invaded the island of Hainan and annexed Tibet in 1950 and built islands in the South

China Sea in the early twenty-first century and put military bases on them. Putin's Russia could move faster to invade the Crimea and the Donbass region of Ukraine in 2014 than the Ukrainian government could. Recently, in February/March of 2022 Russia invaded Ukraine as the rest of the world watched.

Countries that have an autocratic form of government typically do not encourage their citizens to explore new ideas and think outside of the box because this presents problems for those in power. Autocratic governments don't like, and don't reward, free thinkers (divergents) because they question what the government tells them to do or what to believe. The mentality of the autocratic government also crushes the work ethic of its citizens, and the people are taught to settle for less. On the flip side, a republic and/or democratic form of government typically doesn't force conformity on its citizens and leaves the door open for them to be innovative and explore new ideas. Therefore, from a business standpoint, a republic and/or democratic form of government can beat the autocratic governments through technology over time, assuming there is sufficient time before the autocrat invades the democratic country.

During the Second World War, Britain and the other English-speaking countries initially had the English Channel, and later, the Atlantic and Pacific Oceans as buffers. These buffers gave the Allies time to innovate the needed technology and then out produce Germany, Italy, and Japan in weaponry and food. Still, it took the United States a couple of years to get production cranked up and going. Again, technological inventions such as radar, sonar, Ultra, the LST, Mulberries, and the atomic bomb made a huge difference in the outcome of the war. The economic output of the United States, along with these technological innovations saved the day.

It took time for the government and the mindset of the American people to get on board with the idea it was time to fight, not only for ourselves, but for all of humanity.

While the republican form of government is the best long-term solution for the people, nations have to stay vigilant against autocratic nations because in matters of war, or disruptive behavior, they can move faster and stay on task more than a republic can. As Fiona Hill says, "Democracy is not self-repairing. It requires constant attention."[74] The proper checks and balances must be maintained. Autocratic nations don't have to worry about this, and in fact, usually destroy the checks and balances that are in place as part of the process.

After the Second World War, the United States and its democratic allies wanted to get their troops back home and get back to life. Meanwhile, Stalin dictated that Russian troops stay in Eastern Europe and occupy and control the governments there as a future buffer—colonizing the region. Stalin did not have to answer to anyone, he was in control, and he could play the strategic long game without worrying about getting reelected. It took over 40 years for the eastern block of European countries to get out of the direct control of Russian influence. But they are still battling indirect Russian influence and in 2022 Russia's Putin began trying to bring back as much of the old Soviet Union as he could, by invading Ukraine as the first step.

Parliamentary vs the US Presidential Republic

The Presidential Republic (the American form of government) is unique in that there are three distinct and separate branches of government: The Executive Branch, which is run by an elected President, the Legislative Branch (Congress with the House and Senate) and the Judicial Branch, consisting of the courts. All three branches are independent and relatively equal in power. The Legislative Branch passes laws and spending bills. The President can then approve or veto anything the Legislative Branch passes. With enough support, the Legislative Branch has the opportunity of overriding a Presidential veto with a two-thirds vote by both houses. The Courts can then decide if the new laws passed by the Legislative Branch and approved by the President are constitutional. The Courts also have the power to override anything the President does through executive action that it considers unconstitutional or illegal. As well as having the power to approve and veto bills, the President oversees the Executive Branch of the government.

Similar to other Parliamentary systems, our Legislative Branch has a House of Representatives (the Lower House) with two-year terms and a Senate (Upper House) with six-year terms for members respectively. The Senate is critical for stability in the government. In reference to the Senate, The Federalist Papers states: "To recollect that history informs us of no long-lived republic which had not a Senate."[75] The Senate is conceived as an institution that will blend stability with liberty. Should a "perfect storm" in the election arise where one party wins the Presidency and a vast majority of the House, then that party can only win, at most, the open seats available for that term in the Senate (a third every two years), making it more difficult to pass legislation that gives the winning party control of the country.

Furthermore, amending the Constitution requires an additional, time-consuming step that prevents any party that should happen to control the Presidency, the House, and the Senate from abruptly changing the Constitution. The Founding Fathers wanted the Provates to be involved in the constitutional change process, which mandates slow calmness (stability) in the process, for an additional check and balance. So again, one of the positive unintended by-products of the US Constitution is that it slows down constitutional change and must get confirmation through the Provates that any proposed changes are, in fact, a good idea.

New Zealand, like Australia and Canada, started off with a parliamentary system of government with a Governor-General and two houses of parliament, and like them, based it on the Westminster model of Mother Britain. In 1950 however, New Zealand abolished their upper house, leaving them with a unicameral system that developed constitutional issues.[76] When one party controls more than 50% of the seats just about anything is possible and New Zealand found that out between Muldoonism (a short-term approach to problems and ad hoc style) and Rogernomics (a long-term approach to problems and coherent policies), illustrating what can happen when there was no parliamentary check on executive power.[77] In 1993, New Zealand tried to solve the unicameral problem by going to a mixed-member-proportional (MMP) voting, which made it less likely that a single party would have a majority by itself.[78] But that would still not prevent a coalition totally changing the constitution.

In Hungary in 2010, Prime Minister Orban and his Fidesz-Hungarian Civic Alliance achieved a two-thirds majority in parliament. In the decade he's been in power, Orban has used that overwhelming majority to transform Hungary's constitution, institutions, and society.[79]

CHAPTER

6

The Pros and Cons of the Parliamentary System

TRUTH:
For prosperity you need stability and predictability.

It's the government's responsibility to provide an environment with stability and predictability. Otherwise, people and businesses are not able to make long-term plans, only short-term plans. For example, does a business build a new manufacturing facility to expand production with the assumption that the tax rate and interest rates will stay consistent as well as access to new markets, or do they simply remodel an existing facility with all of its existing infrastructure problems and maintain the status quo?

First major flaw of the Parliamentary system.

After an election, typically someone is selected to form a governing coalition. Typically, a coalition of parties resulting in a 51% majority must come together and agree to form a government.

Let's say there are three parties in the election. Party A receives 45% of the vote, Party B receives 45% of the vote and Party C receives 10% of the vote. Who holds the power in trying to form a coalition government? Is it Party A with 45% or B who also received 45% of the votes? Both appeal to large portions of the population, but in actuality Party C with only 10% of the votes holds the power. Minority parties typically appeal to voters for very specific causes. In this example, let's assume that Party C doesn't like nuclear energy and for Party A or B to get into power it must agree to pass legislation killing nuclear power in their country 20 or 30 years down the road. While that scenario seems unlikely, just look at Germany in 2000 when the first Schroder cabinet, which included The Greens, officially announced its intention to phase out nuclear energy.[80] At the end of 2021 three of the remaining six reactors were shut down. The last three reactors are scheduled to shut down at the end of 2022.

The Flaw — Forcing a coalition government gives minority groups tremendous power to get extreme things passed.

Second major flaw of the Parliamentary system.

In the same example where Party A gets 45% of the vote, Party B gets 45% of the vote and Party C receives the remaining 10%. Party A is given the opportunity to try and form a coalition but doesn't take the deal Party C has to offer, and they can't work out a deal with Party B either, so they give up. In this scenario, a new election is called because a coalition government could not be formed. The results of the second election are the same as the first election. Now, Party B is given the opportunity to form a coalition government but also doesn't take the deal Party C has to offer and they also can't get Party A to make a deal either, and also gives up. A third election is called for because a coalition government could not be formed. The resulting vote of the third election results in the same outcome, however this time they are finally able to find a coalition that will work, but only by giving into the demands of Party C. Unlikely as it seems, just look at Israel's three recent national elections: in September of 2019, March of 2020, and May of 2020. Three national elections in less than a year all because the politicians could not form a government.[81]

A fourth election in March of 2021 forced a change in the Prime Minister. Forcing a coalition government gives warring parties the opportunity to create great uncertainty and confusion among the citizens and business.

The Flaw — Having repeated elections not only creates an unstable and unpredictable environment to live in but also a waste time.

Third major flaw of the Parliamentary system.

Governing coalitions can be dissolved at any time and new elections called, creating an unstable environment in which to live, work, and do business. Most Parliamentary systems have one symbolic position often called the Governor-General. Typically, that person can ask someone to form a government, as in the two previous examples, and also has the power to dissolve the government all on their own, for any reason they want. In Britain, this position is symbolically held by the Queen, but in reality, it is the Prime Minister. Margaret Thatcher said, "Calling an election is a big decision, and by constitutional convention it is a matter for the prime minister alone, however much advice is on offer."[82]

Again, quoting the Federalist Papers, "Stability in government is essential to national character."[83] If you doubt the truth of that statement, just consider the following examples fraught with instability:

The track record of Italy's many governments is astonishing. As of 2021, Italy has had 69 governments since the Second World War with an average of one every 13 months.[84] It is impossible to effectively run a government or for businesses and individuals to make long-term plans under those conditions.

When John Kerr, the Governor-General of Australia, did not like the current Prime Minister Whitlam's imperious ways, the Chief Justice Sir Garfield Barwick advised him that he had the power to dismiss the government and encouraged him to do his duty.[85] The Senate was deadlocked for 27 days, but then the Governor-General acted first on November 11, 1975, to dismiss the government and put Malcolm Fraser in as a caretaker and called for elections, resulting in the most serious constitutional crisis in the history of Australia.[86]

Three Canadian examples:

First, in April of 1896, Tupper replaced Bowell, becoming the fifth Prime Minister in five years.[87] Can you imagine the chaos in the United States if we had five presidents in five years?

Secondly, Canadian Governor-General Lord Byng and the Prime Minister Mackenzie King had a dispute in 1925-26. King had formed a minority Government in 1925 only to seek dissolution prior to a motion of censure in the House of Commons in 1926. The Governor-General denied his request but relented after King's resignation.[88]

Third, Pierre Trudeau had the Governor-General Roland Michener sign an order dissolving the House. Pierre Trudeau then returned to the House of Commons and announced that there would be elections on the 25th of June, 1968. The 27th Parliament ended five minutes after it began.[89] Parliamentary forms of government that can call "snap elections" out of the blue, rather than fixed terms, can create uncertainty in life, business, and government.

Brexit:

Another recent example is the British and their exit from the European Union. Boris Johnson was elected Prime Minister and took office in July of 2019; he then called for another general election in December of 2019 resulting in two general elections in the same year.[90] The second round of elections are in contrast to the interests of the people who want their elected officials to do their job and compromise when necessary to ensure stability and predictability in their lives.

Stability in government is better assured if elections for a position in government are for a fixed length of time. Politicians need to take responsibility and do their jobs. Calling for a new election is the politicians' way of telling the voters they didn't pick the right people at the last election.

The Flaw — The parliamentary style that has multiple elections is expensive, a waste of time, and can close a government down. To force a quick election is misguided because it creates instability and unpredictability.

Fourth major flaw of the Parliamentary system.

The Australian, Canadian, and New Zealand governments are based on the British Parliamentary system, which uses the Westminster system of government and has a clear tradition: if you're a member of a cabinet formed by the Prime Minister of the day, you are bound by the principles of collective solidarity and responsibility. If a member of the cabinet has the intention to breach cabinet solidarity, then it is incumbent on the member to inform the Prime Minister and then leave office. Having left the cabinet, that person is then free to challenge for the leadership of the party from the backbench.[91]

Twice in Australian history, the Prime Minister was ousted in a coup: John Gorton in the 1960s[92] and Kevin Rudd in 2010.[93] In Kevin Rudd's case, his own cabinet forced him out in a power play by his primary assistant Julia Gillard. There had been no warning, no trigger or reasons given for the ouster. There wasn't any policy crisis brewing within the government that finally came to a head. No issue surfaced that the public could readily comprehend. The public only had Gillard's vague explanation that, "A good government was losing its way."[94] Gillard then called for new elections. The cold, hard truth was that the 2010 upheaval was about personal political ambition, pure and simple.[95]

The Flaw — The Prime Minster of the country can be ousted from their job without an election or any due process, otherwise known as a coup.

Fifth major flaw of the Parliamentary system.

Again, Australian, Canadian, and New Zealand governments are based on the British Parliamentary system, which uses the Westminster system of government. What is most surprising about the British system is that it is not codified—meaning it does not have a written or formulated constitution.[96]

In America, our founders rejected the English tradition of an unwritten constitution because they wanted to fix things.[97] In Graham L. Paterson's book *The Australian Constitution as it is Actually Written* he provides multiple examples of the Westminster "system," which is made up of unwritten rules called "conventions." Convention is often quoted as the reason for a court ruling. Instead of a codified constitution in the Westminster system, precedence dictates the decisions. Peterson says, "It would not be far wrong to say that ninety-eight percent of the population is totally ignorant of what this [Australian] Constitution actually says."[98] He further says, "It should not have to rely in inferences, on unwritten conventions, on precedent, nor should it include undefined entities and process."[99] In fact, did you know there's no reference to the position of Prime Minister in the Australian constitution?[100] The people of a nation should be able to read and understand what the "primary law" of the country says.

The constitution should define the role of the judiciary, based on the written law. Having met all the great political leaders of the day and made a complete study as he could of English politics, Theodore Roosevelt was convinced that the American governmental system was superior. When asked why, "Because a written constitution is better than an unwritten one."[101] Can you imagine playing any sport where the rules are not explicitly spelled out for both teams and the individuals officiating the game?

In Australia, Prime Minister Howard had broken a century of the Westminster convention in 1996 by axing departmental secretaries of whom he didn't politically approve. Later, Prime Minister Abbott would go on to mimic his hero by conducting yet another public service purge in 2013.[102] These actions demonstrate that the Westminster convention could be ignored when it didn't suit their purpose.

The Flaw — The constitution is not codified and major portions are conventions which are also not written down.

Sixth major flaw of the Parliamentary system.

The Presidential Republic has three separate branches of government; in contrast, the Parliamentary system consists of the Executive Branch and the Legislative Branch that form a coalition up front. The coalition gives them the power to override all the measures passed by the previous administration. Under this system, the executive branch is not separate from the legislative branch, but a subset.

In Australia, after the election of October, 2004, the Howard government also had control of both legislative houses. The controlling body no longer had to justify or compromise on any of the issues before it.[103] Disaster soon materialized for the Howard government and they were soon ousted.

Similarly, Canadian Prime Minister Pierre Trudeau reflected on how quickly the accomplishments he was proud of had been reversed by the Clark government that followed his own.[104]

Today, elections in Hungary and Poland are free, but not fair. Democratically elected strongmen in countries such as Hungary and Poland used parliamentary majorities to push through new laws and constitutional amendments. The necessary checks and balances began falling away.[105] Ruling parties have eliminated checks and balances on executive power. After years of court stacking, the judiciary in both countries were no longer independent.[106]

Because of the backsliding of many countries such as Hungary and Poland, in 2019 Yascha Mounk states, "For the first time since the late nineteenth century, the cumulative GDP of autocracies now equals or exceeds that of Western Liberal democracies."[107]

The Flaw — The Legislative and Executive branches are not separate.

Seventh major flaw of the Parliamentary system.

The Prime Minister and the Cabinet are made up of elected individuals from Parliament.

Prime Minister Margaret Thatcher still had to service her constituency as a Member of Parliament for Finchley.[108]   By convention, all ministers in Great Britain must be members of the House of Commons or House of Lords, and there must be geographic distribution, so no part of the country is left out.[109] In this framework, the Queen approves the cabinet in Britain,[110] unlike the US where the Senate confirms all appointments. In the US Cabinet, the members may come from academia, business, or other elected officials who must give up their current position to take the cabinet post.

The Flaw — Ministers are only chosen from the elected members of Parliament who then have two jobs at the same time. Individuals in academia or business may not be selected.

Eighth major flaw of the Parliamentary system.

In September of 1977, Australian Patrick Gossage's view was, "the Cabinet system paralyzed, rather than facilitated, decision making, and a new framework was imperative."[111]

Margaret Thatcher on the use of a cabinet and how it affected the Dutch Prime Minister, "The notorious instability of coalition governments of the sort he led makes it immensely difficult to get clear decisions and stick to them."[112]

The British Cabinet is a committee made up of elected officials with the Prime Minister as the Chairman of said committee. The committee is also a coalition of multiple party members, and the agenda can often force a breakdown of the coalition and new elections may be needed. Whereas, in the US the President selects the cabinet members to be part of the administration. These cabinet members have no effect on the overall strategy and do not affect elections or the standing of the President. Because the President does not have to have a consensus of his cabinet to make decisions, the President can move faster in the decision-making process.

After Britain had declared war on Germany, Prime Minister Winston Churchill's cabinet wanted him to negotiate a peace deal with Hitler, which meant he was forced to make overtures for peace to Germany through Italy even though he knew it was not the right thing to do. Later, Churchill had to get his cabinet's approval to bomb

Berlin. As a contrast, according to the US Constitution, Congress has sole the power to declare war. However, a President could have said no on the peace overture that Churchill had to consider and as Commander-in-Chief make all the decisions about the use and direction of the armed forces, including dropping the atomic bomb on Japan.

During the First World War, Canadian Prime Minister Borden observed the limits of the British Empire and the relative ease of dealing with wartime Washington. When diplomats could be sidestepped, Americans talked business and made decisions as the British never could.[113]

The Flaw — Management is conducted by Committee/Cabinet rather than one true leader. No one person is responsible or accountable.

Ninth major flaw of the Parliamentary system.

There typically isn't a government-run primary to determine a party's nominee. The party typically has an internal process for selecting their representative.

Any system which allowed British Prime Minster Boris Johnson to sack 21 members from their own party for not supporting him in Brexit, is just wrong.[114] Any system that allows the dominant party to nominate someone for a "safe seat" in the Parliament is also wrong.

Winston Churchill,
Prime Minister of Great Britain
during the Second World War

The Flaw — The party selects who will represent the party in elections, not the people of the party. The individual also does not have to live in the district they represent.[115]

Tenth major flaw of the Parliamentary system.

Parliament can extend its own term as it did in the 1716 Septennial Act and during WWII, 1935-1944.[116]

The United States, even during the Civil War and the Second World War, still had elections.

The Flaw — The Parliament has the authority to stop having elections.

The One major advantage of the Parliamentary system.

Because elections can be called at any time, the Parliamentary system does not allow for politicians to start running for office until they know when the election is scheduled. The benefit is that unscheduled elections greatly shorten the timeframe available to solicit funding, advertise, and run for the office. In the US, elections are scheduled events and anyone may start running for a position one or two years in advance. In the case of the President, it could be even longer.

The Advantage —A shorter election cycle requires less money to run.

Summary

The constitutional form of government in the United States is not perfect; however, with primary elections where the people select the nominee, and not the party, along with term limits for President, the *checks and balance* of the Congress, the Executive branch, the Courts, and the codified constitution make for a more efficient and successful governing process.

As demonstrated, the US Presidential Republic with a liberal capitalist economic system is the best in the world. By using the US Constitution as a starting point, tweaking it to accommodate the Union of Ameristralia, and bringing it into the twenty-first century, is the best *framework* for proceeding forward. That doesn't preclude incorporating different ideas from the other countries into a new constitution in order to make it even better for everyone.

7

The Countries of the Proposed Union of Ameristralia

With the exception of the US, all the countries in the proposed Union have Parliamentary forms of government with two houses, with the exception of Iceland, Greenland, and New Zealand, which have a unicameral (one house) legislature.

Australia

Australia, officially the Commonwealth of Australia, is the driest and flattest inhabited continent on the planet and the sixth largest country by total area. Its population is nearly 26 million.[117] Australia is comprised of six states and ten territories (three internal and seven external sovereign territories offshore). States and territories are self-administered regions with a local legislature, police force, and certain civil authorities, and are represented in the Parliament of Australia.

The six states include New South Wales, Queensland, South Australia, Tasmania, Victoria, and Western Australia. The three internal territories are the Australian Capital Territory, the Jervis Bay Territory, and the Northern Territory. The seven external territories include Ashmore and Cartier Islands, the Australian Antarctic Territory, Christmas Island, the Cocos (Keeling) Islands, the Coral Sea Islands, Heard Island and McDonald Islands, and

Norfolk Island. Territories though, unlike states, rely on federal legislation and additional financial contributions to operate and have less representation in the Senate.

Australia with state boundaries and national and state capitals

In a way, Australia came into existence after the United States declared their independence from Britain in 1776. Britain was forced to stop sending their convicts to the North American colonies and, as a result, opted to send them to Australia, which had a very small indigenous population. The first ship set sail in May of 1787 and arrived eight months later in January of 1788.[118] Some Canadians were also sent to the penal colony in Australia.[119]

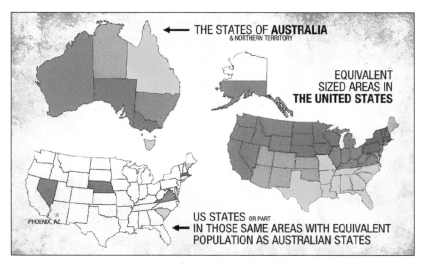

Comparison of Australia and US by Area

Australians often think of their country as the land of second chances. Many convicted and banished individuals from Mother Britain made the boat ride to Australia and were given a second chance to prosper. Many who arrived and had money, or a skill, to support themselves were given a "ticket of leave,"... in essence, a prison parolee, if they behaved themselves. Australia was the first to do this, and it worked.[120]

Initially, New Zealand was a part of Australia and both were the furthest settlements from Mother Britain. During the confederation process, Mother Britain wanted Fiji and New Zealand to stay and join with the Australian colonies from a strategic viewpoint.[121]

Britain withdrew its last garrison from Australia in 1870 and expected the colonies to defend themselves.[122] Subsequent fear of the French in the Pacific forced the Australian colonies to consider working together.

Australia first tried a weak and incomplete Federal Council in the early 1880s because New South Wales was suspicious of Victoria and thus prevented anything stronger.[123] Subsequently, over the next decade, it took two Constitutional Conventions to get the Federation passed.

Like the United States, in the 1800s, just about every Australian settler was well-supplied with firearms and taught how to use them for self-defense and hunting game. Use of firearms also allowed them protection from the native population and outlaws, called Bushrangers in Australia.[124]

Australian author Graham Patterson says that the Constitution of the US, Canada, and Switzerland were used as a reference in creating the Australian "piece of paper"—their Constitution.[125] Australia achieved self-government in 1901.[126]

During the Second World War, Australia expected an invasion by Japan and military planners were prepared to sacrifice the north of the continent as part of their strategy.[127] Ninety-seven Japanese attacks took place on northern Australia in 1942-43.[128] After Australia realized that Britain was unreliable and the United States entered the war in the Pacific, Australia received independence from Mother Britain in 1942.

It is my theory that the United States, as compared to Australia, Canada, and New Zealand, attracted more of the desperate (poor) free immigrants. Time and distance may have been the cause because to get to Australia or New Zealand it took more time (eight months on a ship) and money to get there, whereas the United States was much closer to Britain and Europe.[129] The warmer climate in the United States was better for agriculture than Canada and living in general. France also controlled a good portion of Canada until 1763—to further complicate the immigration issue. The overall living conditions may be a reason why the United States grew faster, bigger, and became stronger, subsequently fighting and winning independence from Britain. Australia, Canada, and New Zealand never fought or declared their independence from Mother Britain. The smaller populations and corresponding weaker economic strength kept the bond with Mother Britain mutually beneficial for both Mother and Siblings for a long time. I suspect after the US rebellion and subsequent independence, Britain learned to treat the remaining siblings a little nicer.

In 1933, Western Australia voted on the question of seceding from the Commonwealth of Australia because it thought it was being neglected.[130] Secession is not a unique desire, or political ploy. In Canada, the Province of Quebec has voted on the question of seceding from the nation on multiple occasions. Some Hawaiians claim their state should be its own country because the United States basically conquered their land. There will always be a minority group in each country or region that thinks it should be its own country.

A couple of interesting tidbits. First, Australia operates on a system of compulsory voting and has fines for those who do not vote.[131] Second, both Australia and New Zealand have a history of requiring compulsory arbitration.[132] Lastly, in 1856, Australia came up with the secret ballot (when voting) and the 8-hour workday.[133]

In 2007, Kevin Rudd changed the wording of the oath of office for Prime Minister and rather than swearing allegiance to the Queen and her heirs, he instead pledged his allegiance to "Australia, her land, and her people."[134] The rest of his ministers were sworn in using the new oath of office.[135] No law or constitutional change was approved, he just did it.

Victoria is the only State in Australia that has fixed Parliamentary terms of office. Their elections are always held on the last Saturday of November every fourth year.[136]

Threats in the Pacific region

Beijing has interfered in the domestic politics of other countries, including Australia, Canada, and New Zealand.[137] Richard McGregor, Australian journalist and author, notes that "Beijing's aim is to develop and dominate land and sea routes that connect Eurasia and the Indian Ocean and thus make China the hub of business and technology all the way to Europe,"[138] and then, "Soon after, China set about executing a long held plan to build large military bases in the South China Sea."[139]

In 2005, a Chinese diplomat named Chen Yonglin defected to Australia and later wrote, "The Communist Party of China has begun a structured effort to infiltrate Australia in a systematic way." The Australian authorities agree. Duncan Lewis, after retiring in

2019 as Director-General of Australia's main intelligence agency, went public with a warning about China's "insidious" agenda. Lewis said that the Chinese were not, "…only in politics but also in the community and in business…basically, pulling the strings from offshore." In 2018, after media accounts revealed a Chinese donor's under-the-table contributions to an Australian senator—who then provided counter surveillance advice to the Chinese donor—the senator was forced to resign his seat. What Australia is experiencing is a version of the strategic corruption that alarmed Americans in the 1930s and led to the passage of FARA (Foreign Agents Registration Act). In 2018, Australia enacted the Foreign Influence Transparency Scheme Act, which is based on FARA but improves on it.[140]

Kevin Rudd believes that Australia does not have the independent capacity to secure their territorial integrity, national sovereignty, or other fundamental national interests of its vast continent in an increasing chaotic region and world.[141] Many countries in Asia, including Australia, fear being left to fend for themselves in a region no longer anchored by US power.[142] At some point, Australia will be required to make a fateful choice between the United States and China.[143] In 2021, Australia signed a deal with the US and Britain to purchase nuclear powered submarines and include them in their fleet; a possible sign of the direction they are leaning.

A landmark treaty between Australia and Japan was signed on January 6, 2022. The Reciprocal Access Agreement (RAA) is a first for Japan with any other country other than the US. The RAA allows the Australian and Japanese militaries to work seamlessly with each other on defense and humanitarian operations.[144]

Superannuation and Budgeting

Australia is very self-reliant and fiscally conservative. I personally give Australia a standing ovation for its superannuation initiative. Superannuation is compulsory for all people who have worked and reside in Australia. The balance of a person's superannuation account is used to provide an income stream when retiring. The Australian government outlines a set percentage of employees' income that should be paid into a superannuation account, on top of standard wages or salaries. Employees are also encouraged to supplement compulsory superannuation contributions with voluntary contributions, including diverting their wages or salary income into superannuation contributions under so-called salary sacrifice arrangements.[145] What a great approach to provide a retirement program. In Britain during Margaret Thatcher's time, the social security budget took up a quarter of government spending.[146] In the US it is around 23% of the budget. Australia's approach is to basically take the government out of the loop and encourage individuals to be autonomous from the government and self-reliant. For the US this would be accomplished by taking the 12% currently going to the government for social security/retirement to go instead to the individual and put into an investment account the individual controls.

TRUTH:
Most people don't have the discipline to put away for the future, they are too worried about today.

Australia's superannuation plan came about in a 1983 agreement between government and unions when they agreed to put 3% of an employee's pay into an employees' superannuation account. Later, in 1992, under the Keating government, the compulsory employer portion came about. Superannuation in Australia will require a 12% contribution rate by 2025.[147]

In Australia, the entire 12% will be from the employer, while in the United States it is about 6% from the employer and 6% from the employee. So the United States has 12% of an individual's pay going to retirement and the employee never sees the money, it's just a line item on their paystub reporting they made a contribution to the government-run system. In Book Two we delve into to this in great detail.

As an example of Australia's financial self-restraint, in 2008, they projected a budget surplus of 22 billion, 1.8% of GDP.[148]

Eight of ten trading partners of Australia went into recession in 2009; Australia was the only advanced major economy not to have fallen into recession.[149]

Canada

Canada has a little over 38,000,000 residents. Canada has ten provinces and three territories, and is the second largest country based on land mass. The provinces consist of Alberta, British Columbia, New Brunswick, Newfoundland and Labrador, Nova Scotia, Manitoba, Ontario, Prince Edward Island, Quebec, and Saskatchewan. The three territories are: Northwest Territories, Nunavut and Yukon Territory. The provinces together collect more tax revenue than the Federal government. Both English and French are the official language of Canada, but English is much more prevalent.

Canada with Provinces and Territories

The British took over Quebec from the French in 1760. The Treaty of Paris in February of 1763 relinquished the French portions of Canada to the British and allowed for the liberty of the Catholic religion, as well as giving special rights to the French language.[150] This one act has hobbled Canada ever since.

The British North America Act of 1867 gave Canada self-rule but did not allow for amendments by the Canadians.[151] The Act assumed the reasonable long-run harmony of the French and English but was not embodied in the act and left it for ensuing generations to rediscover or neglect at their peril.[152] Much like the United States Constitution that pushed the slavery issues down the road for future generations, Canada has the same issue with French-speaking Quebec.

In the 1880s, D'Alton McCarthy, a Canadian parliamentarian, insisted that nations grow from common experiences and language and that Canada must be either British or French—a choice should be made. Geoffrey Marshall, a Canadian constitutional scholar, summarized Canada's experience as, "The world's most complex system of federal distribution, which remains an awe-inspiring example of what is to be avoided by any modern draftsman allocating Legislative powers."[153]

As part of the United States' Articles of Confederation in 1777, Canada was to be admitted by right into the United States and the other British colonies at the discretion of the American States.[154] The drafters of the Articles of Confederation were looking to the future. At the start of the War for Independence from Britain in 1776, George Washington and Benjamin Franklin both tried to make overtures to Canada to join with the original 13 colonies in our fight for independence. After the war was over and the peace treaty was being negotiated with Mother Britain, Benjamin Franklin, as the US negotiator, tried to get Canada to be part of the deal.[155] Obviously, it never happened but the effort was made before and after our War of Independence. There has been an historical and natural evolution of America and Canada into Ameristralia that was never realized earlier by our Founding Fathers.

After the French and Indian War (1754-1763) and the British took control of Canada, there have only been three historical points of friction between the United States and Canada. One was when America invaded Canada in 1775, hoping to get Canada on our side while we were fighting for independence from Mother Britain. The Canadians later drove out the Americans in 1776.[156] The second encounter was in 1812 when President Madison thought he could take over Canada but, after a few battles with the British, negotiated an end to the war with no boundary changes.[157] Lastly, in the 1840s, there was the Aroostock War, which ended in the boundary with Maine being finally settled.[158] In 1871, the Treaty of Washington was signed and all issues between Britain, Canada, and the United States were put to rest in the name of having a lasting peace between Canada and the United States.[159] The border between the United States and Canada is the longest undefended border on the planet.[160] There has always been a close relationship between the peoples of Canada and the United States, which bodes well for an assimilating relationship in Ameristralia.

Canada has a single criminal code as opposed to our fifty-one.[161] Ameristralia should learn from this single code system and I have incorporated the concept into the proposed new Union. In Canada, a majority government is guaranteed five years, although most prime ministers call an election in the fourth year.[162]

In Canada, the reserve powers such, as the dissolution of Parliament, had remained as a matter for the Crown's representative.[163] In 1952, Britain started to appoint a native-born Canadian to the post.[164] In October of 2008, the Prime Minister sought and received 'prorogation' from the Governor-General—the crown's representative.[165] Until 2008, the exercise of the Crown's prerogative had not been perceived to have an effect on the Canadian Federal government.[166]

Others Who Thought About Union

In the late 1800s, Erastus Wiman, a Canadian expatriate and New York millionaire, and Samuel Richie urged a "Continental

Union" of Canada and the United States.[167] Goldwin Smith, a former Oxford professor,[168] believed the logical first step to a transatlantic Englishspeaking union was by the full assimilation of French-Canadians into an American union.[169]

By the end of the 1880s, many agreed with Wilfrid Laurier, a member of the Parliament at that time and Prime Minister later in life, who said, "We have come to a period in the history of this young country when premature dissolution seems to be at hand."[170] Laurier also said, "There are few provinces, if any, in it today that would not rejoice to be out of it," the Dominion of Canada.[171] In 1887, J.W. Longley had been Attorney General in a Liberal government bent on repealing Nova Scotia's membership in the Dominion of Canada. Then, as Erastus Wiman's agent, he traveled the United States promoting Continental Union.[172] However, the time was not right.

Quebec and Trudeau

Prime Minister Pierre Trudeau became convinced and took his stand that Quebec would enjoy a better future inside Canada than separate from it within a renewed Canadian federalism.[173]

In 1965, the Pearson-appointed Royal Commission on Bilingualism and Biculturalism declared that Canada was passing through the "greatest crisis" in its history.[174]

On October 10, 1970, Pierre Laporte, the Quebec Minister of Labour and Immigration was playing football on a field across from his Saint-Lambert home. The Chenier cell of the Front de Libération du Québec (FLQ) kidnapped the Minister.[175] On October 17, 1970, Pierre Laporte's dead body was found after being strangled by the FLQ.[176] This brutal act turned ordinary Canadians against the separatists of Quebec. As Martin Luther King and Mahatma Gandhi preached, non-violence is the best way for the oppressed to make their case.

In 1969, Pierre Trudeau's government issued a White Paper that proposed to abolish the Indian Act and grant First Nations people "equal status and responsibility" to those of the other Canadians. The act was rejected by Aboriginal groups who saw it as an attempt to assimilate them into mainstream society.[177] Again, the Canadian government failed to create an environment where everyone could eventually assimilate into one Canadian culture. French-speaking Quebec and the Aboriginals revere their special status and reject equal status and a blended existence.

In 1959, the Official Languages Act was passed which guarantees the equality of the English and French languages in federal government.[178] In 1974, the Official Language Act was passed in Quebec, also known as Bill 22, making French the official language of Quebec. Bill 22 limited the right of French-speaking peoples, as well as allophones (residents whose primary language is neither French nor English), and anglophones (residents whose primary language is English) to send their children to English schools. Restrictions on advertising only in English were also put into place.[179] In these examples, the government is permanently putting a wedge between the French-speaking and English-speaking citizens of Canada. The end result is no longer a hoped for assimilation of both groups but permanent separation.

In 1978, the Cullen-Couture immigration accord was agreed to, which permitted Quebec to play a direct role in selecting immigrants to its province.[180] Two years later on May 20, 1980, 88% of Quebecers voted: 40.5% voted Yes for separation and 59.5% voted not to separate. Even francophones (French-speaking Quebeckers) said no.[181]

Pierre Trudeau appeared on television on October 2, 1980, and announced his plan to patriate the Constitution unilaterally.[182] April 16, 1981, the "gang of eight" opposing Provincial governors met[183] and Trudeau told them he would seek unilateral patriation. If that request was rejected by the British Parliament, he would put it to the pubic in a referendum as a declaration of independence for a sovereign Canada.[184] November 5, 1981, marked one of Trudeau's greatest triumphs, he got the premiers to agree to a deal.[185] On April 17, 1982, in Ottawa, the Queen signed the Royal Proclamation of the Constitution. Pierre Trudeau declared that at long last Canada had complete national sovereignty.[186]

On October 30, 1995, Quebecers voted again for separation. Ninety percent of Quebeckers voted; 49.4% said Yes and 50.6% said No.[187] An early 2000 poll showed sovereignty support had dwindled to less than a third of Quebecers; most young people seemed to be sick of the issue.[188] Desmond Morton, a Canadian historian, says, "Young Canadians ignore differences of color, culture, and customs," and in America, our youth act much the same way. In reference to Quebec, Morton also thinks that, "Whatever the temptations, geography makes it hard to live apart."[189] The same may be said of the relationship of Canada and the US.

The Quebec business community, traditionally dominated by anglophones, was deeply integrated within the North American context and was fearful of Quebec independence and the socialism of the Parti Québecois. According to a study at the time, eleven home offices had left Quebec in 1975, sixty-one in 1976, and the pace had quickened in 1977.[190] Another study showed that Quebec-based stocks had suffered relatively greater losses than other Canadian or American stocks after the provincial election.[191] In 1978, the board of Sun Life confirmed that the major insurance firm would move from French-speaking Montreal to English-speaking Toronto.[192]

In my view, Canada will have to decide whether everyone will speak the same language, or not. The Union of Ameristralia will stand as one English-speaking nation for the long-term.

Greenland

At one point, the Danish crown lost and forgot about Greenland, which they acquired in 1380 when Norway came under Danish rule. Then, in 1721, a Norwegian clergyman, Hans Egede, persuaded the Danish government to fund a mission to Greenland mainly to convert the descendants of Norsemen to the Lutheran religion. He didn't find anyone there and it marked the beginning of real Danish rule in Greenland.[193]

Greenland is the world's largest island with a population of 56,000. On May 1, 1979, Greenland became a self-ruling

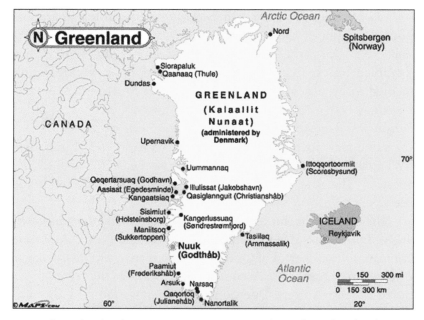

Greenland with major cities in proximity to Canada and Iceland

autonomous territory within the Kingdom of Denmark and has two representatives in the Danish Parliament.[194] Denmark provides an annual block grant of 3.2 billion Danish kroner, but as Greenland begins to collect revenues from its natural resources, the grant will gradually be diminished.

Germany did establish a small weather station on the island during the Second World War. As a result, the United States preemptively invaded Greenland in the Second World War in order to keep Germany from invading and were able to remove the Germans and their weather station.

In 1946, President Harry Truman offered to buy Greenland for $100 million dollars.[195] In 2019, Donald Trump revived the proposal for the purchase of Greenland from Denmark but received a cold shoulder. Land prices briefly rose on the speculation that United States might take over, providing investors a stable and predictable legal environment to do business. Again, people like a stable and predictable environment for investments and the US would have provided that stability. Ameristralia would do the same.

On June 21, 2009, Greenland gained self-rule with provisions for assuming responsibility for self-government of judicial affairs, policing, and natural resources. These provisions are generally considered to be a step toward eventual full independence from Denmark. Additionally, Greenlanders were recognized as a separate people under international law; however, Denmark maintains control of foreign affairs and defense matters.

In 2018, China tried to finance three airports on the island in an effort to get a foothold there.[196] China's Road and Bridges initiative is a strategy to establish a relationship with other developing countries, especially in places such as Africa and Central and South America. Once the relationship is established, then China tries to help extract strategic minerals and resources out of the country for their use and control. Greenland is central to the United States' growing competition in the Arctic with China and Russia. Constant strategic realignment means Greenland cannot be ignored again, as was the case prior to the Second World War. With a population of less than 60,000 residents, Greenland has no means to defend itself and needs a long-term partner for growth and prosperity. Ameristralia is the answer.

In my opinion, Greenland is still a part of Denmark because Greenland has not been offered a better arrangement and, therefore, it has not asked for independence from Denmark.

Iceland

Iceland is home to about 365,000 people and, prior to the Covid pandemic, it was attracting two million tourists a year. There were more visitors in a year than the sum total of all the Icelanders who have ever lived on the island. That is because Iceland had a population that hovered for centuries near 50,000 (much like Greenland) only breaking the 100,000 mark in 1926.[197] According to Orkustofnon, the National Energy Authority of Iceland, Geothermal energy accounts for 2/3 of their primary energy use.

Settlers left Norway and inhabited Iceland in order to escape the tyranny of the Norwegian king.[198] Icelandic culture contains a strange mixture of primitiveness and self-reliance.[199]

The continental Teutonic plates from North America and Europe meet in Iceland.[200]

In the eighteenth and nineteenth centuries, Icelandic farmers rarely stayed at the same farm. Their mobility, both social and geographical, greatly contributed to creating a relatively homogeneous culture with practically a complete absence of dialects.[201]

In 1808, a group of Englishmen advocated the annexation of Iceland by Britain. A ship was sent to Iceland with Jorgen Jorgensen (a former Danish prisoner of war who also acted as an interpreter) and Samuel Phelps who ran a soap factory in Lambeth. The expedition was unsuccessful. A second ship with a British naval vessel escort was sent the following summer. On Sunday, June 25,1809, thirteen armed men stormed the governor's house, captured him, and took him aboard their ship. The British were able to overthrow Danish rule with 13 soldiers and the capture of one person. Iceland was to be an independent country under British rule. After August 22, when the captain of the British naval vessel learned Jorgensen had acted on his own, without being sanctioned by Britain, the captain restored power back to Iceland's governor.[202]

The British could have attacked at any time and taken Iceland.[203] From a military point of view, Iceland was a liability for Denmark because it was too large and too distant to make it worth defending. Britain had the same issue with Canada. But, as with Canada where the British eventually gave into the younger Sibling's and submitted to their requests, primarily for independence and freedom, the Danes eventually gave into the Icelandic demands for independence.

The British invaded and occupied Iceland on May 10, 1940, with the stated purpose to make sure the Germans did not invade as they eventually did in Norway in June of 1940. Some of the British troops included Canadians. On July 7, 1941, the British transferred that responsibility over to the United States with the understanding that the US would leave after the war was over. The United States came with 60,000 men.[204]

British troops finally left Iceland in the spring of 1946. In the following summer, Iceland signed a treaty with the United States to leave in a little over six years because the US needed to keep staff and supplies at the airport in Iceland due to the US presence in Germany in the post-war period after the Second World War. The last American soldier left in May of 1947; however, over 600 Americans stayed at the airport.[205]

When the communists invaded Korea, the United States again signed a treaty with Iceland to station troops there and took over the military defense of Iceland. American forces started arriving on May 7, 1951,[206] and all forces subsequently left Iceland in 2006.

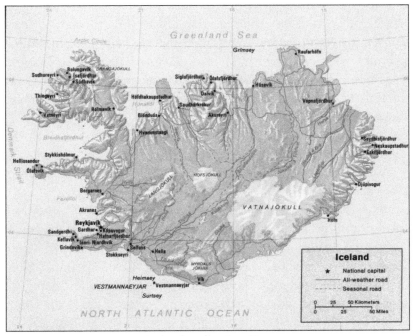

Iceland and major cities

Icelandic schools teach all children Danish and English, as well as Icelandic. Iceland has a purist language policy. No foreign words are used in the Icelandic language.[207] So when the world knows and understands a new word, Iceland would rather make up a new word so that its 360,000 inhabitants can keep their language pure and unique. The French do the same thing. For both Iceland and France this does not make any sense and it doesn't aid in assimilation. If the word "disk" is invented as part of the digital revolution, why create a brand-new different word to confuse people (in France it is the "disque" and in Iceland it is "diskur"). Why not accept the universal new word that everyone knows and understands?

During the Viking Age and Middle Ages, Denmark and Iceland shared a common language, which linked Iceland to the continent. Denmark's lack of interest in Iceland from 1380 until the seventeenth century allowed the Icelanders to evolve their own unique language and a geographic remoteness that distinguished itself.[208] In 1816, Rasmus Christian Rask instigated the establishment of the Icelandic Society in an effort to save the Icelandic language.[209] In the digital age, however, that is becoming more difficult. A recent *Wall Street Journal* article discusses how the digital age is producing young people who speak English when discussing computer games and television. Many young children in Iceland speak English without an Icelandic accent but also speak Icelandic with an English influence now.[210]

One last tidbit: in 1980, Iceland was the first country in the modern world to directly elect a woman as President.[211]

New Zealand

New Zealand has a population of about 5,000,000. From its inception, New Zealand has had a long affiliation with Australia. Originally, it was part of the New South Wales colony.[212] New Zealand also has the territories of the Cook Islands, Nieu (pronounced Nyoo-Ay), the Ross Dependency and Tokelau. The Cook Islands and Niue are self-governing states in free association with New Zealand.

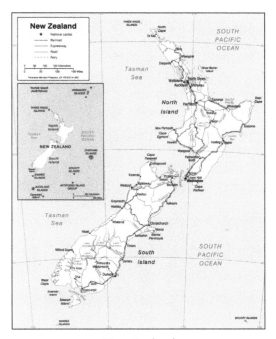

New Zealand

Because of it's geographical distance from Mother Britain, New Zealand developed an emphasis on self-reliance. New Zealand attained constitutional independence by ratifying the Statute of Westminster in 1947, five years after Australia.[213]

Originally, New Zealand had 10 provinces, which were eliminated and replaced with a strong central government as a result of the 1875 Abolition of Provinces Act. New Zealand is officially a bicultural and bilingual country,[214] just like Canada. The other culture and language is the indigenous Maori. In the 1970s, New Zealand built air strips in the Cook Islands, Niue, and Samoa. Consequently, twice as many Cook Islanders live in New Zealand rather than on Cook Island, and the bulk of Nieueans have left their coral outcrop for New Zealand.[215] People tend to migrate toward opportunities.

New Zealand has a long history of unarmed police that dates back to 1886 when its national police force was established.[216]

New Zealand was the first democratic country to give women the right to vote in 1893. Also, New Zealand sacrificed more lives per capita than any other in the Second World War.

Although New Zealand joined the Australia, New Zealand, and United States Security Treaty (ANZUS) in 1951, in 1985 the New Zealand Labour Party pursued policies for New Zealand to be nuclear-free and banned any vessel that had the capacity of carrying nuclear weapons or that used nuclear power. As a result, in 1985, they would not allow the USS Buchanan in its waters creating a cold spell with the United States on defense issues.[217] The United States later took formal steps to suspend the alliance with New Zealand and they went from "ally" to "friend."[218]

United Kingdom

Officially known as the United Kingdom of Great Britain and Northern Ireland it has a population of about 67,000,000. The United Kingdom is comprised of England, Northern Ireland, the Principality of Wales, and Scotland. The Channel Islands (consisting of two bailiwicks) are not part of the United Kingdom, but rather a Crown Dependency. They sit in the English Channel and have a population of about 170,000. The United Kingdom has 14 overseas territories: Anguilla, Bermuda, British Antarctic Territory, British Indian Ocean Territory (Chagos Archipelago, primarily Diego Garcia), British Virgin Islands, Cayman Islands, Falkland Islands, Gibraltar, Saint Helena, Ascension and Tristan da Cunha, the Turks and Caicos Islands, Pitcairn Island, South Georgia, and South Sandwich Islands, Akrotiri and Dhekelia on the island of Cyprus. The total population is 250,000 for all.

Ireland signed the Anglo-Irish Treaty on December 6, 1921, after the Irish War of Independence. Exactly one year later, the Irish free state was a self-governing dominion.

The United States has maintained a "special relationship" with the United Kingdom, our Mother. Long after American independence, the many ties of history, culture, and language still survive, even after two world wars.

The United Kingdom

Mother Britain continues to exert its own independence. For example, in 1973, Britain joined the European Economic Community (EEC). The EEC eventually evolved into the European Union (EU) and grew far beyond an international federation of sovereign states and into something more ambitious and intrusive.[219]

In 1985, Jacques Delores, the President of the EU, emphasized pan-European rules on matters of trade, regulations, and public procurement and put economic and financial connectedness first and political sovereignty second.[220] Margaret Thatcher, when talking about the EU, said that the control of the British economy was transferred from the elected government, answerable to Parliament and the electorate, to unaccountable supranational institutions.[221] Because of Brexit, on January 1, 2021, decades of unencumbered trade and movement of its citizens between Britain and the EU ceased and is one of several changes likely to have big and lasting effects on the British economy. The rights of a British citizen to live, work, or study in any other EU member state also fell away, highlighting the extent of the EU's reach into its citizens' daily lives. EU citizens also lost those rights in Britain.[222]

After the Second World War and the vast devastation in the European countries, the only solution was for government to act as a safety net for its citizens. Almost all infrastructure and businesses were wiped out on the European continent. I believe this is the reason so many European governments lean Socialist today. In credit to the British people and Prime Minister Thatcher, they began the process of returning state-owned business and assets to the private sector and made the turn away from many socialist ideals.[223] Thatcher said, "Unlike the US, Britain had to cope with the poisonous legacy of socialism—nationalization, trade union power, a deeply rooted anti-enterprise culture."[224] Also at the time, Prime Minister Thatcher thought, "What was clearly lacking was a sense of pride and personal responsibility—something which the state can easily remove but almost never give back."[225] She also said, "In particular, welfare arrangements encouraged dependency and discourage a sense of responsibility, and television undermined common moral values that would have united working-class communities."[226]

Margaret Thatcher

In the European Union, in 1992, the Maastricht Treaty radically altered European markets by enshrining specific economic policy choices in supranational agreements that could be changed only by a unanimous vote. The problem was they did not concern themselves much with the possibility of democratic backsliding (removing the checks and balances in governmental systems), which has emerged as the main threat in newer European Union members, such as Hungary and Poland.[227] Dictatorships in countries such as Hungary and Turkey all came to power by winning free and fair elections with an anti-elitist and anti-pluralist message.[228]

Britain has a traditionally short election cycle for campaigning—roughly five weeks—due to the Parliamentary system and can call an election at any moment. Britain doesn't restrict how much money is given to candidates for office but can restrict what the candidate may spend, thus lessening the need for a vast quantity of money to run a campaign.[229] Ameristralia can learn from this in drafting our new constitution and is incorporated in the proposed constitution in Book Two.

As with Australia (Western Australia), Canada (Quebec), and the United States (Hawaii), the United Kingdom had Scotland hold a referendum on leaving the UK in 2014, with Scots rejecting independence by a comfortable margin."[230]

Other Countries are Welcome
All British Commonwealth countries obviously would make a great fit into Ameristralia in the near term. But other non-English speaking countries, including Japan, South Korea, and Taiwan may want to join as a way to ensure their safety and way of life from the mounting Chinese and Russian threats in their region. At one point after the Second World War, Congress received a petition from Japan to make it the forty-ninth state.[231] The petition was prior to the United States adding Alaska and Hawaii as the 49th and 50th states. With the mounting Chinese build up in the South China Sea, it is my guess that China will invade Taiwan in the next few years as it did with the island of Hainan in 1950, or choke it off from the rest of the world until it relents.

Freedom is not free and sitting on the sidelines is not okay, which is akin to people in any country, state, or city who subvert the economy by not paying their rightful taxes that go to help pay for roads, police, courts, schools, sidewalks, and parks. Politicians are often afraid to make the hard choices. Some smaller and/or "neutral" countries have felt compelled to maintain peace and freedom on the planet by not engaging—acting as harmless sheep so as not to be a threat to their neighbors and hopefully be left alone. Political leaders have a fiduciary responsibility to ensure the long-term safety of its citizens. No free riders.

There is truth in Benjamin Franklin's old saying, "If you make yourself a sheep, the wolves will eat you."[232] Tibet was a sheep and China ate it! As a country you cannot assume that if you don't pose a risk to your neighbors, they will leave you alone. With the Russian invasion of Ukraine and the Chinese air incursions over Taiwan, the world is being warned.

Summary

We can learn a great deal through the different history and experiences of these other countries. For example: from Australia, we can include superannuation, which I later call Long-Term Individual Security Accounts (LISAs); from Canada, we can learn to have one penal code for the entire country; from Britain (and other parliamentary systems) we can learn how to have a shorter election cycle for campaigning. These concepts will be applied in Book Two. We learn from the experience of others on how best to do things. The key is we all have a common heritage, and almost all citizens speak English. Success will require that the uniting parties have the same core values. Those core values are enumerated in the next section.

CHAPTER

8

Basic Overriding Core Values And Principles

In life and government there are several overriding core values and principles throughout the world that must be taken into account with any constitutional foundation.

1) The Family Unit

The family unit has been the central cultural focus of all civilizations since the dawn of mankind. Government should not do anything via laws, regulations, or distribution of benefits that would discourage the family unit from forming and staying together. The following are two examples of how the US government discourages the family unit. First, if a couple is married filing a joint return, the tax rate is higher because they are married versus being single. The government recognizes that families have financial *economies of scale* and can afford to pay more, thus penalizing couples for being married. Similarly, a former business acquaintance in Topeka, Kansas, was involved in a car wreck and ended up paralyzed in a wheelchair. In order for my business acquaintance to get the necessary government assistance, he had to divorce his wife and set himself up in an apartment, separate from his wife and kids, in order to qualify for disability assistance, and forcing the now ex-wife to become a single parent in raising her children. Forcing the husband to remove himself from his family, denied him the support they could have provided him. He was forced to sacrifice his day-to-day relationship with his children. Such a practice is wrong on many levels.

John Iceland, a demographer and researcher at Penn State University notes the difference in family structure is the most significant variable in explaining the financial affluence gap. Unable to pool earnings with a spouse, to take advantage of economies of scale, and to share childcare, single parents have a tougher time than their married counterparts in building a nest egg.[233]

In 2014, Rabbi Johnathan Sacks, the former chief rabbi of the United Kingdom said, "The family, man, woman, and child, is not one lifestyle choice among many. It is the best means we have yet discovered for nurturing future generations and enabling children to grow in a matrix of stability and love."[234]

The family unit is important because it provides a framework for the younger generation to learn the norms and customs that keep a society going. A family teaches children to care and honor those who have come before them because they have worked hard to allow the younger generation to be where they are today.

Theodore Roosevelt said, "It is hardly necessary to say that the highest idea of the family is attainable only where the father and mother stand to each other as lovers and friends. In these homes the children are bound to father and mother by ties of love, respect, and obedience, which are simply strengthened by the fact that they are treated as reasonable beings with rights of their own, and the rule of the household is changed to suit the changing years, as childhood passes into manhood and womanhood."[235]

One of the largest impacts on the nuclear family occurred from the late 1950s through the mid-1970s—the interstate highway system. The highway system facilitated an unprecedented expansion of mobility. More than 90 percent of the nation's households have access to automobiles, and by extension, to the nation's highway system. More than any component of that system, the interstate highway system has expanded the options of people to travel within and between their communities. Coupled with air travel, the ability to move to anywhere in the country for education, employment, or other interests often means separation from parents, grandparents, aunts, uncles, and other extended family members—the family support system. Furthermore, economic necessity drove many women to the workplace and many children had to fend for themselves. As a result, daycare became a thriving business.

In December of 2015, the Pew Research Center published its findings on the state of the American family.[236] The family unit of the twenty-first century is distinct from the traditional family of the nineteenth and twentieth centuries. Families are much more diverse and complex as blended families are normalized. Besides the rise in divorce and remarriage rates, birthrates and fertility are on the decline and having children out of wedlock is no longer seen as a taboo.[237]

Parenting is often a tag team event that requires both parents to be actively involved in the children's upbringing. Having both parents living and working together provides economies of scale for the family unit. The caregiver in the family provides the glue that holds the family together, but unfortunately, they are often at a financial disadvantage.

2) Language Assimilation

When someone emigrates to the US they consciously or subconsciously understand that they will have to learn English along the way. Someone wanting to become a full member of society must be willing and able to speak the language of that country. Not learning the language of the country where they have immigrated to, or been brought to, often means they will end up disenfranchised. Being disenfranchised and hiding in the shadows is not only detrimental to the individual and their ability to thrive, but to their family as well.

While there are over one-billion English speakers, only a third consider English their native language.[238] What the billion plus understand is that if you want to be able to move about the planet to learn and work, you must learn English. Plenty of documentation exists showing that young children are able to learn languages at a faster rate. Speaking English around babies and children ensures they will master the language. Embracing English in Ameristralia not only ensures equal access in our society, but using one language is also more efficient for the school system, business, and government and eliminates duplication of signage and materials for agencies and the government. An example of the burden of supporting two languages rather than just one is the province of Quebec in Canada, where French takes precedence over English. Quebec requires French to be spoken and displayed, although, for the most part, the rest of Canada speaks English.

The International Civil Aviation Organization established English as the de facto aviation language for international flights in the 1950s.[239] In the 1950s a Soviet plane carrying Russia's foreign minister to London twice overshot Heathrow Airport and nearly crashed because the pilot struggled to understand the control tower's instructions.[240] The United Nation's specialized agency recognized that a common language—English—is beneficial for safety, efficiency, and security in air travel.

While aviation has formally adopted English as the official language, English has also become the most dominant language in the business world. The prominence of English in most business settings stems from the rise of the Industrial Revolution where the United States and the United Kingdom were the most prosperous over the last two centuries.[241] Companies from around the world rely on English to communicate with other business entities and to reach more customers globally.

After receiving their freedom from Mother Britain's imperialistic ways, many colonies tried to get back to their language roots by trying to discourage the English language in their country, but later realized their error. For example, Sri Lanka, which once passed the Sinhala Only Act to get rid of English in its country, has now restored English to its former official status. The same is true for Singapore, which had replaced English with Malay at one point, and then later launched a Speak Good English movement in 2000.[242] In 1978, China restored English as a permissible foreign language and encouraged it as a part of China's path to prosperity. Today, the top Chinese universities offer hundreds of degree programs in subjects ranging from history to nuclear physics which are all taught in English.[243]

TRUTH:
Language is not the same thing as Culture.

- If you eat a French meal at a nice French restaurant, it can be appreciated and tastes just as good whether you speak French or English.
- Wearing clothing such as a German dirndl or lederhosen is a cultural touchstone for the southern Germans, but also can be worn and enjoyed in any language or any continent to celebrate Germany's traditional Octoberfest.
- French architecture in New Orleans can be appreciated by all who come, no matter what language they speak.

All cultures have their holidays that can be celebrated by families in the traditions of their homelands.

As David Crystal, a British linguist and academic has pointed out, you hear English spoken by politicians from all over the world. Wherever you travel, you see English signs and advertisements. Whenever you enter a hotel or restaurant in a foreign city, most often they will understand English, and there will be an English menu.[244]

3) Competition Creates Accountability
Competition provides the opportunity to make all of us better and gain more accountability in our everyday lives.

Individuals
Anyone exploring the early frontiers of America, Australia, Canada, Greenland, Iceland, and New Zealand learned Nature's

Law. If you don't work, you don't eat, then you and your family perish. The laws of nature provide the ultimate accountability of a person and of a family. You must also put away food and other reserves for any bad times, downturns, or disasters you may encounter in your lifetime. You had to compete with Mother Nature in the Agrarian Age.

Individuals may compete to make a team by practicing harder and longer in order to get better, giving themselves the opportunity to beat out others trying for the same team. If you don't practice, further your education, and make yourself better, the likelihood of making a team, getting into a prestigious college, or achieving the dream job greatly diminishes.

For a while, I officiated grade school aged kids playing basketball. I was amazed when I learned that there would be no score kept. In other words, no winners or losers. Society and nature do not operate that way, and I could see the parents of those young basketball players still keeping score. Business does not work in a scoreless environment either. In life there are always winners and losers, and kids should learn this early on so they are prepared for life and learn to compete. Also, if you lose the game today, there will be another game next week, and so on. You always have a chance to get better and win the next time. Losing provides the hunger to get better. When families play games in the privacy of their homes (Monopoly, Risk, Chutes and Ladders, etc.), they typically play until a winner is declared. I remember watching my granddaughter's first volleyball game. About halfway through the game, the coach instructed the players how to do a "high five" to celebrate a score or good play. She gave them positive reinforcement for scoring on the opponent and reinforcing the concept of teamwork.

Education is important to everyone's financial success. First, and most obvious, is the importance that everyone have, at a minimum, a high school diploma or equivalent. Even so, a high school diploma does not provide unique skills to make a person valuable to an employer. Specific skills are necessary for financial success. For example, more people should explore various trades and get vocational training or enter into apprenticeship programs for careers such as machinist, electrician, welder, plumber, and the like. Not everyone is meant for college. Find your niche in life and be proficient at your trade.

In this competition of life, college or a solid trade is often a necessary hurdle to qualify for many valued jobs. Specific degrees provide certification in architecture, accounting, engineering, law, education, etc. Although general degrees such as Philosophy, Liberal Arts, Social Studies, Political Science, etc., do not provide professional certification. Liberal Arts degrees show the ability to complete complex tasks, assignments, and develop critical thinking skills.

In his book *You Can Do Anything: The Surprising Power of a "Useless" Liberal Arts Education, Forbes Magazine* contributor George Anders' says, "Companies are looking for five key qualities in potential employees: an eagerness to tackle uncharted areas; the ability to solve murky problems; well-honed analytic methods; keen awareness of group dynamics;—and an ability to inspire and persuade others."[245]

Business

If a business holds a monopoly position in the market they are not going to strive to make their customers happy, or innovate in order to provide a better product or service. Utility companies, which quite often are monopolies, are typically heavily regulated to ensure their customers are treated fairly. However, if there are many competitors in the market, customer satisfaction becomes a focus and companies innovate to meet their future needs. The market (where the market allows) and customers, not government, should hold companies accountable, and, when unhappy with a current provider, seek out other businesses offering the same service.

In August of 1997, Bill Gates (co-founded Microsoft) made a $150 million-dollar investment in Apple, which was on the brink of bankruptcy and a competitor. During this time Microsoft was in the midst of an image-tarnishing antitrust fight over its heavy-handed promotion of Internet Explorer during the height of the browser wars with Netscape. As part of the investment, Apple also agreed to drop a long-running lawsuit in which they alleged Microsoft copied the look and feel of the Mac OS for Windows and to make Internet Explorer the default browser on its computers.[246] Bill Gates and Steve Jobs acknowledged that both companies should not have a goal of destroying the other because competition worked to their mutual benefits. For example, when Apple opened the Apple Stores across the country to provide personal assistance to the users of their products, Microsoft eventually followed suit in places such as Overland Park, Kansas and Austin, Texas. Without the competition this would probably never have happened. The competition between Apple and Microsoft is good for the consumer.

American car makers had the market to themselves until the 1960s. The American cars seemed to be designed with planned obsolescence in mind—falling apart after a certain number of years. Then the Japanese entered the car market with inexpensive and qualitybuilt cars. Amazingly, the American market loved cars that were inexpensive and built to last many, many years. The auto industry competition resulted in a vast number of choices for the American consumer and those choices were better built cars that would last for a long time.

Government

Government is a monopoly. If a nation, Provate, or municipality taxes excessively and/or overregulates a business then that business may try to move to another jurisdiction. While a nation, Provate, or municipality may offer lower taxes to entice a company to move to their location as a job creator, that nation, Provate, or municipality should be transparent with their citizens to the trade-offs. As an example, a high-tech company received substantial tax breaks in Austin, Texas, in the 1990s. When the term of those tax breaks ended, the company picked up and moved someplace else, chasing the better deal. The citizens of Austin were the ones stuck with paying a higher tax rate. That same company started up in Ireland because they had a low tax rate, which encouraged the business to move its operations there. A few years later, the company received a better deal in an Eastern European country, shut the Irish operation down, and moved.

Competition is good, even in government, but infrastructure, housing, or other services may be required to support the businesses moving into an area. The citizens of a municipality must decide if they want new businesses to pay the going rate of taxes or if the citizens want to take on any potential tax burden as a tradeoff for the promised economic growth.

In 2010 Australia candidate Julia Gillard, gave her solemn pre-election commitment never to introduce a carbon tax.[247] When she got into office, she had to make a deal with the Green Party as part of a ruling coalition which negated that promise.[248] The parliamentary system required compromise between the parties to get into the office as opposed to America's Presidential system, which would have allowed her to veto any carbon tax as she had promised. The problem with elected officials is that you trust them to do what they say they are going to do, but often they do not follow through. However, before they can be held accountable at the next election—the competition—the damage is already done.

In a *Wall Street Journal* article about accountability, the administrator of the EPA stated:

> "These regulators then invoke science to justify their actions, often without letting the public study the underlying data. Part of transparency [trust] is making sure the public knows what facts and bases the agency is relying on to make its decisions. When agencies defer to experts in private without review from citizens, distinctions get flattened and the testing and deliberation of science is precluded. In the EPA example, transparency [trust] would provide increased opportunities for the public to access the 'dose-response' data that underlie significant regulations and influential scientific information. Dose-response data explain the relationship between

the amount of a chemical or pollutant and its effect on human health and the environment—and are the foundation of the EPA's regulations. If the American people are to be regulated by interpretation of these scientific studies, they deserve to scrutinize the data as part of the scientific process and American self-government."[249]

The citizens must be able to view the detailed background data to determine if games are being played with the data. Here, without the data/information behind the rationale being public—thus submitting the data to competing data—there is no accountability.

People are free to choose where they live and what amenities and/or circumstances they want in that location. The citizens should be telling the governing bodies what their expectations are and what they are willing to contribute, not the other way around. For example, a government body may decrease competition by raising licensing requirements of individuals or businesses. Whether it is a license to cut hair or do carpentry work, the licensing often restricts the supply of labor in the market. The requirement for licensing should correspond to the risk involved.

In Florida in June of 2020, the Occupational Freedom and Opportunity Act was signed by the governor, Ron DeSantis. The focus is on removing unnecessary barriers that make it harder for people to enter certain professions, thus creating more competition. Whole categories, including nail technicians, body wrappers, and makeup artists no longer have to get a license. It was the largest licensing deregulation in Florida's history. In the 1950s only about 5% of American's workers were licensed, but today some 19% are licensed. The regulatory calcification is a major barrier to economic upward mobility.[250] It is up to each individual consumer to decide which vendor to use for a given service and through referrals by friends, research on the internet, and experience find the best provider. Competition in the market will over time weed out service providers who are less qualified.

Education

Parents should decide how their children are educated and where. Public schools are intended to provide basic skills such as reading, writing, math, citizenship, and civility. Over many decades, public schools have been burdened with everything from food security, to child welfare, to de facto parenting. Taxes are used to fund metal detectors and campus police instead of educators and textbooks. Many parents are opting to homeschool their children. An estimated 1.7 million students are homeschooled, which is roughly the size of the Los Angeles and Chicago public school systems combined.[251] There has been a significant increase in charter schools and according to the National Center for Education Statistics, in 2016, about 41% of students enrolled in first through twelfth grade were in schools chosen by parents.[252] The rise in school choice illustrates that competition in education is valued and necessary.

In Denver, a rating system was designed to help parents make more informed choices and steer more resources to underperforming schools (or close them if necessary). The most important issue is choice. Charters have more flexibility in hiring, compensation and curricular policies. That's an existential threat to union control of education.[253] The Denver charter schools have performed well and the Stanford's City Studies project finds impressive test-scores improvement in Denver relative to the rest of the state. One finding was that African-American students attending Denver charter schools posted greater learning gains in reading than students at traditional public schools.[254] Competition in schools makes schools accountable and if they don't produce the desired results parents will move their children to a school that does.

In his book *Neither Liberal Nor Conservative Be*, Larry Bradley states that "practical courses in money management, business ownership, sales, negotiation, statistics and other similar subjects should be part of the curriculum."[255] He also thinks we must have physical education all the way through high school in order to combat obesity. Basically, schools should prepare kids for life.

Employment Autonomy

People don't want to feel trapped in a job.

Some current employment benefits can also be a barrier to employment autonomy. While the employer may be making contributions to a retirement fund, that fund is not the employees until vested in the employer's plan.[256] The vesting schedule, which often covers percentages over years, is a way to keep an employee put—in essence holding the employee hostage. The employee must be willing to stick it out or forfeit those contributions and start over again at another job.

When Social Security was introduced in 1935, life expectancy was lower. Today, workers lack confidence in Social Security because they are paying higher payroll taxes and don't think the program will be solvent by the time they retire. One of the most widely discussed reform plans is to scale back traditional Social Security benefits and replace them fully or partially with a privately managed system of individual retirements accounts. Such accounts could be run independently of Social Security or as an additional component of the existing system.[257]

Consequently, in Book Two I put forth a privately managed system titled LISAs (Long-Term Individual Security Accounts). I propose that both spouses (or partners) share equally in the retirement savings of the other. So of the 11% put into the LISA for a given individual, half would go to the one who earned it and the other half to their spouse, and vice versa if both spouses work. As a true partnership, the couple saves for retirement equally.

For bad marriages (or partnerships) LISAs are a way for either spouse to leave the relationship and have the same financial security to rely on for the transition out of the relationship. LISA removes the impediment of remaining in a relationship for financial reasons.

All working people—whether working for an employer or self-employed—will have a LISA, which is run by an independent third party that they take with them from job-to-job. Employers may opt to make matching contributions into an account as they do for 401(k) programs in the US today. Employers may also make additional pension fund contribution on their own or negotiated with their employees. The LISA approach gives individuals economic autonomy and freedom.

Personal choice in retirement planning should not be surrendered to an employer, union, or the government. Individuals should be free to choose where they work, how they save and spend their money, and how they want to prepare for funding later in life. With the increase of life expectancy decades beyond 65, many people are choosing to change careers or have multiple careers in their lifetime. Instead of a "nanny state," from an early age, children should be taught the value of saving money. Good financial health is as much a personal responsibility as maintaining physical health.

The ultimate goal of Ameristralia is to give people as much financial and personal freedom as possible to fulfill their dreams and give them the best chance of happiness, which is a simple and honorable goal.

4) Risk and Rewards in Society – "The Dream"

The American Dream, or the Australian Dream, Canadian Dream, Icelandic Dream, Greenlander Dream, or New Zealander Dream shares the story of ancestors who left mostly European countries for a better life in a new location, looking for a second chance. Some were seeking a place to practice their religion, some wanted their own land or farm, which was impossible in their home country. Others made the trip over as indentured servants and exchanged a few years of their life for the opportunity to participate in this new "Dream." Some came to escape prison or the gallows.

Yes, there are people who will fail to reach their dream. Only by failing, and the pain that comes with failing, will a person learn and grow. So starting a family, job, business, or a farm may not be successful the first time, but everyone must keep trying and learning in the process. A plethora of clichés fit this scenario— i.e., when one door shuts, another opens, etc. As Larry Bradley says, "Successful people are successful not because they don't have problems. They are successful because they confront the reality of their problems and find a way to turn their circumstances to their advantage."[258]

Another word for passion is to have a *hunger*. When your body, mind, or soul is missing something, it means it has a *hunger* for something and the desire provides motivation to do something to satisfy the *hunger*. Successful individuals will often say they had a *hunger* for their pursuit. That *hunger* was a driving force when they did not accept "no" for an answer: *hunger* for food, *hunger* for love, *hunger* for knowledge, *hunger* for success, *hunger* to help others. That *hunger* motivates us to do something to make it happen. When the *hunger* is satisfied, it provides a sense of accomplishment—confirming there is a purpose in life.

Any manager looking at potential vendors for their company is always hoping to find a vendor that has a *hunger* for their business. If a manager calls three vendors to provide a service and it takes two of them a week to return the call but one calls back within the hour, that tells the manager something. Those responses may mean at least one vendor has a *hunger* for their business and is organized enough to take care of their needs in a timely fashion, while the other two—not so much.

People, businesses, and governments need to learn, grow, and strive to be better. Every society has risks and rewards, but hopefully the *hunger* in life will provide the motivation to be a productive, caring person of society—for the betterment of all.

CHAPTER

9

The Steps for Implementation

The process could easily take six years for the Union of Ameristralia to be approved and implemented by at least the United
States and one other country. Please see a summarized timeline
at the end of this chapter. The United States and participating
nations would have to agree to:

Step One—Preparation
   a) The President of the United States submits enabling
      legislation to the Congress for consideration. The
      President also starts informal discussions with the other
      proposed countries.

   b) The United States Congress passes the enabling legislation
      and agrees to:
      1) take a national public vote within six months after the
         conclusion of the Constitutional Convention to
         indicate approval or disapproval,
      2) have each US Provate approve/disapprove of the new
         constitution based on a vote of the public,
      3) allow illegal immigrants in the US to apply for a
         Temporary Social Security Numbers (TSSNs, or the
         current Green Card system may be used) within the
         first 12 months and the TSSNs will be good for 10

years so they can legally work and pay taxes,

4) anyone (and their spouse and siblings) who has applied for the Temporary SSNs will not be deported,

5) provide funding to finish the wall on our southern border with Mexico and stop any new illegal immigration,

6) all new aspiring immigrants must apply for entrance from outside the country.

c) Any countries agreeing to participate will immediately implement a withdrawal of all tariffs or duties on imports from other agreeing parties of this Union. Identity and safety checks at the border would still remain in place.

d) Over an 18-month period, the United States, with or without the help of one of the other proposed countries, will actively solicit participation from the proposed countries to attend a Constitutional Convention. The purpose will be to write a new constitution, using the United States Constitution as a foundation so that other countries may feel comfortable in joining and participate as equals. If other countries outside of the original group suggested in this book express interest in participating and joining in this process, those inquiries would also be considered on a country-by-country basis.

e) After the 18-months solicitation period has passed and at least one other country has agreed to participate, then within the next 3 months, a date and location outside of the United States for the Constitutional Convention will be agreed upon.

f) Each participating country will appoint an odd number of delegates between 3 and 11 to the convention and an alternate. Delegates should be well versed in history. The delegates will approach this process with an attitude of looking for solutions that can bring this idea to fruition even if it means sacrificing their private feelings, egos, and party interest for the public good and for humanity. No delegate should be appointed who is not in favor of this Union, which is for the people in each of their countries to decide after the convention has completed its task. Delegates should be looking for solutions they think their countrymen will find acceptable. Keeping politics out of the process is key to keeping the proceedings focused on content and results. Each country may also appoint one historian and one journalist to the convention as observers who can document the proceedings. Each country will be encouraged to send at least two Supreme Court Justices to the convention to act as a resource on legal issues and to understand the "letter and spirit" of the constitution.

g) Any of the proposed countries not yet formally agreeing to these proceedings, but still interested in them for the future, may send up to three delegates to the Convention to observe and ask questions as appropriate—but not vote in the proceedings.

Step Two—The Constitutional Convention

a) The Constitutional Convention will last about 180 days and will be chaired by the President of the United States, or someone appointed by the President. The chair will have veto power over the proceedings. The convention may call in advisers as it deems necessary for the proceedings.

b) No private audio and/or video recording devices or cell phones will be allowed at the Convention, but one member of the press and one historian from each country will be allowed to observe the convention and take notes in order to provide documentation of the proceedings for history. The press and historians present may have a camera for still shots only but no flash photography to distract the delegates. There will be an official audio recording of all official sessions. All participants, including the press, historian, and advisors, will keep the proceedings to themselves until the conclusion of the Convention when the new Constitution is presented to the public.

c) If any of the participants' behavior becomes an issue, the chair may have them removed from the proceedings and replaced with an alternate, if available. Sponsoring countries may also recall and/or replace delegates.

d) The Convention will agree on the final proposed constitution and will also decide on parameters of where the new Ameristralian capitol may be located, the look of a flag, and the look of the currency. A contest may be started for a proposed national anthem.

e) A majority vote within each delegation will indicate approval, and if the United States and at least one other country votes in favor of the new constitution that will signify approval of the final document.

Step Three—Post Convention

a) The final agreed upon Constitution will be presented to the people and governments of those countries participating in the process. The proposed Constitution must be approved by the appropriate governmental bodies of each country. The proposed Constitution may not be amended by any country during the approval process because multiple governing bodies will be voting on it at different times.

b) The intention is that the delegates and the Supreme Court Justices who attended the constitutional convention will return to their countries to explain the meaning and spirit of the proposed Constitution to their fellow citizens. The historian and journalist may also provide the same service.

c) Within six months, each country will then hold a referendum on the proposed Constitution of Ameristralia so all eligible citizens in their country may express their approval or disapproval to their political leaders.

d) As a replacement Constitution for the United States, the

new Constitution must be ratified by the United States as appropriate, and if approved, will be put in place regardless of how long it takes for any of the other countries to decide.

e) If the new Constitution does not pass in any of the other countries initially agreeing within 3 years, then the existing tariffs or duties will be put back into place for that country.

Step Four—After Approval

a) An exchange rate for the new currency will be announced. As new currency is released to the public and banks, the old currency will be phased out. The new flag starts flying in place of the old flag. A new national anthem may be selected and put in place.

b) All lands and rights owned by the previous national government will be deeded over to the new Ameristralia government. Current debts and cash will be assumed/transferred. Current federal tax revenue will flow to the new government.

c) After approval in the United States, the existing elected and appointed federal officials will remain in their current capacities until the next regular election is held. However, they may not pass any new legislation, or tax codes—only spending issues will be addressed. At the next regular election, the members of the House of Representatives will be adjusted as described in Appendix B in this book. The Provates will have elections based on those numbers and redraw the districts as prescribed in the new Constitution.

d) After approval and adoption by one other country, a schedule of elections for all offices will be set for all participating countries. At that time, the Parliament/Congress of those other approving countries will cease passing any new laws. However, they may continue to pass spending bills until the new Congress is elected and sworn in.

e) The first President and Vice President of Ameristralia will be elected from those countries that have officially joined the Union during the first prescribed election.

f) Once the new President, Vice President, and Congress of Ameristralia are sworn in, all governmental agencies will begin reporting to a consolidated authority at the federal level. The President will start appointing justices to the Supreme Court of Ameristralia with the approval of the new Senate. Once the new Supreme Court has at least three judges approved, then all other Supreme Courts of the old countries will no longer exist. Greenland/Iceland (as one Provate) and New Zealand will now be Provates within Ameristralia and their national court will now be the highest court in each Provate.

g) After seating all the newly elected positions, the federal legislative bodies of the old countries will cease to exist, except for Greenland/Iceland and New Zealand—their legislatures will now be the Provate legislature.

h) The President will nominate Cabinet Members who will provide the leadership of those consolidating authorities and will be disbursed among the joining countries by the new President.

i) The Senate will decide on the location of the new capitol within the parameters established by the Convention and start allocating funds for its creation. Until completion, Washington D. C. will be the temporary capitol of Ameristralia.

j) All treaties will need to be renegotiated.

Step 5—Post Implementation

a) Other countries in the proposed Union may approve the Constitution of Ameristralia in a delayed fashion. Those countries will all be received with full acceptance whenever they complete the approval process within their country and have elections for representatives to the House and Senate.

b) Other countries not participating in the Constitutional

Convention may ask to join at a later point in time (years, decades or centuries later) and the Congress of Ameristralia may pass the necessary legislation for their acceptance into the Union. Any new country must accept the constitution as written—the time for negotiation is over.

Reasons Behind the Steps for Implementation of the Constitutional Convention

The existing United States Constitution allows for adding new states, but basically assumes they are just extensions of the United States with citizens and immigrants passing through from current states. The proposed Constitutional Convention provides an updated framework for that to happen. The United States Constitution has been a grand document that has worked exceptionally well for almost 250 years-to-date, and is still one of the oldest democratic constitutions in the world. I have taken the liberty of using the existing Constitution of the United States and suggesting alterations to make it more current with special rights and privileges to Provates of different continents—i.e., mandatory seats on the Supreme Court, President, and Vice President from different continents. All issues concerning the dependents (territories, commonwealths, reservations, protectorate, free association, etc...) would also need to be discussed and decided at the Constitutional Convention. Like the United States Constitutional Convention, when the Virginia Plan was offered at the onset of the convention as a foundation for deliberations going forward, the draft constitution presented for consideration in Book Two may be used as a starting point for the discussions.

At the Constitutional Convention it is possible that only a few of the seven countries suggested herein may opt in initially, which is acceptable. A couple of the seven proposed countries may decide to send observers without formally committing to the process, just to observe how things are proceeding. A rare chance exists that another country outside of the original seven proposed countries may want to join the proceedings from the start.

The new constitution would allow all countries to put the past in the past and move forward with a clean slate. The dropping of the tariffs among agreeing parties is a first step for individuals and businesses to begin to see the financial advantages that will be produced by the Union.

Citizenship and our borders must be secured. To solve the physical integrity of our borders (Mexico has vacillated about whether to act as a responsible neighbor), the wall must be completed to keep illegal immigrants out of the country. Also, existing illegal immigrants within our borders must be reconciled with reality. I am suggesting we give them a pathway to citizenship and at the same time set rules in place that any future immigrants must apply for entry into our country from outside of our country—you cannot come in illegally and then apply after you get here.

At the United States Constitutional Convention, John Dickinson, a Pennsylvania delegate, notes that, "Reason may mislead us; experience must be our guide."[259] My interpretation of Dickinson quote means we must sometimes look past ideology and use our actual experiences and the experiences of other countries to guide us.

In the current Constitution of the United States, the framers intentionally left many things vague. For example, they didn't elaborate what powers the President would have, but rather simply said, "executive power shall be vested in a President." And in other areas the framers used broad terms in phrases such as "necessary and proper" or "privileges and immunities" or "commerce among the several states."[260] These broad phrases allow the constitution the flexibility to grow and evolve over time. But now that time has passed and we have the necessary experience, it is time to tighten up the language where appropriate.

After the Second World War, the Japanese politicians failed to write a constitution to the satisfaction of General MacArthur, so he had one drafted in nine days.[261] The constitution was so well done that it has not been amended in more than 60 years.[262] It is my hope that the suggested changes in Book Two for the existing United States Constitution will facilitate the direction and timely completion of the process. I am suggesting that the Constitutional Convention be given about 180 days to complete its task. Our original Constitutional Convention consisted of 74 people of which 55 people participated from 12 colonies who met from May-September. Rhode Island never participated and New York dropped out halfway through the process. The remaining 11 colonies took 10 months to ratify and adopt the constitution. Ratification went through colonial constitutional conventions rather than the legislatures. It worked. I propose the state legislatures within the US use the public referendum as the hurdle for ratification of this new constitution. Let the people speak and be heard.

The various parameters for the new capital will no doubt be discussed, which might be something like:

1) not within 100 miles of D.C. or,

2) not east of the Mississippi River in the United States, except for maybe Michigan and Minnesota or,

3) not in the United States.

The first flag could simply be a world map with the participants colored in and the first currency could use symbols from the old countries; a Crown, Eagle, Kiwi, Koala Bear, Maple Leaf, and a Viking.

Like the Virginia Plan, Book Two presents the proposed changes to the constitution of the United States and, like the Federalist Papers, tries to explain the reasoning for some of the changes. Some of the Basic Overriding Core Values and Principles, which I identified in the previous chapter, are incorporated. Some suggested changes are meant to simply provoke discussion on certain topics, but not deliberated in this text.

A new constitution would also ensure that country specific amendments as, for example, Greenland and Iceland are recognized. The constitution will also allow for a negotiated assistance for other countries wishing to join. Appendix A of Book Two provides the proposed constitution in its entirety without commentary for everyone's consideration.

The process will be quite daunting and may motivate our adversaries to take provocative actions to try and distract the participants in this process. What follows below is an estimated timeline for the process:

Timeline

Year	Month	Action
0	January	US President asks Congress to draft enabling legislation to start the process
0	January	US President begins informal discussions with six other proposed countries regarding the Union
0	July	Congress finalizes and passes required enabling legislation
0	July	US President begins formal solicitation of other countries over following 18 months
2	January	Accepting countries select location/time for a Constitutional Convention
2	July	Constitutional Convention held at selected time and location
3	January	The new Ameristralia Constitution is presented to participation countries for their approval
3	July	The completed designs for currency and flag are presented for approval
4	January	US gives final approval for new Ameristralia Constitution
4	January	New flag and currency receive final approval and introduced for use
4	January	LISA begins in US
4	July	At least one other country approves the Union Constitution
4	July	Dates set for first elections
5	April	Primaries are held
5	October	General Elections held
6	January	New President, Vice President and Legislature sworn in

Historic Parallels To Show The Way Forward

As Machiavelli said, "It should be borne in mind that there is nothing more difficult to arrange, more doubtful of success, and more dangerous to carry through than initiating changes in a state's constitution."[263]

Australia's first referendum was held on the 3rd and 4th of June in 1898, but Queensland and Western Australia refused to take part. Despite this, the referendum went ahead in the four other colonies of New South Wales, Victoria, South Australia, and Tasmania. Without the two largest parts of the Australian continent being involved, Queensland and Western Australia, it was questionable as to what sort of federation could be achieved.[264] When New South Wales did not receive the votes to pass the referendum it seemed the federation would not go forward.[265]

After the referendum failure, the respective Premiers made six compromises—one being the location of the new capitol—a second referendum was scheduled between April and July of 1899. Victoria, South Australia, New South Wales, and Tasmania voted for the federation in 1899 with Queensland delaying their vote until they saw which way New South Wales would vote. The following September, Queenslanders endorsed the federation. Western Australia still refused to take part until they voted on it on July 31st of 1900. So Western Australia was not an original participant to the accord.[266]

A similar situation will most likely occur with this proposed Union. Some countries, states or provinces may say yes, while other countries, states, or provinces may say no or refuse to vote. Then with time, as others see that things are moving forward, they will opt into the Union. Many Americans probably think that the writing and ratification of the United States Constitution consisted of calm reflection and choice. But the ratification debates were, as the scholar Michael Faber recently put it, a "knock-down, drag-out fight."

The process was not smooth, and failure was always on the horizon. The proposed Constitutional Convention will be no different. It took 10 months for 10 colonies to ratify the US

Constitution in 1787-88, with 9 being the key threshold. North Carolina took until November of 1789, and Rhode Island finished in May of 1790.

Naysayers will say that these countries that are thinking about coming together are too different. But as a corollary to our original 13 colonies, Washington told Lafayette, in February 7, 1788, "It appears to me, then, little short of a miracle, that the Delegates from so many different States (which States you know are also different from each other), in their manners, circumstances, and prejudices, should unite in forming a system of national Government, so little livable to well-founded objections."[267] But danger from other nations was the impetus and strong glue that bound us together, as is the case today.

By agreeing to these procedures, it demonstrates that all the parties are determined to find solutions, which will allow all the parties to move forward, within the framework, toward success.

After the United States Constitutional Convention, Elbridge Gerry, a delegate who refused to sign the Constitution, was burned in effigy in Massachusetts. George Mason of Virginia, who also withheld his signature, was encouraged by the mayor of Alexandria to leave town shortly after his arrival, given the great threat to his personal safety. Mobs forced Anti-Federalists in Pennsylvania to return to the State Assembly, where they hurriedly set a date for the state's ratifying convention.[268]

For any large governing body, whether it is Congress or a Constitutional Convention, the larger the assembly may be, the greater chance that passion will prevail over reason. For the cohesion of the group, that is the reason for suggesting between three and eleven delegates from each country to make it a more manageable size. The United States Constitutional Convention had 55 delegates who showed up from the 12 colonies, or about 4.5 per colony. The seven proposed participants times nine appointed delegates (an assumed average) equal a total of fifty-four. The smaller size encourages everyone being on the same team. The larger the size, the more the group will spilt into different factions.

The importance of the convention staying on course cannot be overstated. The French Revolution was hijacked and taken in a different direction than originally intended. The same is true in Russia when the Czar was toppled. Russia was on the road to a democracy when Lenin hijacked the proceedings and the country. So in this Constitutional Convention there will be an American chairing the convention with veto power if things go astray, as a safety check.

Conclusion

As with the failure of the politicians from the original 13 colonies who, during the United States Revolutionary War, failed to provide the necessary funding for defense during our early years, it demonstrated that politicians could not be trusted to accomplish what was actually required. However, in their defense, the framework was missing to help make that happen. The original Articles of Confederation could only ask the colonies to contribute men and monies to keep the fight going. Hence, the United States Constitution was agreed upon and could now demand men and monies for the defense of the 13 colonies. A better framework was put in place—a Union, not a loose confederation.

So now in the twenty-first century, a constitution exists that was created almost 250 years ago when transportation and technology didn't allow for standardized systems and controls to be in place. Each State was doing their own thing, and if the national government thought something was "fishy" they could overturn elections for national offices and decide what was right and what was wrong. If the presidential election was in dispute or there was no winner after the first ballot of the Electoral College, then Congress could step in and decide.

In the current environment, politicians are too concerned about the next election in two years and not thinking of the long-term solutions that need addressed. Or they leave long-term solutions off the table so that it can continue to fester, for political purposes, for the next election. As citizens, we don't try to fix these unresolved issues because as citizens we can't—all we can do is vote. We don't have the power to act unless we run for office and get elected. Therefore, in Book Two, I have presented several common-sense long-term solutions that many in our political leadership have failed to address. The Constitutional Convention and resulting Ameristralian Constitution will provide the missing *framework* to allow these solutions to be addressed, an acceptable solution found, and then implemented.

In a *Foreign Affairs* article, former Secretary of State Madeleine Albright says that people are not "giving up on democracy, they are generating a steady stream of proposals for its improvement, including more rigorous term limits, reforms of campaign financing, equal access for candidates to the media, ranked-choice voting, … shorter campaigns, and steps to make it simpler … to establish new political parties."[269] Many of the ideas Madeleine Albright has suggested are incorporated in Book Two.

In the current environment, our autocratic enemies are focused on subverting the moral leadership and defense of democratic nations while the world stumbles along and doesn't address our problems. Similarly, prior to the Second World War, when Germany, Italy and Japan overtly moved to attack and occupy their neighbors and other territories, the world sat by and did nothing. When it was almost too late to stand up and say NO, Mother Britain and others finally did rise up and fight. But Britain and the other English-Speaking countries (Australia, Canada, India, New Zealand, and the United States), with the neutral help of the English Channel, and the Atlantic and Pacific Oceans, were finally able to prevail, but costing about 70 million lives in the process. After the Second World War we created the United Nations in hopes it could bring peace and prosperity to the world. Unfortunately, it has not worked, just look at the UN's response to the Russian invasion of Ukraine in 2022. Nothing!

Prior to the First World War there were the Napoleonic Wars (1803-1815) then a gap of 90 plus years prior to the First World War starting in 1914. For 90 years people remembered the death and destruction and avoided war. People and leaders forgot. Coming into the twenty-first century, blatant attacks on foreign nations was an inconceivable notion. In 2023, it will have been 78 years since the last great war, the Second World War. Again, people and leaders have forgotten about the death and destruction. Some leaders (i.e., Russia's war in 2022 with Ukraine and with China's intentions over Taiwan) get aggressive about growing their countries and others get lazy about fighting for peace. History works in cycles—it repeats itself—and I fear bad things are on the horizon. We must be prepared to fight for peace. Peace through Strength for Humanity.

I am suggesting that Australia, Canada, Greenland, Iceland, New Zealand, United Kingdom, and the United States come together and create the Union of Ameristralia. The Constitutional Convention being proposed will improve the American Constitution and simultaneously bring everyone together as Ameristralia; will simultaneously provide a *framework* and process so solutions for our long-term defense and prosperity may be addressed and implemented.

Ameristralia is a great **idea!**

"There is no greater power on earth than an idea whose time has come."[270] —Martin Luther King, Jr.

The **time** for **this idea** *has come.*

BOOK TWO

The Current US Constitution
and the Federalist Papers

The current Constitution of the United States, the foundation for our government, has been in place since 1787. Alexander Hamilton, John Jay, and James Madison, three of the Founding Fathers, wrote a series of essays published serially in popular New York newspapers of the time, which came to be known as the Federalist Papers. The essays were written as an attempt to convince the State of New York to ratify the Constitution.

James Madison's essay entitled "The Structure of the Government Must Furnish the Proper *Checks and Balances* [italics added] Between the Different Departments" (essay No.51) states, "In framing a government which is to be administered by men over men, the great difficulty lies in this: you must first enable the government to control the governed; and in the next place oblige it to control itself."[271]

The columnist Shelby Steele writes:

In a democracy, the legitimacy of institutions and of government itself is earned and sustained through fidelity to a discipline of democratic principles. These principles strive to ensure the ennobling conditions the free societies aspire to: freedom for the individual, the same rights for all individuals, equality under law, equality of opportunity and inherent right to 'Life, liberty and the pursuit of happiness.' Freedom, then, is not a state-imposed vision of the social good (say, a classless society); rather, it is the absence of any imposed vision that would infringe on the rights and freedom of individuals. In a true democracy freedom is a higher priority than the social good.[272]

Steele goes on to say, "Freedom is what *follows* from a discipline of principle—equal treatment under the law, one man one vote, freedom of speech, separation of church and state, the litany of individual rights and so on."[273]

American historian Gordon Wood puts it this way: governments "were never [the] full embodiment of the society," rather, "all governments are limited agencies of the people."[274]

Some of the highlights of the proposed changes to the US Constitution are:

- Assimilating and evolving into speaking a single language: English
- Equal rights for all
- Term limits for all elected officials
- Financial audits of federally elected and appointed officials
- End gerrymandering
- Uniform election laws
- Congress cannot overturn elections
- Fix the Electoral College
- Congress must approve all federal agency rules
- Benefit of doubt goes to the citizens or businesses over the Government
- Government is no longer the insurer of last resort for natural disasters
- Universal Identification Card, (no voter registration necessary and no census)
- Immigration reform

- Right to die for the terminally ill
- Right to work
- Control over your own retirement monies
- Guaranteed vacation and maternity leave
- All employers will provide medical insurance
- Reestablish trust in the media
- Equal rights and responsibilities for individuals living in territories, commonwealth, protectorates, or reservations
- Require a balanced budget
- School choice

What follows is the proposed template for the new constitution. The template is not cast in stone, but rather a starting point that will prompt discussions on a wide variety of topics.

The delegates to the Constitutional Convention from each country represented may go through all parts of this proposed constitution and decide on the best wording and approach for each item, or whether it needs to be included at all. Or, some other document might be used as a starting point.

As the author of this book, I have spent countless hours on the topics covered in this book, however, I am not an attorney, let alone a constitutional attorney. All the language is intentionally not "legalese" in nature so that the average person can understand the meaning of the text. If the Constitutional Convention converts some or all the text to a more legal format, that is their prerogative.

Most of the proposed changes to the constitution are toward the end of Book Two, starting with Article 5. So please be patient and please read on to the end.

The New Federalist Papers and the Proposed Ameristralia Constitution

Below is an explanation for the format used for the suggested changes to the current United States Constitution.

The **bolded black text** is the original United States Constitution with Amendments.

The Amendments have been inserted into the document, as appropriate, rather than at the end. The Amendments have also been edited down to fit in the appropriate spots and have been identified when they surface in the text. They are also listed in the Index at the end of the book for easy reference. The 12th, 15th, and 23rd Amendments have been ignored because I have chosen to totally rewrite them. They dealt with the Electoral College and Voting Rights.

The **bolded purple text** are the suggested modifications to a new constitution and the amendments. A justification for the changes is in regular black text and font. Some of the Articles and sub-sections of the original Constitution have been altered in the Ameristralia version. Some have been removed and others have been added to meet current needs. As a result, the numbering of articles and sections has been changed accordingly. Appendix A will provide a clean version of the Ameristralia Constitution with no commentary.

The Constitution of Ameristralia

Preamble, First paragraph:

We the People of Ameristralia, in Order to form a more perfect Union, establish Justice, [e]nsure domestic Tranquility, provide for the common [D]efen[s]e, promote the general Welfare, and secure the Blessings of Liberty to ourselves and our Posterity, do ordain and establish this Constitution for Ameristralia.

"We the people" creates the *framework* for the base authority of the document. As stated in the Declaration of Independence, "… we are endowed by our Creator with certain unalienable Rights, that among these are Life, Liberty and the pursuit of Happiness."

Preamble, Second paragraph:

We the people believe a common language is essential for a cohesive society. Therefore, English is the official language, and all organizations, businesses, and governmental bodies will use only English and the English alphabet of 26 letters for all advertising, ballots, contracts, documents, forms, websites, and other official written communications when interacting with the public.

English is currently the common language of Australia, Canada, New Zealand, the United Kingdom, and the United States. English is the most spoken language in the world by number of speakers and the third most spoken native language in the world after Standard Chinese and Spanish. English is one of the official languages in 60 countries.

English currently is the language of academics the world over and used by all international pilots and airports. Countries, such as Germany, use English for many of their college level programs. In Germany as of November 2020, more than 1,700 Master's study programs from 220 different universities are taught in English.[275] Germany obviously knows English is important in learning and a needed skill set in international academics and business.

English is widely understood and spoken in Greenland and Iceland. Greenland has their Greenlandic language (spoken by less than 57,000 people in the world), but its citizens are required to also learn Danish and English. Iceland's official language is Icelandic (spoken by about 314,000 people in the world), but Danish and English are also compulsory subjects in school. Greenland and Iceland will need to make the official switch to English in order to be part of the Union.

All the written documents for organizations, businesses, and government will only be in English. Conversations whether personal, organizational, in business or government may be in any language comfortable for the people involved. But no organization, business, or governmental department is required to provide a translator for someone who does not speak English.

When a government recognizes and grants special rights for languages other than its official language, conflict and misunderstanding may arise. For example, The Charter of the French Language in the Province of Quebec is a law that makes French the usual language of business in Quebec, although the rest of the Canada speaks English. This specialized law creates barriers between employers and workers, and negotiations between companies.[276]

According to the Canadian Census Bureau, 26 million people (75%) of Canadians speak English, eight million people (21%) speak French and six million (18%) are bilingual. However, 84% of the French speakers live in Quebec.[277] Canadians, complaining of "constitutional fatigue," attempted to fix the problem through the Meech Lake and Charlottetown proposals, which failed to win approval.[278] The failure to reach agreement has caused a journey without an end in the quest for a constitutional settlement on the French-speaking Quebec issue. French-speaking Quebec now sees themselves not as a minority in Canada but a majority in Quebec.[279] Canada provides the best example of why it is necessary to speak one language throughout a country.

Other examples are New Zealand that has Maori as an official language alongside English, or Puerto Rico which also has Spanish as an official language. In these examples, the question is: should federal employees be required to speak French, Spanish, Maori as well as English in order to provide service to anyone in the country? Should the constitution also be written in French, Spanish, Maori as well as English? One official language can eliminate friction in society, schools, business, and politics. The KISS principle, first introduced by the US Navy, with a slight modification, Keep It Simple & Straightforward, is an important principle to apply here.

While societies, associations, and groups have the right to preserve their languages and customs as they see fit, for the long-term good of society overall, a federal system based on Provates and one based on a single language needs to be reconciled. Reconciliation occurs through facilitating assimilation over time. When people immigrate to Australia, Canada (less Quebec), New Zealand, the United Kingdom, and the United States everyone comes knowing they will eventually need to learn English in order to thrive in their new home. If French-speaking people in Quebec do not want to assimilate into the Union by refusing to learn English, then they have the option to opt out and create their own country surrounded by English-speaking folks.

In 1620, Pilgrims arrived in North America. The Pauquunaukit Wampanoag Indians watched them almost starve to death because the Pilgrims had no idea of how to live in this new land. The tribe wanted to help the Pilgrims, but they didn't speak the same language. In the Spring, the Indians sent an emissary, Samoset, who greeted them in broken English. A few days later, Samoset brought Squanto with him. Squanto not only spoke better English, he had lived in London.[280] Squanto was able to pass their Indian knowledge on to the settlers. Because they were able to communicate, the Pilgrims, instead of perishing, thrived. Members of the human race need to be able to speak with each other.

The proposed Ameristralia Constitution decrees that all written materials and forms will be in English but does not say a word about what language people speak—that is intentional. For example, in my wife's case, when she was growing up, her family spoke German in the home, but they did their best to speak English at school and work. At social gatherings with other German immigrants, they all spoke German. The same would be true with the new constitution. In Quebec, French-speaking families would continue to speak any language they'd like at home, social situations, or business, but all written materials and forms will be in English. In Ameristralia this means that customer call centers have the option of speaking any language necessary to help customers with their problems, but if a form needs to be filled out, it will need to be in English. But the call center will not be required to staff people that speak non-English languages.

Foreign nouns used in language are permissible, but the descriptors must be in English. For example, Filet Mignon is French and may be used, but then you can describe the steak and how it is was prepared in English. As another example, France was the first to teach ballet and the French words are accepted as the universal standard. So you can talk about an Arabesque move in ballet and then describe it as an extension of the dancer's leg off the floor to the back in English.

Preamble, Third paragraph,

We the people believe in the family unit and the government should do nothing that disincentivizes a family unit from forming and staying together. Part of the common culture is the realization that we are free individuals and responsible for our own actions. Therefore, we must be self-reliant, and we all have a responsibility to work hard in order to provide for our family with the goal of each generation getting a little further ahead.

In Chapter 8 of Book One, I discussed the importance of the family unit and how it passes the information and values necessary for each generation to move forward and have it a little better than the previous generation. However, family units are not something that can be mandated by the government. Regardless of whether parents choose to stay together or not, it will continue to be the responsibility of each parent to conduct themselves in a way that provides for themselves and their minor children.

The Pilgrims were early immigrants but many others followed. The Louisiana Purchase and other land acquisitions allowed for immigrant settlers to head west for the vast emptiness beyond. They had a *hunger* to find land to settle and raise a family. In these new territories, typically, government was too far away to either impose its will upon them or offer its benefits. Instead, the overriding power was Mother Nature and her Law of Nature that taught the settlers to work hard, have supplies for the winter, learn, conform or die. In essence, pioneers had to assimilate with Mother Nature. They were free of government intervention and had the freedom to live in any way that allowed them to be successful. That culture—some called Manifest Destiny—held a belief that our citizens had the Divine right to expand its dominion and spread democracy and capitalism across the North American Continent. Free enterprise, capitalism, and honest rewards for hard work can allow almost anyone an opportunity to be successful. The early settlers in Australia, Canada, Greenland, Iceland, and New Zealand had similar experiences.

In 1931, James Truslow Adams coined the term "American Dream" in his book *Epic of America*. He wrote, "...that dream of a land in which life should be better and richer and fuller for everyone, with opportunity for each according to ability or achievement."[281] Obituaries are rife with the stories of people who came to the United States with nothing or from impoverished families who went on to do great things in our country. The American Dream is possible because of the existence of the United States and the free enterprise system. The free enterprise system enables businesses and individuals to create, produce, market, and sell products and services based on supply and demand. Then the businesses that do a better job of providing a product or service thrive and the businesses that do not eventually die.

Nathan Nguyen was born in Vietnam in a house of straw with a dirt floor prior to immigrating to the US in the early 1990s and here is what he says about the American Dream:

> If achieving the American Dream is at least somewhat related to money, then understanding how to create, maintain and grow wealth are the timeless keys to unlock it. What makes the rich different from the broke (poor is a state of mind) is having the skills to turn income into assets, that can increase in value and generate more income. I believe it is imperative that we prepare all students with skills that empower them to achieve and sustain financial independence. We must educate them on these topics while they're in school so that they are ready for the financial responsibilities of adult life and can focus on achieving their own version of the ever-evolving American dream.[282]

As we approach the mid twenty-first century, it will be necessary to define financial independence. As a society, we have done this before when we transformed from a largely agriculturally based country to the Industrial Revolution. We can do it again as we move further into the Technology Revolution where coders will be the new assembly line workers, where Long-Term Individual Security Accounts (LISAs) supersede company or union pensions, and government programs help everyone achieve the "Dream" through creating equity in growing assets that can be used when it is needed. In Article 5, Section 3, I'll discuss Long-Term Individual Security Accounts (LISAs) that provide a mechanism for financial independence.

There are many examples of people who started with nothing and made a success of themselves. Here are a few examples:

Christel DeHann, born in 1942, was an immigrant from Germany. She was working as a secretary in 1974 when she and her husband, Jon, devised a business creating Resort Condominiums International Inc. (RCI), in Indianapolis, Indiana, with an initial investment of about seven thousand dollars. RCI acted as a brokerage service for owners of vacation properties that allowed people to swap timeslots so they could try out different resorts rather than returning to the same timeshare each year. Although a novelty at first, the swapping option became a strong selling point for timeshares. Ms. DeHann won control of RCI after her divorce and expanded it globally, eventually selling it for more than $625 million in 1996.[283]

Joan B. Johnson, the daughter of a railroad porter, was born October 16, 1929, just in time for the stock market crash. She met her husband, George Johnson, in high school. George went to the bank and tried to borrow $250 to start his own business and was turned down because it was too risky. He turned around and applied for a $250 loan for a family vacation and was approved, but used it to start the company. Successful people find a way around "no." Joan kept the books of the company, handled hiring and scheduled production of the original product line of Ultra Wave, which became the biggest supplier of hair-care products for the African-American market. In 1971 it became the first African-American owned company listed on the American Stock Exchange. After a divorce in 1989, Joan took control of the company. In 1993 she sold Ultra Wave for $70 million.[284]

Walt Disney had his first job as an artist in Kansas City with Gray Advertising but was let go six weeks later when the firm lost a big client. In the process, he learned the skills he needed to create cartoons and a couple of years later, started Laugh-O-Gram Films. Disney slept in his studio and subsisted on canned beans. While that business failed, he learned from this experience. Disney moved to California. His parents took out a mortgage to invest in their son and his uncle lent him the use of his garage, a great example of family taking care of family. Unfortunately, his first major cartoon character, Oswald the Lucky Rabbit, was seized by his distributor because of a poorly written contract. He shortened Oswald's ears and lengthened his tail, creating a mouse his wife called Mickey. Walt was a "Project Entrepreneur," which means he took the earnings from one project to then feed the next project. Walt moved on to his first full length animated movie in 1937: *Snow White and the Seven Dwarfs*. Project entrepreneurs don't use their earnings to buy big yachts, instead they put the money into the next project. Later, after taking his daughters to an amusement park, Walt thought he could come up with something better. Overextended and short of cash, he founded Disneyland and he borrowed on his life-insurance policy. He also had to get help from the American Broadcasting Company and Western Publishing to complete the financing. Walt had worked hard and suffered, but in the end he persevered.[285]

Dwight Eisenhower's father owned a general store in Kansas, which ultimately failed, so he went to work as a laborer. Dwight's parents eked out a modest living and invested all their hope in their sons' careers. They encouraged all seven of their sons to compete with each other and their contemporaries. Dwight's first choice was to enter the United States Naval Academy but his scores were not good enough so he opted for the United States Military Academy at West Point. Dwight later became Supreme Allied Commander in Europe during the Second World War, and ultimately, the 34th President of the United States.[286]

Whether it is an article in a business magazine, the obituaries in a local paper, the *Wall Street Journal,* or postings on websites such as www.legacy.com, there are many, many examples of someone who had an idea, learned to adapt it with the world around them (assimilated), and through hard work and perseverance became successful—often times with the help of their family. The common culture is to work hard and persevere.

Preamble, Fourth paragraph,

We the people believe that we treat all men and women equally under the law without regard to ethnic background, skin color, or religion. While men and women are equal, they are biologically different and as such deserve their own separate bathrooms, locker rooms, and living arrangements if they so desire.

The 1972, Equal Rights Amendment for women failed to be passed by twelve of the US states which doomed it to failure. The fourth paragraph of the Preamble establishes legal gender equality for women and men.

Assimilation, or compromise, is a natural reoccurring event. Assimilation is interrupted when a government gives any group of citizens special or exclusive rights. Whether it is not giving full rights to women versus men, or one ethnic group or religion being suppressed by another. It isn't right.

Ian Haney López, a law professor at the University of California, Berkeley, conducted focus group interviews with Latino voters in the run-up to the election in 2020. He found that half minimized the importance of ethnic background and said they believed Latinos can get ahead through hard work, or they considered themselves more akin to European immigrants who eventually became part of the mainstream. Haney López says, "History suggests that the mainstream shifts and grows as assimilation propels once-marginalized groups up the socioeconomic ladder." It's what happened after the Second World War to Italian and Polish Catholics and Eastern European Jews whose parents arrived a century ago in the last great immigration surge. Evidence suggests that assimilation is now happening among Hispanics and Asians as they intermarry with Anglo-Americans. Today, more than one in 10 babies born in the United States have one Anglo-American and one non-Anglo-American parent.[287]

In France, the government does not officially track the ethnic background of its population. French society aspires to be colorblind. Humanity also aspires to be "color-blind." For those who are from European descent, it may be difficult by appearance to identify ancestry. Unless attire is involved, religion is nearly impossible to identify by appearance alone. Those of African or Asian decent over the centuries have not always been given the opportunity to blend into the society where they live. In 1967, sixteen states still forbade interracial marriage in the United States, and it took a ruling by the Supreme Court (Loving vs Virginia) to finally strike down the discriminatory practice. History shows that social norms and acceptance tend to lag behind legislation. In 1968, many Southern States would not broadcast Petula Clark's television special because, during a duet, she touched Harry Belafonte's arm. Now, more than fifty years later, interracial couples in society, entertainment, and advertising are the norm.

It is true that as human beings we all belong to the human race with a common origin. Regardless of where we are born, or to whom we are born, each person shall be treated equally under the law. Racism and bigotry are human constructs. When they are allowed to take hold in a society, they subordinate a group to be seen as "other." The tendency to discriminate in a culture based on perceived differences is as old as mankind. The promise of the human race is that we have the intellect and hopefully the morality to reject it.

TRUTH:
Love is Blind.

Although Thomas Jefferson told a group of Indian leaders from the Delaware, Mohican, and Munries tribes on December 21, 1808, "You will mix with us by marriage, your blood will run in our veins, and will spread with us over this great island,"[288] it took almost 160 years for government to evolve past the point where it tries to impose an old morality on the lives of individuals. Over time, assimilation of the different ethnic backgrounds will happen because love is blind.

Government will not impose a vision upon the people. Freedom is the absence of any government-imposed vision that would infringe on the rights and freedom of individuals. For freedom to work there must be a discipline of principles driving society.[289] The role of government is to create a level playing field for everyone to compete and to not give anyone any special privileges that will give them a leg up or allow them to hold others down.

Affirmative Action was enacted as part of the Civil Rights Legislation with an intent to level the playing field. In the first half of the twentieth century, there were still many laws on the books in many states that promoted segregation and blocked access to equal services (i.e. separate water fountains, bathroom, white's only public swimming pools, and poll taxes). Unfortunately, Affirmative Action has been used as a sledgehammer, instead of productive public policy, and has undermined the original purpose of ensuring equality.

For example, the federal government recently found that Yale participated in admission discrimination based on ethnic background, violating federal civil-rights law. Ethnic background was the "determinative factor" in hundreds of admissions decisions each year. The federal government found that the majority of applicants, Asian-American and Anglo-American students, had one-tenth to one-fourth more likelihood of being admitted than African-American applicants with comparable academic credentials.[290]

Martin Luther King said:

That is why, even amid great struggle, Black Americans responded by building their own institutions and businesses. Great universities, medical schools, hotels, restaurants, movie companies and even a flight school sprung up. All of this was self-financed—and made possible by two-parent families, churches and other cultural institutions that provided shelter against the outside storm of racism. Like all Americans, blacks have triumphed over their circumstances only when they have adopted bourgeois virtues such as hard work, respect for learning, self-discipline, faith and personal responsibility.[291]

These five characteristics of hard work, education, self-discipline, faith, and personal responsibility will prevail for any group of people, even when it is blunted by obstacles in life. Everyone faces obstacles, and the response to those obstacles defines us as individuals. Being defeated or learning from the experience to achieve success is entirely up to the individual.

Preamble, Fifth paragraph,

The government will consist of three separate but equal branches of government: Legislative, Executive, and Judicial.

Power is distributed and no single branch can exert direct control over the citizens. The distribution of power is the unstated basis for the heart and soul of the constitution—it provides the necessary *checks and balances* in government.

John Jay said, "Nothing is more certain than the indispensable necessity of government, and it is equally undeniable, that whenever and however it is instituted, the people must cede to it some of their natural rights in order to vest it with requisite powers."[292]

Article 1 - Legislative Branch

Section 1,

All legislative Powers herein granted shall be vested in the Congress of Ameristralia, which shall consist of a Senate and House of Representatives.

Section 2,

1: The House of Representatives shall be composed of Members chosen every second Year by the people of the several Provates, and the Electors in each Provate shall have the Qualifications requisite for Electors of the most numerous Branch of the Provate Legislature.

2: No person shall be a Representative who shall not have attained the age of thirty Years, and been seven Years a Citizen of Ameristralia. They must also be an Inhabitant of the Provate and Congressional District from which they will be chosen.

The original wording says, "and who shall not, when elected, be an Inhabitant of that State in which he shall be chosen." I have changed the wording from "shall not" to "must." In today's language, the original wording seemed to be contrary to the intent.

The age requirement was raised from 25 to 30. At 25 some people could graduate college and run for a position in the House, leaving no time to experience the real world prior to taking office.

3: Representatives (deleted per the 14th amendment, "and direct Taxes") shall be apportioned among the several Provates which may be included within this Union, according to their respective Numbers, which shall be determined by counting all Ameristralia citizens having been issued a federal identification card. The actual Enumeration shall

be made within three years after the first Meeting of the Congress of Ameristralia. The Number of Representatives in the House shall be three times the number in the Senate and the proportion shall be so regulated by Congress based on population, but each Provate shall have at Least one Representative; and until such enumeration shall be made, the Provates will be allocated as shown in Appendix B. Each Representative will have one vote.

Stricken in part is "and excluding Indians not taxed, three fifths of all other persons." The original text counted slaves as three-fifths of a free person and Indians were not included either—they were their own "nation." (Per the 14th Amendment, section 2, ratified in July of 1868.)

In the United States the Reapportionment Act of 1929 fixed the number of House of Representatives at 435.[293] Census enumeration and reapportionment practices weren't set in stone at the founding. With the new Ameristralia Constitution it will no longer be necessary for a census every ten years. The proposed constitution also prescribes the number of Representatives based on the number of Senators. So as Ameristralia continues to grow in Provates over the coming decades and centuries, the formula determining the number of Representatives in the House is already set.

Australia currently has 151 Representatives and 76 Senators. Canada's distribution of representatives is 338 Members of Parliament and 105 Senators.[294] The United States currently has 435 Representatives and 100 members in the Senate. So Australia has basically a 2 to 1 ratio of Parliamentarians to Senators, Canada about a 3 to 1 ratio and the United States is about a 4 to 1 ratio. The proposed ratio of 3 to 1 is a reasonable middle ground. The UK has 650 in the House of Commons compared to 769 in the House of Lords. Basically 1 to 1 which is an outlier when compared to the others.

Modern federalism began with the United States in 1787. The House has power distributed based on population and the Senate has power distributed by giving equal power to each Provate. Provates with a large population, such as New York, could have considerable weight in the House, but not in the Senate. Smaller population Provates have the ability to force compromise in the Senate. Following the American example, a federal constitution was adopted in Canada in 1867 and Australia in 1901.[295] It is the essence of Federalism that power from geographic territory and power from the population be divided.[296] Federalism acknowledges diversity and gives it constitutional expression.[297] It will also help protect the other countries joining in the Union so that the large population mass in the United States doesn't dominate in the Congress. But just like any other country, people in the cities have different needs from those in rural parts of the country. The US and the other countries in this proposed Union have diverse populations also and we will all move forward together. We all want life, liberty, and the ability to pursue happiness in a fair, safe and stable environment.

4: When vacancies happen in the Representation from any Provate, the Provate will schedule a special election for a replacement if there is sufficient time prior to the next scheduled round of elections for that position.

The proposed change does not allow a Provate to appoint someone to an empty seat. An election must be held, whether for a Senator or for a member of the House of Representatives.

A common practice in many locales is for an elected individual of Congress to step down from their position so that a Governor of the same party can appoint their replacement. An incumbent is much harder to defeat during the following election versus an open field where no one is the incumbent and the people get to choose the replacement. The current practice helps the party to keep the seat under their control and then the replacement is beholden to the party rather than the people.

When a vacancy occurs in a legislative body of over one hundred individuals it doesn't present a problem for the legislative body. Life moves on. Now elected officials will be motivated to serve their full term rather than to resign early.

5: The House of Representatives shall ch[oo]se their Speaker and other Officers; and shall have the sole Power of Impeachment.

Section 3,

1: The Senate of Ameristralia shall be composed of two Senators from each Provate, elected by a vote of the People in the Provate, for six Years; and each Senator shall have one vote.

(Amendment 17, item one, ratified in April of 1913.)

Amendment 17 made the election of individuals to the Senate a public vote of the people, rather than being selected by the legislature of the Provate.

2: Immediately after they shall be assembled in Consequence of the first Election, they shall be divided as equally as may be into three Classes. The Seats of the Senators of the first Class shall be vacated at the Expiration of the second year, or the second Class at the Expiration of the fourth Year, and the third Class at the Expiration of the sixth Year, so that one third may be chosen every second year. At the time of Union, if the Provate already has two Senators with six-year terms then they will assume the positions with the established time frame as long as it conforms to the goal of having one-third of the members being elected every two years.

In the United States, the existing Senator will assume the new positions. As other nations join, their Senators may also assume their positions as long as the goal of one-third elected every two years is maintained. If not, then an arrangement will be put into place to ensure that happens.

3: No Person shall be a Senator who shall not have attained to the Age of thirty Years, and have been nine Years a Citizen of Ameristralia. They must also be an Inhabitant of the Provate in which they will be chosen.

The original wording says, "and who shall not, when elected, be an Inhabitant of that State in which he shall be chosen." I have changed the wording from "shall not" to "must." Again, this is for clarity because the original wording seems contrary to the intent.

4: This item is deleted. It read "The Vice President of the United States shall be President of the Senate, but shall have no Vote, unless they be equally divided."

The Vice President will no longer have duties in the Senate. The Vice President's primary task is to assist the President and to be prepared to assume the office if needed.

Having the Vice President hold an office in the Senate also is contrary to the philosophy of the separation of powers of the different branches in the government.

5: The Senate shall ch[oo]se their Speaker and other Officers. (Deleted is the wording "and also a President pro tempore, in the Absence of the Vice President, or when he shall exercise the Office of President of the United States.")

Again, the Vice President will no longer have duties in the Senate. The Vice President's primary task is to assist the President and to be prepared to assume the office if needed.

6: The Senate shall have the sole Power to try all Impeachments. When sitting for that Purpose, the[re] shall be [a]n Oath or Affirmation. When the President of Ameristralia is tried, the Chief Justice shall preside: And no Person shall be convicted without the Concurrence of two-thirds of the Members present.

7: Judgment in Cases of impeachment shall not extend further than (deleted is "to") removal from Office, and disqualification to hold and enjoy any Office of honor, Trust or Profit under the Union of Ameristralia: but the Party convicted shall nevertheless be liable and subject to Indictment, Trial, Judgment and Punishment, according to Law.

Section 4,

1: (Elections for Senators and Representatives has been deleted and moved to Article 5, Section 2, several pages later.) **The terms of Senators and Representatives** shall end at noon on the 3rd day of January, of the years in which such terms would have ended if this article had not been ratified; and the terms of their successor shall then begin.

(Amendment 20, item 1, ratified 4/26/1933.)

2: The Congress shall assemble at least once in every year, and such meeting shall begin at noon on the 3rd day of January, unless they shall by law appoint a different day.

(Amendment 20, item 2, ratified 4/26/1933.)

Section 5,

1: ("Each House shall be the Judge of the Elections, Returns and Qualifications of its own Members, and" is deleted.) **[A] Majority of each [House] shall constitute a Quorum to do Business; but a smaller Number may adjourn from day to day, and may be authorized to compel the Attendance of absent Members, in such Manner, and under such Penalties as each House may provide.**

The first sentence was deleted because it gave Congress (a political body) the ability to overturn an election. Later in the proposed Constitution we have the Provate Secretary of State as the sole authority for declaring the winner for any race in their Provate.

2: Each House may determine the Rules of its Proceedings, punish its Members for disorderly Behavior, and, with the Concurrence of two thirds, expel a Member.

3: Each House shall keep a Journal of its Proceedings, and from time to time publish the same, excepting such Parts as may in their Judgment require Secrecy; and the Yeas and Nays

of the Members of either House on any question shall, at the Desire of one fifth of those Present, be entered on the Journal.

4: Neither House, during the Session of Congress, shall, without the Consent of the other, adjourn for more than three days, nor to any other Place than that in which the two Houses shall be sitting.

Section 6,

1: The Senators and Representatives shall receive a Compensation for their services, to be ascertained by Law but at no time more than six times the average per capita income of the average citizen, and paid out of the Treasury of Ameristralia. No law varying the compensation of the services of the Senators and Representative shall take effect until an election of Representatives shall have intervened. They shall in all Cases, except Treason, Felony and Breach of the Peace, be privileged from Arrest during their Attendance at the Session of their respective Houses, and in going to and returning from the same. (deleted, "; and for any Speech or Debate in either House, they shall not be questioned in any other place.") Housing or a stipend may be provided for members of Congress.

(Amendment 27, ratified 5/5/1992.)

A maximum upper limit for compensation is set. The current Median Income Per Capita in the United States is around $32,000/year. So six times that number would limit the pay to around $192,000/year. The Senators and Representatives currently get paid $174,000/year. Leaders in the House and Senate currently make $193,000.

With the creation of a new capital city it may make sense to have government-provided housing, like on many military bases, or provide a stipend, which then gives representatives the option of finding their own housing.

The deleted sentence provides individuals in either House

protection from what they have said in either House. The portion of the constitution "and for any Speech or Debate" allows our elected representatives to put their speeches into the record and then later use them on the campaign trail preventing anyone from being held accountable for the content of their speeches. In essence, current members could out-right lie and not be held accountable.

2: No Senator or Representative shall, during the Time for which they were elected, be appointed to any civil Office under the Authority of Ameristralia, which shall have been created, or the Emoluments whereof shall have been [i]ncreased during such time; and no Person holding any Office under the Union of Ameristralia, shall be a Member of either House during his Continuance in Office.

The item prevents members of Congress from holding multiple offices at one time.

3: Elected officials in Congress are not exempt from the laws and regulations they pass.

Congress must be ruled by the same laws they pass. Otherwise, they are immune to the bad side effects of anything they pass. James Madison stated that, "They can make no law which will not have its full operation on themselves and their friends, as well as on the great mass of society. This has always been deemed one of the strongest bonds by which human policy can connect the rulers and the people together. It creates between them that communion of intent and sympathy of sentiments."[298]

Section 7,

1: This item is stricken: "All bills for raising Revenue shall originate in the House of Representatives; but the Senate may propose or concur with Amendments as on other bills."

Both houses should have the ability to originate any and all bills. In 2021, the Senate first passed a Bipartisan Spending bill and then sent it to the House for Approval. The House wanted the Senate to originate and pass the bill first so the House would know what they would accept.

2: Every Bill which shall have passed the House of Representatives and the Senate, shall, before it becomes a Law, be presented to the President of Ameristralia; **If the President approves, the President shall sign it. If not signed, it will be returned with Objections to the chamber where it was originated to be recorded and considered. After reconsideration, two thirds of that chamber shall agree to pass the Bill, it shall be sent, together with the Objections, to the other legislative chamber, by which it shall likewise be reconsidered. If approved by two thirds of that chamber, it shall become a Law. But in all such Cases the Votes of both Houses shall be determined by Yeas and Nays, and the names of the persons voting for and against the Bill shall be entered on the Journal of each House respectively. If any Bill shall not be returned by the President within ten Days (Sundays excepted) after it shall have been presented to the President, the same shall be a Law, in like Manner as if had been signed, unless the Congress by their Adjournment prevent its return, in which case it shall not be a Law.**

3: Every Order, Resolution, or Vote to which the Concurrence of the Senate and House of Representatives may be necessary (except on a question of Adjournment) shall be presented to the President of Ameristralia; **and before the Same shall take Effect, shall be approved by the President, or being disapproved by the President, shall be repassed by two thirds of the Senate and House of Representatives, according to the Rules and Limitations prescribed in the Case of a Bill.**

4: No bill or legislation may exceed 1,000 pages, must address a single issue, and legislatures in each House must be given seven days for consideration prior to voting.

Too often, legislators pass bills that are too long for anyone to take the time to read and thoroughly understand. The press also has no time to examine such legislation prior to passage, to make the contents known to the public. The bill/legislation should be 1,000 pages or less so the material can be digested, understood, and then passed. If the bill/legislation needs broken up into small pieces, so be it.

Another issue is that too many times, legislators propose legislation, which includes multiple issues (riders) so that one party can set up the other party to vote "no" on the bill and defeat it. That way, the other party can claim in the next election that the member from the other party voted against "xyz," which was only a small portion (rider) of the bill. By slipping the controversial issue/rider into the larger bill, the factual claim can be made that so and so voted against the "xyz," when in reality, the individual voted against the larger bill/legislation only because they could not vote on a particular rider in the bill. For accountability and transparency, bills and legislation need to be on a single issue and free of any non-pertinent riders.

Section 8,

1: The Congress shall have Power To Lay and Collect Taxes, Duties, Imposts and Excises, to pay the Debts and provide for the common Defen[s]e and general Welfare of Ameristralia; **but all Duties, Imposts and Excises shall be uniform throughout** Ameristralia. After a second country joins Ameristralia and until new laws are passed setting a common standard, the President may set these policies;

After a second country joins the Union, then the realignment of internal barriers, and differing tariffs and duties, could present immediate issues and also give foreign companies a quick way to bypass tariffs and duties of one former country into the new Union. In this situation, the President will have the power to establish those rates until new legislation is passed.

Taxes outside the parameters of this constitution may be adjusted by the President until the Congress has a chance to pass the necessary legislation.

2: The Congress shall have Power to borrow Money on the credit of Ameristralia. **Passing bonds for special projects or purposes is permissible – but not more than one year in three, unless in times of war.**

If bonds are issued to provide a stimulus in a downturn in the economy, that is permitted but only once in a three-year stretch. Obviously, the interest payments on those bonds will need to part of the budget going forward.

3: To regulate Commerce with foreign Nations, and among the several Provates, the federal government shall have primary regulatory and criminal authority over any business, or crimes committed, that involves multiple Provate jurisdictions. The federal authorities also have primary jurisdiction over bank robberies, kidnappings, digital software, social platforms, pipe-lines, electrical transmission lines, rivers, lakes, waterways, ports, harbors, and international airports.

With a two-thirds vote of Congress and approval of the President, this list may be expanded, so that the federal government takes primary jurisdiction over more items.

The transmission of liquid or gas energy pipelines or any electrical transmission lines used in the distribution of energy will be the sole responsibility of the federal government to govern. The federal responsibility is to ensure the safe and efficient movement of this power between Provates. The government may not deny a permit if the movement of the energy is needed to supply energy to another portion of the Union, but it may redirect the placement of those lines. In essence, this keeps one Provate from starving another Provate from the energy it needs in order for its citizens and businesses to flourish.

There may be an industry that is so widely and inconsistently regulated between various Provates that everyone feels the federal government should take over jurisdiction. Let's use the example of an insurance company. Let's assume the capitalization requirements and governing constructs are such that one Provate let's just about anyone operate as an insurance company, as compared to other

Provates. The wide disparity in capital requirements may be deemed unfair or unwise and some will think it needs fixed.

A Board should be established for the regulation of social media and software companies. This should not be left to the Provates.

4: To establish a uniform Rule of Naturalization and uniform Laws on the subject of Bankruptcies throughout Ameristralia.

    a) Existing 1) citizens, 2) inhabitants of territories, commonwealths, reservations, protectorates 3) or any family (spouse and siblings) living, working, and paying income taxes inside Ameristralia is automatically considered a citizen with full privileges at the time of adoption.

    b) Congress will set a number for immigrants (or refugees) wishing to enter the country each year and Congress and the President will ensure there are physical barriers where needed on land borders and sufficient Coast Guard assets to prevent illegal immigration from the water. All immigrants and refugees must apply for entrance into Ameristralia from outside Ameristralia. Each year the President may approve 25 individuals to stay in the country and apply for asylum from within Ameristralia.

    c) After a second country joins Ameristralia, and until new laws are passed, setting a common standard/policy resides with the President;

Any illegal alien families living and working in the country, filing an annual tax return, automatically become citizens once the new constitution is passed. The proposed enabling legislation in the US will give Temporary (10 years) Social Security Numbers to illegal immigrants (or Green Cards) so they can work and later prove they worked and meet the criteria set above.

It is possible that members of visiting sports teams, cultural performers, or diplomats, once they get here, will claim political asylum from their home country. The President will have the power to accommodate these individuals rather than have them go home, or go to a third country, and apply from there.

After a second country joins in Ameristralia, and until new laws are passed by the Congress, the President may set an immigration standard for Ameristralia because it may take several months for Congress to address all the issues with the startup of the Union. This allows the President to take executive action that will expire once Congress passes the necessary legislation.

5: To coin and print Money, regulate the Value thereof, and of foreign Currency and use the Metric System for the Standard of Weights and Measures. No currency other than the Ameristralian dollar may be used in Ameristralia's commerce.

In the Federalist Papers, Madison admits not dictating the use of the dollar was an oversight on his part.[299] Dictating the use of the dollar will help ensure that all monies earned and spent are in Ameristralia's currency and are not part of an unregulated, fringe economy, such as Bitcoin or Dogecoin, even though industry titans such as Mark Cuban and Elon Musk are now accepting Dogecoin in their business enterprises. Cryptocurrencies are to be treated as a foreign currency or an investment, not legal tender within Ameristralia.

In the 1970s and 1980s there was an international push to get all countries on the metric system. Australia was largely successful in making the switch. Canada also tried to make the switch but still uses both because of the proximity to the United States. The United Kingdom uses a combination of both based on the application. New Zealand made the switch in the 1967, but still uses the Imperial system is some areas.[300]

In 1975, the United States passed the Metric Conversion Act and started to make the switch to the metric system under President Carter, but didn't make any major changes because it was voluntary. Bottling is one of the areas that started to make the conversion. So now you can buy a 2-liter bottle of Dr. Pepper Zero or a 1.75-liter bottle of Jamison Irish Whiskey. However, a can of Dr Pepper Zero is still in a 12-ounce can.

Lack of standardization can cause serious problems and the United States' rejection of the metric system has led to problems. For example, in 1983, an Air Canada Boeing 767 lost power midair because its field load of fuel had been mistakenly calculated in pounds, not kilograms. The landing was the first "dead stick" landing of a commercial jetliner. Luckily, the Captain happened to have a glider-pilot license along with ten years of experience. In another example, years later, a probe destined for Mars disintegrated on landing because United States software had used pounds rather than kilograms.[301]

6: To provide for the Punishment of counterfeiting the Securities and current Coin and Currency of Ameristralia;

7: Establish Post Offices and post Roads;

8: To promote the Progress of Science and useful Arts, by securing for limited Times to Authors and Inventors the exclusive Right to their respective Writings and Discoveries;

9: To constitute Tribunals inferior to the [S]upreme Court; subordinate Tribunals will have no more than 5 judges each and the Supreme Court will have 9 judges;

The current United States Constitution does not specify the number of individuals on the individual courts. The number of Justices on the Supreme Court has changed six times before settling at the present total of nine in 1869.[302]

In 2020, there was talk of packing the bench with new judges to offset the conservative judges appointed by President Trump. By specifying a number, it prevents the current party in power from packing the court with new justices, thus providing the necessary constitutional *check and balance* that is missing to counter any misguided activity from the Legislative and Executive Branches when one party dominates.

10: To define and punish Piracies and Felonies committed on the high Seas, and Offen[s]es against the Law of Nations;

11: To declare War, grant Letters of Marque and Reprisal, and make Rules concerning Captures on Land and Water;

The powers in 10 and 11 are unique because it gives the government, via the constitution, jurisdiction over "captures" in international water and other lands. The power resembles that of Mother Britain and the imperial ways of the past.

12: To raise, provide and maintain military forces. (Stricken is "Armies, but no Appropriation of Money to that Use shall be for a longer Term than two Years;")

Originally, the founders thought there wouldn't be a need for a standing army, but time has shown that is not the case.

13. This item is stricken "To provide and maintain a Navy;

Item 12 above now covers both items.

14: To make Rules for the Government and Regulation of military forces; (Stricken is "the land and Navy;")

By taking out "land and Navy," it broadens the framework of all military forces.

15: To provide for calling forth the Militia to execute the Laws of the Union, suppress Insurrections and repel Invasions;

16: To provide for organizing, arming, and disciplining, the Militia, and for governing such Part of them as may be employed in the Service of Ameristralia, **reserving to the** Provates **respectively, the Appointment of the Officers, and the Authority of training the Militia according to the discipline prescribed by Congress;**

17: To exercise exclusive Legislation in all Cases whatsoever, over such District/City (not exceeding ten square miles) as may, by Cession of particular Provate, **and the Acceptance of Congress, becomes the Seat of the Government of** Ameristralia, **and to exercise like Authority over all Places**

purchased through eminent domain **by the Consent of the Legislature of the** Provate **in which the Same shall be, for the Erection of Forts, Magazines, Arsenals, dock-Yard,** right of way for transportation and utility service, **and other needful Buildings; And** also natural gas pipelines, electric transmission lines, electrical generation, mass transit corridors, etc., for the establishment of the new Capital city.

The changes provide additional authorization to make sure the new capital has the infrastructure necessary to operate effectively.

The original wording gives the Provate a veto over having the new federal capital put in their jurisdiction. Restricting a Provate veto may be something to discuss at the Constitutional Convention. Anyone living within the capital could still be a resident of the Provate it's located in, and the district will be a city (controlled by the federal government) within the Provate.

It also provides Congress the ability to approve right of ways for utilities and transportation (highways and airports), and electrical generation outside of the City.

18: To make all Laws which shall be necessary and proper for carrying into Execution the foregoing Powers, and all other Powers vested by this Constitution in the Government of Ameristralia, **or in any Department or Officer thereof.**

Section 9,

1: This item deleted: "The migration or importation of such Persons as any of the States now existing shall think proper to admit, shall not be prohibited by the Congress prior to the Year one thousand eight hundred and eight, but a Tax or duty may be imposed on such Importation, not exceeding ten dollars for each person."

Item one of section nine was part of the grand compromise to bring the 13 colonies together, which prevented Congress from stopping the slave trade before 1808. By setting a date, it was an acknowledgment that at some point in the future, slavery would come to an end and left the issue for later generations to tackle. As it happened, the federal Act Prohibiting Importation of Slaves of 1807 took effect on January 1, 1808. At this point, the Southern States knew it was just a question of time before slavery was abolished and the country began the slide towards the Civil War, which started in 1861.

2: The Privilege of the Writ of Habeas Corpus shall not be suspended, unless when in Cases of Rebellion or Invasion the public Safety may require it.

3: No Bill of Attainder or ex post facto Law shall be passed.

4: In any given year, every organization, business or individuals' income will pay a minimum of 1% and a maximum of 20% in income tax to the federal government, unless in time of war. Income for organizations and businesses is defined as revenues minus expenses. Religious, Charitable and nongovernment Educational institutions will be subject to a 1% federal income tax.

> a) The federal government may only raise revenue through a tax on income (wages earned, governments benefits received, inheritance/gifts/lottery/ gambling proceeds, interest, dividends, capital gains), nominal one-time usage fees, duties, tariffs, bonds issued, mineral royalties on federal land, and fines.

> b) Provates and local governments, together, may not charge individuals, organizations, or businesses more than 5% on income. Provates and local governments may only raise revenue by a tax on income (wages earned, government benefits received, inheritances/gifts/lottery/gambling proceeds, interest, dividends, capital gains), sales taxes, real and personal property taxes, nominal one-time usage fees, bonds issued, fines, and

mineral royalties within the Provate. Property tax rates may not be higher for commercial properties than residential properties.

c) Inheritance, gifts, lottery and gambling proceeds will be tax-free on the first one million dollars when the money goes into a person's LISA. The first million not going into a LISA will be taxed at the normal Federal and Provate rate and any monies received over that amount will be taxed 60% at the Federal level and 15% at the Provate level.

d) Everyone over the age of 18, and all organizations and businesses, must file an income tax return each year.

(Amendment 16, ratified 2/3/1913, which gave the government the right to tax income.)

Every citizen, organization, and business must contribute something for the common good of the country. An incorporated business, under the law, is considered to be the same as a person except that businesses do not have the right to a vote. Maintaining the same income tax rates and property tax rates between residential and commercial property ensures some fairness between the entities.

Federal, Provate, and local entities may not circumvent the cap on taxes by instituting fees. Such fees would be deemed illegal if they are not nominal one-time fees. For example, if a citizen is charged a fee for a service provided by a municipality such as trash service, and the citizen is not given the opportunity to use a private company for the same service, then that fee is an illegal tax. The service fee is required of all property owners whether they use the service or not, making it illegal because it is not a one-time fee. For example, in Kansas City, Missouri, the trash service the city provides is not charged for separately, but rolled into an individual's property taxes. Property taxes are a legal tax. A trash service fee is not like a nominal one-time fee to use the National Park system. Visiting a National Park is an individual choice where only attendees pay the one-time fee, which is a legal tax to maintain the park. Toll roads are another example of one-time fees that fit the definition.

Franchise taxes on the utility bill would not be legal because it is not on the list of approved taxes, but having a sales tax on the utility bill would be allowed. However, extra taxes placed on a utility bill have the potential to hurt low-income folks the most.

To receive any benefits from the government, the current US philosophy is that an individual must deplete their own resources first (including any pride and dignity) and then the government comes in to help out. I have known a couple of families who have depleted the assets of a loved one just so the loved one can qualify for assistance in a nursing home. It becomes a game. In the new framework all working citizens will have assets for retirement and these assets (LISA, Long-Term Individual Security Accounts, covered later in Article 5, section 3.) may not be touched by the government or by the courts which will require a new mindset on how benefits are distributed.

Everyone should receive the same dollar amount in benefits, whether a day care subsidy or hospice benefits at death or any other benefit, without any income or asset qualifications. In a hypothetical example where the government wants to help all young families with daycare, let's assume the benefit is $500/month/child and both Family A and B have two children. Let's also assume Family A makes $50,000/year and is in the 1% tax bracket and Family B makes $100,000/year and is in the 20% tax bracket.

Family A gets $1,000/month ($12,000 annually), and 11% goes to their LISA, $1,440, and they pay the 1% income tax on $10,560 ($12,000 − $1,440), or $105.60. All income and benefits are subject to LISA contributions and covered later in more detail.

Family B gets the same $1,000/month ($12,000 annually), and 11% goes to their LISA, $1,440, and they then pay the 20% income tax on $10,560 ($12,000 − $1,440), or $2,112.

The net result for Family A is a net benefit of $10,454.40 after paying a tax of $105.60, with $1,440 long-term benefit that goes into their LISA. As a net result, Family B receives a net benefit of $8,448, after paying the $2,112 in taxes each year with $1,440 long-term benefit that goes into their LISA. See the chart below for a summary.

	Family A	Family B
Benefit which is taxable	$12,000/annually	$12,000/annually
11% goes into LISA	$1,440	$1,440
Net Benefit after LISA	$10,560	$10,560
Benefit is taxed at	1%	20%
Tax is	$105.60	$2,112
Net Benefit	$10,454.40/year	$8,448/year

Married parents spilt the benefit, while a single parent (primary caregiver) receives the entire amount. No one has to prove they are poor or destitute to get help. No one has to play games (staying single rather than getting married, which disincentivizes the family unit) in order to qualify and then receive the benefit. If there is a way to beat the system, smart people will do it. The government helps everyone equally and that assistance is recognized as income, taxed accordingly, and the LISA contribution is required.

The result is that Families A & B get the same benefit, but Family A pays $2,006.40 less in taxes than Family B. They both have two kids and they both get needed help from the government because all new families struggle with the costs of raising children.

Also, because the benefit shows up as income to each family, it gets counted when determining poverty levels, whereas currently it does not. The current official poverty measure has existed for about 50 years and is widely used, but it does have limitations. For example, the official measure looks only at pre-tax money income and does not examine the impact of government taxes and non-cash benefits on a family's well-being. The official measure also generally does not take the value of assets into account, though a recent change in measurement now considers distributions from retirement savings as income.[303]

As part of the Covid-19 Relief Bill, the administration wanted to help families with children. Some families received $250-300/child/month as a tax credit, if their joint income was less than $150,000. As stated before, a tax credit does not show up as income to the family and the family could still be classified or appearing as "poor" when in reality they may not be. All financial assistance must be counted as income—no more tax credits.

Taxing government benefits such as unemployment benefits is nothing new for the Federal government. Provates, such as New York, already tax unemployment benefits.[304]

Under these proposals, no hidden taxes, such as Value Added Taxes, are permitted nor any new tax type that might be thought up. Taxes may only be levied once on a product at the point of sale—sales tax. Revolutionaries rejected indirect taxes (i.e., Value Added Taxes) on the grounds that they would be a burden on all, regardless of income, and therefore a particularly heavy burden on the poor.[305] Also, no government body may charge a person, organization or business for their regulatory actives, like audits or inspections.

In 2019 after the Administration's tax cuts, the US had the lowest global tax rate, except for three other countries, Chile, Ireland, and Mexico. The tax burden in the US fell to 24.3% of GDP. The US tax rate was 10% below the 2018 Organization for Economic Cooperation and Development average of 34.3%. Taxes in France and Denmark are nearly twice as high as the US.[306] Ireland has a 15% income tax on businesses. When Margaret Thatcher took office in Britain the top tax rate was 83%, with a base rate of 33%.[307] A great example of how bad things can get with the tax code when maximum rates are not established.

In Canada, Prime Minister Borden is associated with introducing the income tax to Canada in 1917, which was presented as a temporary measure.[308] But the Canadian temporary income tax survived the Second World War and grew dramatically in size and bite.[309]

A consistent Provate income tax (and a cap) for businesses may greatly reduce the risk of one Provate from trying to provide incentives to poach a business from another Provate. Regarding businesses, the only other major tax would be property tax on the building they occupy and the cost of regulatory compliance. For the individual, the personal tax rate may influence their decision on the Provate in which they live and work.

Rather than taxing essential businesses (daycare, grocery store, utility companies, etc.), the Congress may decide to levy only a 1% tax on these essential businesses to make their products and services more affordable to everyone. The alternative is to tax them at the regular rates and then turn around and give benefits to everyone for daycare, groceries, and utility bills as we do now in the US.

There are too many examples in the US of inequitable taxation as well as the propensity to keep taxing. For example, for decades Connecticut's lack of an income tax lured New York workers and businesses to that Provate. Then in 1991, Republican Governor Lowell Weicker introduced an income tax, promising it would fix the Provate's fiscal issues. It didn't, and the original 1.5% rate has since been raised five times to today's 6.99%. The progressive tax ratchet is always up.[310] The thought of cutting benefits/expenses never occurs to most politicians. Politicians want to buy more votes.

In 2020, the State of New York, which has an income tax, spent $5,231 per resident. If New York spent at Florida's level per resident, the Empire State would save $56.7 billion each year. If Illinois were to trim its state's per resident spending to match Texas', it would save taxpayers $22.3 billion a year—and there would be no need for any income tax increase. Californians could save $64.6 billion annually if the state matched New Hampshire's per capita spending. If New York and Illinois spent like Florida and Texas, they could save enough to put away the tin cup, claiming they need to raise more taxes. Other high-tax, high-spending states include Connecticut ($6,745 per resident), Delaware ($8,383), Hawaii ($8,054), Iowa ($5,422), Maryland ($4,997), Minnesota ($5,000), Oregon ($7,154), Pennsylvania ($4,305), Vermont ($5,884), Virginia ($4,804), and Wisconsin ($6,300).[311]

As a side note, sometimes government or regulatory bodies force companies to charge and/or offer optional products in order to help the "less fortunate." Because they have been deemed "impoverished," the subsidy is not seen as a tax. The phone bill is a good example where there are special fees/taxes as in the Federal Universal Service Charge, which are supposed to support schools, libraries, and rural health care facilities. In the Union, companies will not be required to charge an extra fee (tax) so they can subsidize service for someone else, as mandated by law, which is actually a hidden tax on other customers of the company. That practice would now be illegal.

Inheritance and gifts will be tax-free on the first one million dollars received when it goes into an individual's LISA with a 50/50 split; however, there should be accommodations for a family farm or business in this scenario. The second million will be taxed at normal rates and any monies received above that will be taxed at the higher rate (60% federal and 15% Provate for a total of 75%). Each generation should have the expectation of working and finding their success in life on their own and not from the previous generations' work. Society is providing the proper *incentives* and expectation for each generation.

Everyone must file an annual income tax return—no exceptions. I know of a young man who started a business and planned not to file a tax return for the business, thinking he could just slip through the system and not get caught. Although illegal, he was willing to take that calculated risk. I was able to convince him otherwise. Filing a signed return should not be seen as a detriment. If taxation is equitable, and devoid of loopholes, and filers still lie, then they can be held accountable under the law. Filing a signed return replaces a need for a census because, once a year, each household is verifying where they live, and the members of the family are identified.

5: No Tax or Duty shall be laid on Articles exported from any Provate. However, Congress has the authority to deny exports of specific products and services to particular countries.

6: No Preference shall be given by any Regulation of Commerce or Revenue to the Ports of one Provate **over those of another: nor shall Vessels bound to, or from, one** Provate, **be obliged to enter, clear, or pay Duties in another.**

7: No Money shall be drawn from the Treasury, but in Consequence of Appropriations made by Law; however, if Congress fails to pass a budget for the coming fiscal year in the appropriate time, then the President will have the power to pay the country's bills. The President may not exceed expenditures from the previous year's budget for each department and has the latitude to spend less than the amount for the previous year. The exception would be defense spending where the President can increase defense spending by the amount that is cut from other domestic programs; **and a regular Statement and Account of the Receipts and Expenditures of all public Money shall be published from time to time.**

Each department will receive a financial audit each year, looking for fraud, monies not spent, and lack of controls in the systems. The exception would be defense/security spending for non-traditional purposes.

If the Congress fails to pass a budget out of incompetence or as political leverage with the President, the country must be able to operate. For example, in the 1970s, the Opposition which controlled the Australian Senate refused to authorize expenditures in the hopes it would force an election.[312] The US Congress has been known to play similar games.

Sometimes, Congress funds policing actions (wars) as an outside budget item. By allowing defense spending to increase, the military will always be properly funded. Providing for the defense of the country is the primary responsibility of, and was a major motivator for, the various states coming together as one country—the United States of America. The same objective holds true with Ameristralia.

Departments within the government should have non-partisan auditors assessing the controls and potential fraud in any given department, as well as any unspent monies. The audit applies to the defense/security, but obviously there are some non-traditional (secret activity of NSA, CIA, etc.) that would fall outside those parameters and not need to see the light of day.

8: All budgets passed will be balanced, i.e. projected revenues and projected expenses will be equal. In the event of a projected overage or shortage at the end of the fiscal year, the amount of overage or shortage will be rolled over into the next budget. Congress has five years to implement.

The last year for a budget surplus in the US was in 2001. After the 9/11 attacks in 2001 there was deficit spending to fund our war on terror and the rest is history. Since then, both parties have been spending enormous amounts of money with no end in sight. The American people and other countries wishing to join the US in Ameristralia will want the US to get its financial house in order. However, during the transition, there may be a need for special spending to bring everything together, thus the five years allotted for implementation.

9: No Title of Nobility shall be granted by Ameristralia: [a]nd no Person holding any Office of Profit or Trust under them, shall, without the Consent of the Congress, accept (deleting the word "of" here) any present, Emolument, Office, or Title, of any kind whatever, from any King, Queen, Prince, or foreign State.

Presently, if a US President receives a gift from a foreign government, it then becomes property of the government. Gifts are considered a gift to the American people. In many Presidential libraries you will find a display of gifts that other countries have given to that President.

If Mother Britain should join the Union, then if someone already has a title, say, Queen of England, that is okay. But no one from the joining Provates would receive any new titles. No new kings, queens, or knights will be allowed.

Section 10,

1: No Provate shall enter into any Treaty, Alliance, or Confederation; grant Letters of Marque and Reprisal; coin or print **Money; emit Bills of Credit;** (deleting "make any Thing but gold and silver Coin a Tender in Payment of Debts"); **pass any Bill of Attainder, ex post facto Law, or Law impairing the Obligation of Contracts, or grant any Title of Nobility.**

2: No Provate **shall, without the Consent of the Congress, lay any Imposts or Duties on Imports or Exports, except what may be absolutely necessary for executing it[ ]s inspection Laws: and the net Produce of all Duties and Imposts, laid by any** Provate **on Imports or Exports, shall be for the Use of the Treasury of** Ameristralia; **and all such Laws shall be subject to the Revision and Contr[o]l of the Congress.**

3: No Provate **shall, without the Consent of Congress, lay any Duty of Tonnage,** (delete "keep Troops"), **or Ships of War in time of Peace, enter into any Agreement or Compact with another** Provate, **or with a foreign Power, or engage in War, unless actually invaded, or in such imminent Danger as will not admit of delay.**

Each Provate has their own militia, i.e., the National Guard. The US Constitution made allowances for that in the above section. Here each Provate is given that right up front, without Congress acting or taking away the right.

Article 2 - Executive Branch

Section 1,

1: **The executive Power shall be vested in a President of Ameristralia. The President shall hold Office during the Term of four Years, and, together with the Vice President, chosen for the same Term, be elected, as follows.**

When speaking of the President, as was done here, they often used masculine pronouns such as "he" or later "him", etc. They never considered that a woman could also be President. I have changed it here and throughout this document so it is gender neutral. Either the "President", "their", "they", or "he or she" is used throughout.

2: **The Electoral College system will be used for the election of the President and Vice President. The voting for the Electoral College will be done in the Senate and the Senior Senator of each Provate's delegation will cast all votes, one for each Senator and one for each Representative of the Provate, for the winning candidate based on their Provate's election for the office. If the Senior Senator is absent, then the Junior Senator will cast the appropriate votes. If no representatives are present from a given Provate then the Speaker may cast the votes for the Provate.**

All of a Provate's votes will go for just one candidate. If there isn't a winner after the first ballot, then Rank Choice voting comes into play for each Provate. In case of a tie, a coin toss will determine the winner.

The above proposed text supersedes the 12th Amendment to the constitution which was ratified on 6/15/1804.

The Electoral College forces presidential candidates to campaign in all parts of the country and appeal to a broader coalition of voters. The current United States constitutional system gives Provates broad control over their Electoral College process. Provates appoint electors "in such Manner as the Legislature thereof may direct."[313] The process should be defined to take out all ambiguity and standardize the process for each Provate. Currently, if someone is not selected in the first round of voting in the Electoral College, then Congress gets to pick the President and Vice President. The proposed changes will take Congress out of the process and puts the necessary *checks and balances* into the Constitution so that the will of the people prevails.

The Electoral College in the United States was set up so that larger Provates with bigger populations would not dominate in electing the President and Vice President. The smaller Provates, whether in size or population, did not want to be put at a disadvantage or overlooked. The approach forces parties to pay attention to all parts of the country and address the issues of the entire country. The same would be true for Ameristralia. The Electoral College would ensure that the former United States, due to its population size, does not dominate the voting for President and Vice President in the Union of Ameristralia.

In Canada in 2019, Prime Minister Justin Trudeau won reelection with just 33% of the vote while the second largest party only won 34.4% of the vote. In Canada, as well as the United States, the candidates with an "efficient" distribution of voters wins. Both systems force parties to compete beyond regional strongholds for voters and go after voters in all regions, and or have positions attractive to a greater audience.[314] This is the beauty of the Electoral College in the United States where better distribution of the votes helps pick a winner, much like in Canada.

The Electoral College will also have a bearing on the elections in Ameristralia with its widely disbursed geographic area and diverse populations. The needs and issues of the entire Union will need representation. Recognizing that each Provate on each Continent may have different, specific needs, the Electoral College will better address this situation than a straight counting of popular votes for president.

For example, today in the United States if Party A won 70% of the votes in all the big cities on both coasts and totally ignored the

AMERISTRALIA

issues of the rest of the nation, it could probably win the election if one-person one-vote were the law of the land for President. In another example, in Ameristralia, if Party A won 70% of the former United States vote and ignored the issues of the rest of Ameristralia, it could probably win the election. The goal is to have people running for the Presidency with programs and positions that will benefit everyone, not one group or region over the other.

There have been unfaithful deviations in the electors selected to vote in the US Electoral College. For example, in the 2016 election, one Colorado elector was replaced when he cast a vote for Ohio Republican John Kasich instead of Hillary Clinton. Also, in 2016 a Washington elector could have been fined for voting for Colin Powell instead of Hillary Clinton. In fact, 10 of 538 presidential electors in the 2016 Electoral College attempted to cast votes for people other than their party's presidential nominee. For this reason, I propose that one Senator from each Provate cast all the votes in the Electoral College for their Provate.

In most cases, in the US, the Electoral College winner also won the nationwide popular vote. The last three exceptions were Benjamin Harrison, in 1888; George W. Bush, in 2000; and Donald Trump in 2016. Donald Trump lost the popular vote to Hillary Clinton by 2.1%, or roughly three million votes. However, in the Electoral College he won by racking up 304 electoral votes to Clinton's 227.[315] If Clinton would have campaigned for the necessary electoral votes (i.e., in Wisconsin) rather than trying to drive up the popular vote in places such as California, where she knew she was going to win, the elections may have turned out differently.

The 1876 election for President produced no winner in the Electoral College. So there was the Compromise of 1877 to resolve the issue of who would be President. Governor Hayes came to an understanding with a group of Southern representatives in a series of conferences. The upshot of these conferences was that the Republicans agreed to abandon the three remaining Republican governments in South Carolina, Louisiana, and Florida, in favor of the Democratic claimants. The US Army was also taken out of

163

the South where they were protecting African-Americans trying to realize their new found freedom, thus ending the Reconstruction Era. The Southern Democrats would let the Republican nominee win the election for President by promising to defeat their party's filibuster, assist in completing the count, and see that Hayes was peacefully inaugurated.[316]

The Compromise of 1877 led to the Electoral Count Act of 1887 (ECA). The law was intended to resolve contested presidential elections, but in the twenty-first century, it has mainly been used by partisans in Congress to exploit the ceremonial process of counting electoral votes. Some Democrats took advantage of the ECA to cast doubt on legitimate results in 2001, 2005, and 2017, and Republicans did the same in 2021. Yet the ECA allows Congress to unnecessarily interfere with Provate decisions. Members of the House and Senate can claim electoral votes are not "regularly given" or "lawfully certified," holding up the count and disqualifying electors if a majority in both houses agrees.[317] The entire process needs to be defined here so there is no ambiguity and the people decide, not politicians.

3: The terms of the President and Vice President shall end at noon on the 20th day of January.

(Amendment 20, item 1, ratified 4/26/1933.)

If, at the time fixed for the beginning of the term of President, the President elect shall have died, the Vice President elect shall become President. If a President shall not have been chosen before the time fixed for the beginning of their term, or if the President elect shall have failed to qualify, then the Vice President elect shall act as President until a President shall have qualified; (Deleted, "and the Congress may by law provide for the case wherein neither a President elect or a Vice President elect shall have qualified, declaring who shall then act as President, or the manner in which one who is to act shall be selected, and such person shall act accordingly until a President or Vice President shall have qualified.") **if neither the President elect or Vice President elect shall**

have qualified by the day prior to taking office, then the senior Senator in leadership from their party shall appoint a successor President.

(Amendment 20, item 3, ratified 4/26/1933.)

This text takes away the ability for Congress to decide by law what the succession will look like. Succession is put into the Constitution so it cannot be changed. The previous paragraph deals primarily with the President Elect. Similarly, the language for the sitting President and Vice President is duplicated in the following paragraph. In both paragraphs the legislatures pick a successor, a political body. What if the House is controlled by the party that lost the Presidential election? Should they be allowed to pick the new President. I am suggesting the senior Senator in leadership from the party that won the Presidential election select a successor that best reflects the will of the people.

4: (Deleted, "The Congress may by law provide for the case of the death of any of the persons from whom the House of Representatives may choose a President whenever the right of choice shall have devolved upon them, and for the case of death of any of the persons from whom the Senate may choose a Vice President whenever the right of choice shall have devolved upon them.") If neither the President or Vice President shall have qualified to hold office, then the senior Senator in leadership from their party shall appoint a successor President

(Amendment 20, item 4, ratified 4/26/1933.)

This text takes away the ability for Congress to decide by law what the succession will look like and succession is put into the Constitution so it cannot be changed.

5: (This section is deleted, it said, "The Congress may determine the Time and choosing the Electors, and the Day on which they shall give their Votes; which Day shall be the same throughout the United States.")

The Electors shall meet in the Senate Chamber on Tuesday six weeks after the election at 1:00 p.m. for casting the votes for President.

Selection of electors in the Electoral College is specified in the Article 2, Section 2, of this document. However, a senator will now cast all of the votes for each Provate, simplifying the process.

Formerly, this item described how the electors will vote in the Electoral College and how that information is transmitted to the "Seat of Government." The old language is replaced by this new item and the item before it, which lays out the rules for voting in the Electoral College.

6: No Person except a natural born Citizen, or a Citizen of Ameristralia, at the time of the Adoption of this Constitution, shall be eligible to the Office of President; neither shall any Person be eligible to that Office who shall not have attained to the Age of thirty[-]five Years, and been fourteen Years a Resident within the Union of Ameristralia.

7: No person shall be elected to the office of the President more than twice, and no person who has held the office of President, or acted as President, for more than two years of a term to which some other person was elected President shall be elected to the office of the President more than once. (Then deleted, "But this article shall not apply to any person holding the office of President when this article was proposed by the Congress, and shall not prevent any person who may be holding the office of President, or acting as President, during the term within which this article becomes operative from holding the office of President or acting as President during the remainder of such term.").

(Amendment 22, item 1, ratified 2/27/1951.)

When the constitution for the Union is ratified in the US, the sitting US President assumes the role until the first Union election can be scheduled. It is assumed that this would be within two years. Term limits for the President, Vice President, and members of Congress do not start until the first Union election takes place.

8: In Case of the removal of the President from Office or their Death or Resignation the Vice President shall become President.

(Amendment 25, item 1, ratified 2/10/1967.)

9: Whenever there is a vacancy in the office of the Vice President, the President shall nominate a Vice President who shall take office upon confirmation by a majority vote of both Houses of Congress.

(Amendment 25, item 2, ratified 2/10/1967.)

10: Whenever the President transmits to the Speaker of the Senate and the Speaker of the House of Representatives their written declaration that they are unable to discharge the power and duties of his office, and until they transmit to them a written declaration to the contrary, such power and duties shall be discharged by the Vice President as Acting President.

(Amendment 25, item 3, ratified 2/10/1967.)

11: Whenever the Vice President and a majority of either the principal officers of the executive departments or of such other body as Congress may by law provide, transmit to the Speaker of the Senate and the Speaker of the House of Representatives their written declaration that the President is unable to discharge the powers and duties of their office, the Vice President shall Immediately assume the powers and duties of the office as Acting President.

Thereafter, when the President transmits to the Speaker of the Senate and the Speaker of the House of Representatives their written declaration that no inability exists, they shall resume the power and duties of their office unless the Vice President and a majority of either the principal officers of the executive department or of such body as Congress may by law provide, transmit within four days to the Speaker of the Senate and the Speaker of the House of Representatives their written declaration that the President is unable to discharge the powers and duties of the office. Thereupon Congress shall

decide the issue, assembling within forty-eight hours for that purpose if not in session. If the Congress, within twenty-one days after receipt of the latter written declaration, or, if Congress is required to assemble, determines by two-thirds vote of both Houses that the President is unable to discharge the powers and duties of the office, the Vice President shall continue to discharge the same as Acting President; otherwise, the President shall resume the powers and duties of their office.

(Amendment 25, item 4, ratified 2/10/1967, which has two paragraphs.)

12: The President shall, at stated Times, receive for their Services, a Compensation, which shall neither be increased nor diminished during the Period for which they shall have been elected, and shall not receive within that Period any other Emolument from Ameristralia, but said compensation will never exceed 14 times the average per capita income of the average citizen.

> **a) Vice Presidents compensation will never exceed eight times the average per capita income of the average citizen.**

> **b) The government will provide a residence for the President and another residence for the Vice President and while in office the equivalent of their full pay will be put into their LISA, tax free.**

> **c) After leaving the office of President, the President will receive a salary, security staff and administrative staff for 12 years.**

Compensation is structured similarly to the compensation of the Congress. The intent of Ameristralia's legislators is for them to be public servants and for them to be compensated as such. The most equitable approach is if incomes increase throughout the country then their pay may also be increased.

In 2020, the President received an income of $400,000, plus an expense account of $50,000. The current per capita income is about $33,000 and 14 times that is $462,000.

In 2020, the Vice President was paid $235,000, eight times $32,000 equals $256,000.

13: Before they enter on the Execution of their office, they shall take the following Oath or Affirmation: "I do solemnly swear (or affirm) that I will faithfully execute the Office of President of Ameristralia, and will to the best of my Ability, preserve, protect and defend the Constitution of Ameristralia."

Section 2,

1: The President shall be Commander in Chief of the Army, Air Force, Coast Guard, Marines, Navy, and Space Force of Ameristralia, and of the Militia of the several Provates, when called into the actual Service of Ameristralia; they may require the Opinion, in writing, of the principal Officer in each of the executive Departments, upon any Subject relating to the Duties of their respective Offices, and the President shall have Power to grant Reprieves and Pardons for Offen[s]es against Ameristralia or any Provate, except in Cases of Impeachment.

The President is the Commander-in-Chief of all armed forces, within any constraints established by Congress. The Space Force will probably not be a military force initially but rather a policing force and may also have the necessary weapons against a possible asteroid strike, enemy satellites, or missiles.

Currently, the President may only pardon someone for a federal crime, not any crime at the Provate level. The proposed Constitution later dictates that there be one penal code across all Provates. Therefore, depending on the circumstances, a conviction for a person can be at the Provate or Federal level.

2: The President shall have Power, by and with the Advice and Consent of the Senate, to make Treaties, provided two thirds of the Senators present concur; and shall nominate, and by and with the Advice and Consent of the Senate, shall appoint Ambassadors, other public Ministers and Consuls,

Judges of the Supreme Court, and all other Officers of Ameristralia, whose Appointments are not herein otherwise provided for, and which shall be established by Law: but the Congress may by Law vest the Appointment of such inferior Officers, as they think proper, in the President alone, in the Courts of Law, or in the Heads of Departments.

All treaties, ambassadorships, and other public officials will need to be renegotiated and resubmitted.

3: The President shall have Power to fill (delete "up") all Vacancies that may happen during the Recess of the Senate, by granting Commissions which shall expire at the end of their next Session.

All presidential nominees must be voted on within 90 days of nomination. For the Secretaries of Defense and State, or a Vice Presidential nominee, they must be acted on within 30 days. If the President has nominated two people to fill a particular vacancy and both are rejected, then the President may nominate any new person to fill the position without the necessary approval.

The Senate is prevented from stonewalling a President they don't like and are simply being obstructionist. If the President uses this option to fill a position and the individual is bad for the country, then the Congress always has the option to impeach the appointed person or the President.

The short time window given for the Secretaries of Defense and State are necessary for the safety and security of the nation. Delaying action on their nominations would be detrimental to the nation. The same applies for a vacancy for Vice President.

4) All individuals appointed to board or commission positions will not have terms longer than six years. The President may not fire an existing board member or commissioner. No political party may occupy more than fifty percent of the seats on a board or commission.

Appointed Cabinet or Department heads may be fired at any time by the President.

For example, the commissioner of Social Security was asked to resign in 2021 after the new President was sworn in, but he refused. He was then fired by the new President, although statutes said he could only be fired for neglecting his duties or malfeasance. A Justice Department legal opinion concluded that because of a recent Supreme Court ruling, the commissioner could be fired by the President at will.

If a board or commission member is not performing their job then they may be removed through impeachment.

5) The President, with the consent of Congress, may negotiate with other countries that express an interest in joining the Union. All countries will conform to Ameristralia's standards over an allotted time frame, and some may need financial assistance for the necessary transition.

Conversions may be necessary, but are not limited to standardization of roads, railroads, measurements, electrical standards, medical, and retirement systems. The debt burden of the interested country must also be addressed.

The reunification of East and West Germany in 1990 provides the best example. There had to be allowances and considerations made for East Germany to rejoin with West Germany after the Iron Curtain collapsed, ending Communism.

6) If the President invokes powers in case of an emergency, that emergency power may not last longer than twelve months.

The intent is to provide for some undefined emergency and then give sufficient time for Congress to provide the proper authorization. The emergency, (i.e., a pandemic) may keep going, but the President's power to act unilaterally does not.

Section 3,

The President shall from time to time give to the Congress Information o[n] the State of the Union, and recommend to their Consideration such Measures as the President shall judge necessary and expedient; the President may, on extraordinary Occasions, convene both Houses, or either of them, and in Case of Disagreement between them, with Respect to the Time of Adjournment, the President may adjourn them to such Time as the President shall think proper; the President shall receive Ambassadors and other public Ministers; the President shall take Care that the Laws be faithfully executed, and shall Commission all the Officers of Ameristralia.

Section 4,

The President, Vice President, and all civil Officers of Ameristralia, shall be removed from Office on Impeachment for, and Conviction of, Treason, Bribery, or other high Crimes and Misdemeanors.

The President and Vice President may not be charged for any ordinary criminal charges while in office.

Article 3 - Judicial Branch

Section 1,

1: The judicial Power of Ameristralia, **shall be vested in one [S]upreme Court, and in such inferior Courts as the Congress may from time to time ordain and establish. The Judges, both of the [S]upreme and inferior Courts, shall hold their Offices during good Behavior** until the age of 80, **and shall, at stated Times, receive for their services, a Compensation,** which for the Supreme Court will never exceed nine times the average per capita income of the average citizen and **which shall not be diminished during their continuance in Office.** A residence or stipend will be provided for each justice on the Supreme Court.

   a) Lower federal courts pay will never exceed six times the average per capita income of the average citizen.

   b) For the first 60 years the members of the Supreme Court, when possible, will be distributed as follows; 3 from North America, 3 from Australia/New Zealand and 3 from outside of those first two areas, if such areas exist.

   c) The justices on the respective courts will select a Chief Justice to lead their respective courts.

There is no current age where a justice must retire. While life expectancies are increasing and there are able-bodied septuagenarians and octogenarians, it is reasonable to establish a maximum age of service.

In New York, both the state constitution and state statute say judges can serve beyond the age of 70 if they have the mental and physical capacity to continue the work.[318]

The current justices on the United States Supreme Court will fill the nine seats initially for Ameristralia. After the US and one of the proposed countries have approved this Union and the new President and the new Congress has been elected, the Supreme Court will be filled, giving time for others to join the Union and have potential Justices nominated to the bench. After three justices have been nominated and approved by the Senate, the existing nine members of the US Supreme Court will be dismissed and may be offered a lower court appointment. As stated above, for the first sixty years, the Supreme Court will have three seats reserved for individuals from North American; three seats reserved for Australia and New Zealand; and the three remaining seats will be for any other areas that join Ameristralia from outside of these two identified continents (Greenland, Iceland, Caribbean, Hawaii, or the United Kingdom) and, if not, be at large seats. After six years has passed, the original date of the Union being formed, if there are open seats on the bench, the President will nominate enough justices to fill all nine seats.

A fixed number of seats are set in place and a certain number of seats for each area within Ameristralia are allocated so that after the Union is established, the Provates will have an extra layer of assurance during the transition phase. The assurance will remain in place for sixty years after the formation of the Union.

Currently in Canada, by custom, three of their justices must be trained in the civil law and come from Quebec, the other three come from Ontario, with two representing the western provinces and one coming from the Atlantic provinces. In Australia, the justices overwhelmingly come from Sydney and Melbourne.[319]

Once the new federal Supreme Court is in place with at least three justices, then all the other existing federal Supreme Courts will be disbanded. Lower Federal District Courts may stay in place with necessary adjustments.

In 2019, the Chief Justice of the Supreme Court made $277,700 and Associate Justices made $265,000. So nine times the average per capita income equates to $288,000.

2: Judges will rule on the issues before them based on the Ameristralia Constitution and the laws as they were originally written and conceived. Being a judge requires the ability to decipher between the letter and "spirit" of the Constitution and laws passed by Congress.

a) Judges may not impose solutions or accept plea deals by the government that allows the court or government to, in essence, legislate from the bench, but rather stop illegal activity. Sentencing should be based upon legal course of action, restitution, rehabilitation, and burden on the government.

b) All acts and/or laws passed by Congress and any regulatory rules promulgated by regulatory agencies must always be logical, fair, and reasonable, and when based on science, thoroughly researched and the underlying data made available to the public.

Judges may not concoct reasons why something is good or bad. As authors, Barnett and Bernick say in their recent book on the 14th Amendment, "[The judges] also must not abuse their delegated powers by using whatever discretion that original meaning gives them to pursue their own extralegal ends, goals, purposes, or objects, rather than serving the interest of their principals. Where the letter of the Constitution is unclear, fidelity to the Constitution's design requires that judges, legislators, and other constitutional decision makers turn to the law's original spirit."[320]

For example, the 1872 *Slaughterhouse Cases* debated the citizenship between federal and state inhabitants. The primary reasoning of the US Supreme Court was that the Privileges or Immunities Clause of the 14th Amendment is limited to federal citizenship rather than extending to state citizenship. The opinion by Justice Miller in the *Slaughter-House Cases* effectively redacted the Privileges and Immunities Clause in the 14th Amendment from the Constitution.[321] Rejecting the clause should not have happened because doing so also eliminates the separation of powers when the Congress, President, and the Provates pass a Constitutional Amendment and the Court chooses to ignore the will of the people.

The Obama administration often used a "sue and settle" strategy to bypass Congress. Some 137 new Clean Air Act regulations were imposed as a result of legal settlements with green groups.[322] Many of these settlements provided funds for parties not involved in the litigation. In 2013, for example, $1.3 billion was not just used for paying the 91 plaintiffs in the case, but rather thousands of folks, not claiming discrimination, were also paid.[323] Forcing Congress to approve all regulations may also stop this tactic. In 2021, the administration, through "sue and settle," was going to give illegal aliens a proposed $450,000 per child to parents who were separated from their children.[324]

The 1938 Food, Drug, and Cosmetic Act authorizes the FDA to regulate the "standards of identity"[325] of hundreds of food products to ensure uniform labeling. Ever wonder why some foods taste and look the same regardless of the brand?

Let's take ketchup for an example. The FDA requires ketchup to have a pH of 4.2±0.2 and lemon juice "may be used in quantities no greater than necessary to adjust the pH." The consistency must also be such, "that its flow is not more than 14 centimeters in 30 seconds at 20 °C." Manufacturers have more leeway with hummus and pickle relish.[326] The intent may have originally been for products to be uniform, but hundreds of variations and thousands of pages in the Federal Register later, the requirement now serves mainly to fatten trial lawyers who can sue manufacturers if their labels don't conform to government specifications. As a result, some low-fat ice creams are labeled frozen dairy desserts.[327]

More recently, the debate is about what constitutes milk in terms of animal base (cow, goats) and plant base (almond, soy). The examples go on and on from French salad dressing to pre-packaged cherry pie. Food safety is important, but should grocery store desserts be federally sanctioned? Is that reasonable and fair? Today we have basically unlimited products with almost any flavor you want.

3: In decisions between individuals or businesses and the government, the individual or businesses will receive the benefit of the doubt on the interpretation of regulations promulgated by the government.

Not doing this puts the citizen or business always at the mercy of the government's interpretation of what the law means. If the law is murky, the rules/regulations/laws need to be written so the intent is clear.

Section 2,

1: The Judicial Power shall extend to all Cases, in Law and equity, arising under this Constitution, the Laws of Ameristralia, and Treaties made, or which shall be made, under their Authority;-to all Cases affecting Ambassadors, other public Ministers and Consuls;-to all Cases of admiralty and maritime Jurisdiction;-to Controversies to which Ameristralia shall be a Party;-to Controversies between two or more Provates;-between a Provate and Citizens of another Provate; -between Citizens of different Provates;—between Citizens of the same Provates claiming Lands under Grants of different Provates, and between a Provate, or the Citizens thereof, and foreign States, Citizens or Subjects.

If other parties to a treaty are not fulfilling their obligations, then Ameristralia will not be bound by the treaty.

The courts are, therefore, prevented from enforcing a treaty when the other country does not comply.

2: In all Cases affecting Ambassadors, other public Ministers and Consuls, and those in which a Provate shall be Party, the [S]upreme Court shall have original Jurisdiction. In all the other Cases before mentioned, the [S]upreme Court shall have appellate Jurisdiction, both as to Law and Fact, with such Exceptions, and under such Regulations as the Congress shall make.

3: The Trial of all Crimes, except in Cases of Impeachment, shall be by Jury; and such Trial shall be held in the Provate where the said Crimes shall have been committed; but when not committed within any Provate, the Trial shall be at such Place or Places as the Congress may by Law have directed.

All courts and trials will be recorded.

The government must be transparent and accountable to the citizens of the country. The courts are no different than police officers performing their duties. There is no proposed level of quantity and quality established. The recording could consist simply of one camera covering the entire room and four microphones—one for the judge, the witness, the prosecution, and one for the defense.

Section 3,

1: Treason against Ameristralia, shall consist only in levying War against them, or in adhering to their Enemies, giving them Aid and Comfort. No Person shall be convicted of Treason unless on the testimony of two Witnesses to the same overt Act, or on Confession in open Court.

The Founding Fathers thought it would be too easy for a single person to come forward and perjure themselves in order to get someone convicted of treason. Therefore, they required two individuals to come forward in order to convict someone.

2: The Congress shall have Power to declare the Punishment of Treason, but no Attainder of Treason shall work Corruption of Blood, or Forfeiture except during the Life of the Person attainted.

"Corruption of Blood" is an old English phrase to punish the dependents of those in power who got stripped of their titles and land. So the government not only punished the dad (presumably) but also punished the children for the acts of their dad. Just a fun fact.

3: Any elected, appointed, or staff person who has publicly or privately (with two witnesses) stated that they are going to go after a person, organization, or business based on their party affiliation, or a political cause they support, may not be allowed to harass that person or business through law enforcement or the courts, and they will forfeit their position.

As in the case with Treason, it takes two people to go on the record in order to prove this has happened. The intent is to take politics out of law enforcement.

4: **The Judicial power of** Ameristralia **shall not be construed to extend to any suit in law or equity, commenced or prosecuted against one of the** Provates **by Citizens of another** Provate, **or by Citizens or Subjects of any Foreign State.**

(Amendment 11, ratified 2/7/1795)

Article 4 - Provate Relations

Section 1,

1: Full Faith and Credit shall be given in each Provate to the public Acts, Records, and Judicial Proceedings of every other Provate. And the Congress may by general Laws prescribe the Manner in which such Acts, Records, and Proceedings shall be proved, and the Effect thereof.

2: The Provates' primary responsibilities are to provide and adequately maintain physical infrastructure (roads, bridges, park, etc.), safety (policing, fire protection and sanitation), schools and universities, voting systems, and lower courts and jails.

3: The Provates do not have authority to establish different standards than the federal government has already set.

Item 2 establishes in writing some of things that a Provate has primary jurisdiction over and in Item 3 what it does not. For example, in California they have acquired the ability to set separate EPA rules for their Provate. The federal government sets the standards for everyone, not the Provates.

The federal government may have four different kinds of standards. First, a minimum standard like the minimum wage. Second, a maximum standard like the speed on a highway. Third would be a band the Provates could work within, like allowing the Provates to legislate the age for purchasing hard alcohol – 18 to 21 years of age. The fourth kind of standard is federal standard that a Provate has no authority to change, like an EPA standard.

Section 2,

1: The Citizens, Organizations or Businesses of each Provate shall be entitled to all Privileges and Immunities of Citizens, Organizations or Businesses in the other Provates.

A Provate, or city, may not penalize or restrict an individual, organization, or business from traveling to other Provates or cities. In 2020, there were Provates, cities, and businesses that tried to penalize businesses and individuals in other Provates because of voting laws that were passed in a given Provate.

2: A Person charged in any Provate with Treason, Felony, or other Crime, who shall flee from Justice, and be found in another Provate, shall on Demand of the executive Authority of the Provate from which they fled, be delivered up, to be removed to the Provate having Jurisdiction of the Crime.

Anyone fleeing the country to escape prosecution, gives up their citizenship and their ability to return.

3: (This item is deleted. "No Person held to Service or Labour in one State, under the Laws thereof, escaping into another, shall, in Consequence of any Law or Regulation therein, be discharged from such Service or Labour, but shall be delivered up on Claim of the Party to whom such Service or Labour may be due. Neither slavery nor") [I]nvoluntary servitude, except as a punishment for crime whereof the party shall have been duly convicted, shall not exist within Ameristralia, or any place subject to their jurisdiction.

(Amendment 13, ratified 12/6/1865.)

Here the founding fathers used "held to service or labour" as code words synonymous for slavery.

Section 3,

1: New Provates may be admitted by the Congress into this Union; but no new Provate shall be formed or erected within the Jurisdiction of any other Provate; nor any Provate be formed by the Junction of two or more Provates, or Parts of Provates, without the Consent of the Legislatures of the Provates concerned as well as of the Congress, except as otherwise noted in this document.

Later, we discuss the Channel Islands, Gibraltar, and Cypress and allow for them to be merged with another Provate if appropriate, *with both parties' approval.* For example, say Spain years later decided to join the Union. It would be logical for Gibraltar and Spain to be one, but with the hostility towards each other in the past that may not be realistic.

We also suggest that Hawaii act as the lead in assimilating all the other Pacific Ocean islands and the District of Columbia reverting back to Maryland. That portion of the District of Columbia that resided in Virginia was retroceded back to Virginia in March of 1847.

2: The Congress shall have Power to dispose of and make all needful Rules and Regulations respecting the territory or other Property belonging to the Ameristralia; and nothing in this Constitution shall be so construed as to Prejudice any Claims of Ameristralia, or of any particular Provate.

Section 4,

1: Ameristralia shall guarantee to every Provate in this Union a Republican Form of Government, with three separate branches of government; Executive with a Governor, Legislative and Judicial; and Ameristralia shall protect each of them against Invasion; and on Application of the Legislature, or of the Governor (when the Legislature cannot be convened) against domestic Violence.

2: Judges in the Provates, at any level, will not be elected, but rather appointed. However, Judges may be removed by a vote of the people.

Judges are supposed to be impartial and rule based on the law of the land. Running for judicial office and campaigning saying you have the latitude to do certain things for voters to make them happy, is contrary to the job description. A judge's only job is to enforce the constitution and interpret the laws on the books. There should be no attempt at legislating from the bench or trying to make voters "happy."

In some areas, Texas for instance, they have "Judges" who act as county administrators. They are not judges in a court. In these instances, the county administrator's name for the office needs to be changed so there is no confusion.

3: Remote, isolated and inaccessible areas of a Provate may receive special consideration by the respective Provate.

Circumstances such as voting, collecting DNA samples, providing schools, law enforcement, and so forth, may require unique solutions, or people in these areas may just want to be left alone. For example, indigenous people on their own land may not want anything to do with the government. The Provate will make that determination.

Article 5 - General

Here begins many of the changes that will bring the constitution into the twenty-first century.

Section 1, Identification Cards

1: The federal government will provide all identification cards and/or drivers licenses for free as well as license plates for vehicles for a fee. Anyone a) already a citizen, b) inhabitant of a territory, commonwealth, reservation or protectorate, c) or any family (parent and siblings) living, working, and paying income taxes in Ameristralia will be considered a citizen at the time of the acceptance of this constitution and will be issued a government identification card.

A citizen must have a federal government identification card in order to work, attend a school, rent a room, rent property, rent a car, vote or receive any benefits.

A non-citizen must have a Green Card in order to work in Ameristralia. For foreign travelers who want to rent a car, hotel room, or a house short-term, a passport is sufficient. For foreign exchange students or those wishing to attend college, a passport is also sufficient.

The provision includes previously illegal immigrants who will now be citizens, assuming someone in the family is working and paying income taxes.

Local driver's license offices will now report and be administered by the federal government. The same will apply to departments issuing license plates. There will also be no need for anyone to sign up for the Selective Service, for a potential draft, because the government will already have the information.

2: At birth, a DNA sample will be taken from the child, as well as from the mother and father (if he is available). At age 16 (when applying for a Driver's License/ID card), and at death, another DNA sample will be taken to validate the

identity of the person. The federal government will verify the consistency of the sample each time. New immigrants will also provide a DNA sample upon arrival.

Congress will setup and sufficiently fund a Census and Identity Theft Agency to track and monitor the DNA, fingerprints, physical and mailing address, where they work, criminal history, and appropriate licenses. Should inconsistencies arise, or identity theft take place, they will be investigated and resolved.

States' rights have been at the core of the United States since its inception. There are some who will find the centralization of driver licenses, vehicle registrations and tags, and DNA tracking not only an overreach by the federal government but an assault on their privacy. I understand. While founded on American principles, Ameristralia will also adopt practices of other democracies and evolve with technological advances. But with the number of Provates going from 50 to 80 or so, the "bad guys" will focus on the weakest link to attack our internal systems. With one system centrally controlled, it is hoped there are no weak links that can be exploited. Centralized standards provide for consistent quality control.

When fingerprints became the means to identify people and criminals in the nineteenth century, the practice was seen as revolutionary. DNA is the logical evolution of using unique biological markers. Whether it's the remains of a person found in the woods years or decades later, or a child raised by a kidnapper, DNA will help. In the case of a missing child who applies for their first driver's license/ID, or turns 16, these kids will be identified and reconnected with their parents and the guilty parties arrested. Identifying a parent will be easier and ensures the necessary child support is paid by forcing said parent to be accountable. The Agency data should also be able to identify the parents of abandoned children. Persons who are being "trafficked" may be easier to identify.

Although people may share the same eye and hair color, or have the same blood type, their DNA is unique and can be useful in more accurately solving crimes. Not only can DNA evidence point to a suspect, if there is no match, it may be able to rule out a suspect or even exonerate someone.

In some cases, advances in DNA testing has allowed law enforcement professionals to solve decades-old cases. Current database technology, which allows for DNA profiles to be stored and quickly searched, is not much different than the Integrated Automated Fingerprint Identification System (IAFIS), a computerized system maintained by the Federal Bureau of Investigation (FBI) since 1999. It is a national automated fingerprint identification and criminal history system.[328] Fingerprint matching is used not only by law enforcement but for job and volunteer placement and firearms purchases.

Furthermore, the military already collects fingerprint and DNA samples. The TSA's Global Entry program also takes fingerprints.

DNA from incoming immigrants may validate that all their children are theirs and not being smuggled into the country. Children lost in the system can be reconnected with family. DNA collection could also be a deterrent to criminals if they know their DNA is in a database.

Death benefits (hospice, or other benefits) should be made regardless of income or assets. Providing these financial incentives puts the government in a position to receive timely death information with DNA samples. The additional information will help further negate the need for a physical census.

Identity theft is becoming a big issue in our society and the government needs to have systems in place to help individuals regain their proper identity. The government has a fiduciary responsibility to help citizens reclaim their identity and put the perpetrators in jail.

3: Individuals will be required to notify the federal government when they move. The Post Office will also notify the federal government of any address changes as a double check.

> **a) The federal identification (ID) cards will allow anyone to move from Provate to Provate without having to get a new driver's license, license plate or register to vote.**

b) The federal government will notify the respective Provate when someone new has moved into or out of their jurisdiction.

The notification will allow the Provate to charge the necessary property taxes on any vehicles coming into their Provate. The Provate then can also update their local voter rolls.

I have moved over a dozen times and the time and hassle of getting a new driver's license, car tags, and registering to vote was very time consuming. A centralized approach will make it easier for anyone and their family to move within the confines of Ameristralia.

4: Individuals will get replacement ID cards every 10 years, starting on their 20th birthday and an updated photo will be added. Every person over 16 is required to have their Identification Card/Driver's License on them or in close proximity. Under 16, then the parent is responsible for their children's identification cards. Visiting or working foreigners are required to have their passport in close proximity.

Starting at age 20, required taxes and LISA contributions must have been paid for all prior applicable years in order to receive the new/replacement ID card.

Under this proposed schedule, an individual will receive an ID card at birth (that the parents hold), 16, 20, 30, 40, 50, 60, and every 10 years until the death of the individual. Obviously, for new legal immigrants they will be inserted into this schedule based on their arrival.

Requiring taxes and LISAs to be up-to-date forces compliance and everyone paying their rightful share in society.

5: Every time someone's ID card has been read by a government entity (voting, traffic stop, applying for benefits, attending school, death certificates, etc.), or a business verifying the citizenship of a prospective employee, or landlords renting property, that information will be passed on to the federal government electronically on a real time basis,

when possible. Provates and other federal departments will link, and share data, to the appropriate national databases.

These procedures will allow the government to stop conducting a census count every ten years. The government will be tracking the existence of a person each time they interact with the government and/or some businesses. Contrary to what citizens want to believe, the government already does a good deal of individual tracking.

In most places, people can hide out in the open in the crowd of humanity without being detected. However, the use of cameras and other sensors already exist in cities, towns, and businesses all over the country, and is growing. Redefining the expectation of privacy.

The new tax collecting agency for Ameristralia will pass monthly information to the Census and Identify Theft Agency for confirmation of employment. If a person's address and monthly tax withholdings show the person is working in Sydney, New South Wales and their ID is shown to have voted in Toronto, Ontario, then more work may need to be done to verify it is the right person. Or, if the citizen is arrested for a non-violent drug charge and their ID (or connected databases) verify they are employed, then that person can be released, rather than held in jail. More details on this later in the Individual Bill of Rights.

As a citizen, you realize that often times in government, the left hand doesn't know what the right hand is doing. Agencies and departments must share data in order to know what is going on with its citizens. Also, as a citizen, why do I have to fill out a new form for every department giving the same data over and over again? I want the data to already be there and they should already know who I am after I present my ID.

6: An up-to-date federal ID is also required in order to receive a government benefit or stipend, the individual (or their spouse if they have dependent children) must be working if physically and mentally able.

Everyone should work and pay taxes for the mutual benefit of society. If someone is not willing to help themselves by working, then why should the government help them? Working even a part-time job qualifies as contributing to the greater good and helping yourself.

For example, there are many jobs an amputee is qualified to perform. Through technology, individuals who may have lost a limb(s) in the past and were unable to work, now have the ability to rejoin the workforce and provide for themselves. Medical insurance, with or without the help of the government, should provide quality prosthetics for those individuals and devices such as wheelchairs. These steps are necessary in order to integrate back into society and the workforce.

Individuals with mental or physical disabilities should be reverified every ten years. With emerging technologies, these individuals may have an opportunity to reassimilate back into society and make contributions.

If someone is able to live by themselves, although they may not have a typical home, it also means they have the skills and intellect to work. Focusing on peoples' abilities and what they need to be productive allows people to be treated with dignity rather than being marginalized.

Section 2, Elections

The intent of the next Section on voting is to make the Constitution legally "thick" and not open to Judicial interpretations. If there is anything left unclear in the proposed wording for Elections, it needs to be clarified and made exact so that there is no question of the meaning or of any situation that is not covered.

Currently, there are no standardized rules for operating polling stations and running elections. Lack of standardization creates opportunities for political parties in power to change the rules to benefit their party, which must never be allowed to happen. In several states this has already resulted in basically one-party states, such as California, New York, and Rhode Island on the coasts and

Nebraska and Oklahoma in the Midwest. One party states are a threat to democracy.

Elections must be standardized and codified in the Constitution and operated fairly to protect our democracy through permanent *checks and balances.* There must also be a chain of custody for the ballots to insure there hasn't been any tampering.

1: All elections will be held on the third Monday of April and the third Monday of October each year. Early voting will take place for the 9 consecutive days prior to the actual election day. Polling places will be open 7:00 a.m. to 7:00 p.m. on Election Day and 9:00 a.m. to 3:00 p.m. for the 9 days of early voting. All times are local time.

> **a) Federal Primaries will be held in April and Federal General Elections in October of even number years.**
>
> **b) Provate, special, and local elections will typically be held in odd numbered years but may also be held in even number years.**
>
> **c) In case of a pandemic, or other declared emergency, the number of days for early voting will increase to 16 consecutive days prior to the actual election day.**
>
> **d) Congress will determine the dates for Presidential Primaries because they are the exception to the rule. Voting will be on one given day with no early voting, 7:00 a.m. to 7 p.m.**
>
> **e) Poll watchers from multiple parties will be allowed.**

We don't want to have voter fatigue in the election process. It is hard enough to encourage people to get out and vote without throwing a lot of additional elections into the mix.

Voting will take place for ten consecutive days, which also includes two Saturdays and two Sundays. In the case of a pandemic, it will add seven additional days of early voting. If an individual can't find a time to vote in person during that timeframe, the individual probably isn't excited about voting.

The 9:00 to 3:00 for early voting is proposed because of perceived staffing needs over that timeframe. These times allow the regular full-time employees to man/supervise the polling station in the confines of a normal eight-hour day, for early voting. Then there are the four weekend days that have to be staffed.

Presidential Primaries are unique because of the condensed timeframe between primaries and the fact that candidates may drop out at any time during the process, complicating the voting process. The voter doesn't want to vote early only to find out that one or more of their three choices (as in Ranked Choice Voting, which will be discussed at length later) has dropped out of the race.

2: Provates, and their counties, will have primary responsibility for running all elections. All ballots will be cast in person without assistance in the voting booth after presenting their federal identification card and verifying the physical address is in their jurisdiction and that the identification card has not been used for voting elsewhere. Backup databases of voter rolls and who has voted will be updated daily in case of internet failure.

    a) All cast ballots, whether made on paper or made via a terminal at the polling center, will result in a paper ballot the voter can read and verify for self-auditing purposes prior to being submitted/cast and also be machine readable for accurate and faster results.

    b) All voting for any public office at any level of government must be done in secret.

    c) Each polling center will have an accumulator(s) that reads the paper ballots as they are submitted/cast and accumulates the results. All ballots will be saved for at least eighteen months for audits.

    d) Each day the accumulators at each polling center will print off a summary of the raw results on paper for auditing purposes, as well as, a raw electronic version sent to the 1) Provate Secretary of State, 2) appropriate county office, and 3) an acceptable news service office (selected by Congress) within an hour of the last vote being cast. Besides the number of first place votes cast for each candidate, it will

show the split for the second and third choice votes of that candidate – as done in Ranked Choice Voting. After the election, the accumulators and ballots will be taken to a central facility for storage and possible auditing.

e) The respective County and Provate Secretary of State will then review the results for accuracy and accountability. After the appropriate local officials feel everything is correct, the Provate Secretary of State will certify the results of the election no later than three weeks after the election. After the results are certified by the Provate Secretary of State, any entity may audit the ballots under the supervision of local authorities.

f) No voting results (whether early voting, mail, or actual voting day) may be shared with the public or political parties until all polling stations are closed in each Provate on the last day of voting. Raw results may be shared at that time.

g) Neither Congress or Provate legislatures will have the authority to overturn the election results. A federal court may invalidate, correct, or require an audit after the results have been certified.

h) Provisional ballots for individuals with 1) an identification card without the proper physical address, or 2) if the identification card has already been used someplace else, or 3) if the internet is down and no back up database is onsite to verify 1 and 2 above, will be later researched to determine if valid.

i) No polling data will be provided to the public within four weeks of election day.

j) Releasing exit polling after the Provate has closed all polling stations is permissible.

k) Voting in a) remote, isolated, or inaccessible areas, and b) voting for the legally blind, or c) for individuals who are physically unable to mark a ballot on their own, all will be left to the discretion

of the respective Provate to manage, as long as in all cases the results can be reported prior to the last polling station in the Provate closing.

What is not explicitly said here is that a political party may no longer run their own primary voting process. So, the mass chaos associated with the 2020 Iowa caucuses will never happen again. The Provate and their counties will run all elections.

The current problem is that the Constitution does not give Congress the authority to regulate and/or standardize elections. Congress has some power, but it is limited to Federal Congressional elections and the Presidential Electoral College.[329] By adding it to Ameristralia's Constitution, it standardizes the process to ensure the process is secure and reflects the wishes of the citizens. During the early years of the United States, the central government had no experience with multi-state elections. Previously, the distances and lack of technology of the various states, which were too far from the federal government, made it difficult to direct and standardize the voting process. Now with technology, standardization is not only possible, it is necessary—for accountability and to ensure the necessary *checks and balances* are built into the system.

Because of the International Dateline, Provates in Australia, or Hawaii, and New Zealand will vote first. However, results cannot be shared until all polling stations are closed in each Provate. The interim results of any Provate should not be allowed to influence the voters still waiting to vote in that Provate.

All electronic voting equipment at precincts must return to voters notices of under voted ballots—when someone casts fewer votes on a ballot than is allowed—so the voter can correct them prior to submission. Obviously, an electronic voting machine would not allow overvoting (too many votes for the same office/person).

Provisional ballots will be given out, which permit voters to cast a ballot that can later be counted once it's established that the voter is a legal resident and hasn't already cast a ballot. As a result, no voter is turned away on Election Day or denied the right to cast a ballot as long as they have a current federally issued identification card.

Sending the preliminary unaudited summarized voting results to an appropriate news service each day will keep local officials accountable for the certified results reported later. By example, if the unedited summary results show 10,000 votes at one location and then later 12,000 get certified, everyone will know something is wrong. Currently, all of this happens behind the scenes, usually by part-time employees.

In the 2020 election in New York, New York, there were 135,000 plus extra ballots cast than voters. It turns out that the dummy ballots used in a test were not taken out of the system prior to the actual voting.[330] If others would not have been paying attention, the wrong count could have been certified. An outside organization is needed, a news service and/or Provate Secretary of State, looking over the shoulder of county officials as a double check.

Currently in the United States, the House of Representative has final say on its members' elections and the Supreme Court has held that courts can't intervene in those decisions according to the US Constitution's Article I, under section 5, 1.[331] Under this scenario, the House of Representatives, and the party in control of that body, have power to overturn the results of the election. In the proposed Ameristralian constitution, the House of Representatives, a political body, does not have the authority to change the results, but rather a neutral/nonpolitical body as the court system will be used.

A study by economist John Lott finds that 46 of 47 European countries require government issued photo IDs to vote. The exception is Great Britain (although not Northern Ireland). In 2021, Prime Minister Boris Johnson's government said it would make photo IDs mandatory in response to a 2016 Royal Commission report. As the BBC summarized it, authorities had turned a blind eye to electoral corruption via mail-in ballots in the UK because of a desire for political correctness.[332] We cannot let the desire for political correctness to drive our decision-making process.

The US Justice Department has a voter fraud unit. Unfortunately, voter fraud happens on a regular basis. The key phrase they use is that there is "no widespread voter fraud" that would have affected the outcome of the election. In the 2020 election in North Dallas, there was an individual caught fraudulently submitting mail-in ballots for the mayoral election in Carrolton for the race in which he was running. The individual was charged with 84 counts of mail application fraud and 25 counts of possessing an official mail ballot. Fortunately, there was someone smart enough to recognize what he was doing and notified authorities.

Obviously, in voting for President, a small number of fraudulent votes may not affect the outcome, but in local and some Congressional elections, an extra 100 votes could make a huge difference. In 2020, an Iowa vote came down to a difference of 6 votes (196,964 v 196,958) for the House of Representatives.

In 2021, two Georgia election workers were fired for shredding about 300 registrations forms, and in Michigan three women were charged with fraud. One of the Michigan women worked at a nursing home and filled out absentee ballots and forged residents' signatures.[333]

The proposed system is one that will keep elections from being tied up in the courts after every election or in the Congress as they decide which Provate to trust for the results.

For individuals in remote, isolated, or inaccessible areas, the respective Provate may determine what proper procedures will be. A few examples may include:
   a) a small island in the Pacific that has 100 residents and only has one flight a week that delivers mail and supplies.
   b) an island with no air service and the only access is via a boat.
   c) someone living above the Article Circle in a small community, or by themselves, or without roads for access or mail service.

In all of these examples, there may be a need for special treatment. The Provate may decide what is proper in these circumstances. It may be that the individual(s) doesn't want anything to do with society, and that is their choice/right.

3: An absentee ballot will be allowed for individuals stationed or working out of the country and their physical address in Ameristralia is for that voting location. Absentee

voters may not request a ballot earlier than 90 days prior to the election. The county clerk will have verified the voter's signature on their ID, physical address in Ameristralia, foreign mailing address, and employer against the federal rolls prior to sending the ballot out.

Completed absentee ballots must be received by 5:00 p.m. on the Monday prior to election day (one week prior to election day) by mail or package service from a foreign country. Signatures will be manually verified upon receipt of the completed ballot. Voters will not be able to fix ballots that do not qualify.

In 74% of European countries they ban absentee ballots except for citizens living abroad. Another 6% limit them to voters in the hospital or the military, and they require third-party verification and photo ID.[334]

If a person is working or serving in the military overseas, then they get to vote absentee because their ID will show the physical address of their home in Ameristralia. The mailing address on their ID would be their foreign address. However, if they are living abroad and not working (retired), then their home (physical and mailing address) is no longer Ameristralia and they are not able to vote until they return to Ameristralia to live or work.

The UK, which allows postal voting, has had many notable mail-in ballot fraud cases. In Viktor Orban's Hungary, which has the loosest mail-in voting in Europe and doesn't require photo IDs to obtain those ballots, the ruling party won 96% of overseas mail-in votes in 2018. The liberal group Open Democracy notes that fraud is possible because "there is little scope for verification of identities, or to check that people are still alive."[335]

In Torrance, California, an individual stole the mail from a mail carrier. The Post Office didn't know the mail was stolen from one of their vehicles. As part of the theft there were 300 ballots for the 2021 election in California. The only reason police knew it happened was that the thief passed out in his car with the mail in his possession. With no chain of custody for the ballots, no one knew they were missing. The example given earlier of an election in Iowa that turned on six votes might have been greatly altered if 300 votes went missing. Also, in 2020 a state Senate election in Pennsylvania turned on 300 mail ballots that voters forgot to date. A House primary vote in Florida was decided by five votes, with 1,400 mail-in ballots thrown out.[336] In Texas, in 2022, during primary voting, 27,000 ballots were flagged for rejection, or 17% of mail-in votes.[337]

Unless working out of the country, voting in person is the only way to make sure everyone's vote gets counted correctly, without any question of the votes being cast.

In the proposed constitution, individuals who have a ballot that does not qualify, i.e., missed the deadline, signature does not match, etc., have no redress because of the time parameters.

4: Paid advertising, except non-electric billboards, for candidates are restricted to a period of 61 days prior to the Primary or General election, to the day before the election itself. Only one advertisement per 30-minute segment, per TV/Cable/Streaming channel is allowed.

a) Two out of three advertisements in a given day must be strictly about their candidate and their policy positions. All advertising for a candidate must identify the party affiliation of the candidate.

b) Attack advertisements about the opposition candidate must be factually based and honest. Candidates and organizations running attack ads for individuals running for a federal office may run them by the Bipartisan Commission for Elections and Media (with co-chairs from two opposing parties, and no party occupying more than 50% of the seats) set up by the federal government and must approve/disapprove them within two business days. If approved by the Bipartisan Commission for Elections and Media the candidate or organization running the ads may not be sued, but the Bipartisan Commission for Elections and Media can be sued on an expedited

basis for judicial review. If the candidate or organization runs unapproved attack advertisements, then they may be sued if not factual and honest. All ads will predominately display whether the Commission has approved or not approved of the attack ad.

c) Attack ads may not contain information about donors or organizations that support the opposition candidate, and the ads must identify the party affiliation of the sponsoring organization.

d) Any advertisements to notify people about rallies or gatherings that do not contain any messaging about positions are always permitted. Bumper Stickers and Yard signs are always permitted.

e) No foreign money will be accepted by any candidate or organizations participating in the election process.

f) Individuals or organizations may not accept money from foreign sources and then turn around and funnel it to a candidate. No foreign individual, organization or business may directly pay for advertisements for any candidate or cause.

g) Producing Deepfakes will be a felony crime requiring time in prison.

Non-electronic billboards (billboards where someone must physically hang a new advertisement) are acceptable and may be hung a few days early and stay up through election day. Electronic or rotating billboards are acceptable for political campaigns but must be turned off on Election Day and fall into the 60-day window.

All advertisements for a candidate must identify the party affiliation of the candidate. Truth in labeling is required. It has been my experience that many politicians try to hide or mislead voters by their message and lack of party identity.

In most Parliamentary systems, the time allowed for running for office is limited because of the ability to call an election with very short notice. Conversely, the campaign period for President in the US in 2016 lasted nearly 600 days, compared to the official campaign period in the UK, which is approximately five weeks.[338]

Reducing the timeframe that television and other advertisements may be aired will decrease the need for vast sums of money to finance a campaign and may also create a more level playing field for all candidates. Advertisements in a given 30-minute segment may be from 15 seconds to two minutes in length. A candidate running for office is not prevented from campaigning or doing interviews—radio, print, social media, or television— anytime they want. Candidates may pass out bumper stickers and yard signs anytime during the campaign.

The Soviet Union secretly subsidized the Labour Party in the UK in 1929, which subsequently won enough votes in parliamentary elections to form a government. The Soviet Union also sought to help Adlai Stevenson in 1960 and Hubert Humphrey in 1968, both running for President. Fortunately, both candidates declined the offer. [339]

Deepfakes are a current concern and are discussed in greater detail later in this book.

5: Ads for a candidate or a cause must identify sponsorship. It must be clear which party they support (as opposed to a PAC, organization, or cause with very ambiguous names), as well as a website with details. Sponsorship must be in a font large enough to be easily read on the page or screen.

Note: Advertisements for a cause or a party may run year-round, but again, no foreign money.

6: Each Provate will determine the age of majority at between 18 and 21 years old. The age of majority determines when a citizen has the maturity to exercise their full rights such as voting, drinking alcohol, purchasing a weapon, and taking legal drugs. Any Ameristralian citizen above the age of majority with a federal ID and not currently incarcerated is eligible to vote in the district and Provate they live.

(Amendment 19 ratified on 8/26/1920 gave women the right to vote.)

(Amendment 24 ratified on 1/23/1964 eliminated the poll tax.)

(Amendment 26 ratified on 7/1/1971 lowered the voting age from 21 to 18.)

If an individual is not mature enough at 18 to drink beer or hard alcohol, purchase a gun or drive an 18-wheeler, then they may not be mature enough to vote. Also at 18, just graduating high school, individuals don't have any worldly experiences in which to make judgements about life, government, or the makeup of a good politician. They might have ideas (some based on parental opinions), but no life experience in order to make an independent judgement.

Did you know that the frontal cortex of the brain is the last part of the brain to fully mature?[340] It's not fully functional until a person's mid-twenties. The frontal lobe marks the cognitive maturity associated with adulthood. Something to think about when it comes to adult activities such as voting.

7: A political party may be registered at the Provate level by paying a $10,000 annual fee to the Provate's Secretary of State, or at the Federal level by paying a $100,000 annual fee to the Secretary of State of Ameristralia. If the party has registered at the Provate or Federal level, then any individual running for an office in that Provate will be put on the ballot for the office they are running as a representative of that party in that Primary. Individuals with no party affiliation may run for any office and they will be under the Independent designation, no fees required.

The fee is simply to verify seriousness of a party and not intended to keep any serious party from participating in the process. If money is a problem for a new party, then their candidates may run as an independent.

8: Congress will establish the filing dates for Federal offices, except for the Vice President where the party selects the candidate. Presidential candidates only have to file once at the Federal level with the Secretary of State of Ameristralia in order to be on the ballot of all Provates for the Primary, and the party will notify the Secretary of State of Ameristralia of their candidate for the General election. When possible, the candidate selected for Vice President will be from a different continent than the Presidential candidate.

The current process where each Presidential candidate must register in each Provate and pass each individual hurdle makes it very difficult and confusing for a candidate wishing to run and it wastes a lot of time and money.

When Abraham Lincoln was running for the office of President the first time, he was not on the ballot in a single Southern state south of Virginia.[341] Provates must not be allowed to pick and choose which candidates are on their ballots.

9: The Primary for the President will be held in a sequence of individual Provates because of the geographical challenges in a national campaign covering multiple continents. The first Primary will be in South Australia starting in January, followed by Alberta, Iowa, Scotland (then one of any new continents added later), and then Congress will dictate the sequence of regional Provates from that point on—giving preference for geographic neighbors and/or common media markets.

The tally from all these individual primaries will be passed on to the respective parties and the party will then decide who is going to represent them in the general election.

    A) The Bipartisan Commission for Elections and Media will reimburse candidates and staff for airfare between continents up to $1,000,000 for the Primary and another $1,000,000 for the General election.

    B) If more than one individual is running as an independent, then Ranked Choice Voting will also be used. The Bipartisan Commission for Elections

and Media, which is set up to look at and approve political advertisement, will decide which Independent will prevail. The Independent Candidate for President will announce who they have selected for their Vice President in a timely manner.

Early voters must be given an opportunity to meet the candidates face-to-face in close informal settings to determine the true character of the candidate. Large crowd events allow the candidate to hide behind the podium and give speeches without any close give and take with the voters. There should be one Presidential primary on each continent (two for North America) prior to the regional primaries taking place. Congress will set the dates of the primaries.

During the 2020 election for President, many States (Kansas was one of those States) did not hold a Republican primary because Trump was running for his second term. Each Provate is going to have a primary and each party must participate. The lack of voting in the 2020 Primary in Kansas for Republicans meant that they were disenfranchised during the Primary because they could not vote for the candidate of their choice. The party picked the candidate for them even though there were others running against Trump.

After the completion of the primaries, the Party is charged with picking the candidate at their convention because some of the candidates may have dropped out in the process, complicating the voting and nominating process.

10: Every elected office in the country shall first have a primary election where the members of each party will have the opportunity to determine the consensus majority choice to run for the party in the general election. Individuals without a party affiliation will run as an Independent.

Blanket Primaries and Open Primaries (sometimes called Jungle Primaries) where all the candidates for one office, regardless of party affiliation, are thrown together at the Primary election are unfair to smaller parties and will no longer be tolerated.

11: Upon arrival at the polling station for the Primary election, the Voters will notify the staff of the Party they intend to participate with for voting, or if they are independent.

There will be no need to pre-register and identify a party affiliation.

12: Voters may identify their top three choices for an office and Ranked Choice Voting will be used in the primary election to determine the winner for each party. When two candidates are left with no one having the majority, the candidate with the most votes wins the party's nomination to the general election.

In the rare case of a tie, a coin flip will decide the winner.

Ranked Choice Voting is an electoral system that allows people to vote for multiple candidates in the party for the same position during a primary, in order of preference. Under the current system, as a voter, you don't want to waste your vote on someone you don't think will win (but you like) and you don't want to be forced to choose between the lesser of two evils. With Ranked Choice Voting, a voter may fill out the ballot with their first choice, second choice, or third choice for each position. So you give your first choice to the candidate you like (but may not have much of a chance to win) and then your second and third choices so you still get to provide input into who wins the nomination.

Rank Choice Voting may also provide an incentive for candidates to not bad mouth one another in hopes of getting their opponent's voters to select them as their second or third choice.

The candidate with the majority (more than 50%) of first-choice votes wins outright. If no candidate gets a majority of first-choice votes, then it triggers a new counting process. The candidate who did the worst is eliminated, and that candidate's voters' ballots are redistributed to their second-choice pick. In other words, if you ranked a losing candidate as your first choice, and the candidate is eliminated, then your vote still counts: it just moves to your second-choice candidate. That process continues until there is a candidate who has the majority of votes, or the most votes in the final round of voting.[342] If the voter doesn't identify their second or third choices, that is their right.

Alaska and Maine are the only Provates in the US to have established the use of Ranked Choice Voting for all congressional and Provate elections. Many large cities in the US use Ranked Choice Voting, including St. Paul, Minnesota, and four cities in the California Bay area.[343] In 2021, New York, New York, had their first vote using Ranked Choice Voting. As of this writing, 50 US cities have adopted Ranked Choice Voting, with more coming.

Example

Assume that there are four candidates for mayor from Party A in a hypothetical city. The table that follows presents the raw first-preference vote totals for each candidate.

Raw first-preference vote tallies in a hypothetical mayoral race		
Candidate A	475	46.34%
Candidate B	300	29.27%
Candidate C	175	17.07%
Candidate D	75	7.32%

In the above scenario, no candidate won an outright majority of first-preference votes. As a result, the candidate with the smallest number of first-preference votes is eliminated: Candidate D. The ballots that listed candidate D as the first preference are adjusted, raising their second-preference candidates. Assume that, of the 75 first-preference votes for Candidate D, 50 listed Candidate A as their second preference and 25 listed Candidate B. The adjusted vote totals would be as follows:

Adjusted vote tallies in a hypothetical mayoral race		
Candidate A	525	51.22%
Candidate B	325	31.71%
Candidate C	175	17.07%

On the second tally, Candidate A secured 51.22 percent of the vote to represent Party A in the general election, thereby winning the primary election.

13: Each party and the winning Independent will then present their candidate in the General election. Voters may identify their top three choices for each office and Ranked Choice Voting will also be used in the General election to determine the winner. If two candidates are left and a majority is not achieved, the candidate with the most votes wins the election for that position.
In the rare case of a tie, a coin flip decides the winner.

Ranked Choice Voting is an acceptable method of eliminating the need for runoff elections, during the primary and general election.

Australia has a preferential voting system, also known as Ranked Choice Voting.[344] After implementation the major parties started to shrink in size and other parties started to proliferate.[345] Ranked Choice Voting may allow more than two parties to participate, as is currently the situation in the United States. Competition is always better and is a way to provide accountability for the voters because now they may have more than two choices.

In the United States, the two-party system has been co-opted by the radical fringe on both sides and exacerbated by the media. The election process has become a tribal rather than a political system.

In the essay "Publius," James Madison wrote that holding the Union together by the establishment of a Constitution allows for the reduction of what he termed factions—a group of citizens motivated by a common passion that is counter to the well-being of the citizenry as a whole.[346] A benefit of the republic as a form of government is to mitigate factions because it advances that a higher number of representatives guard against the attempts of the few to wield power. Rank choice voting ensures that a few do not have a stranglehold on the two-party system, allowing for more parties to share into the process.

14: No elected official in the Executive or the Legislative Branch of any Government may hold the same office for more than thirteen years or run for the same office again if reelection will put their tenure in that position over thirteen years, except for the President and Vice President of the Union who have stricter limits. The thirteen-year clock begins after the first election under the new constitution.

Term limits have been bounced around for decades. After FDR died, Congress passed term limits for the President but stopped there. FDR was elected President four times. However, the legislators didn't want to put a restriction on their ability to stay in office. Current legislators have become professional politicians and have entrenched themselves to become the governing class in our country. There needs to be "new blood" regularly infused into these institutions and term limits are the answer. When leaders stick around too long, Graham Paterson rightly notes that, "leaders begin to see themselves as rulers rather than servants to the people."[347]

Later, we discuss existing members of Congress rolling over into the new government of Ameristralia, in which case the thirteen-year limit does not start counting until the new government is in place.

The 22nd Amendment dictated two terms in office of President and also allowing for a couple of extra years in situations where the Vice President takes over for the President in mid-term.

TRUTH:
Without term limits, some politicians will remain focused on retaining power, not serving the people.

Most politicians do not have the inherent self-control to limit regulations or the amount of taxes they levy against their voters. Therefore, a constitution needs to set those limits to constrain the government. What makes the United States Constitution unique is that it was created by the people, for the people, and was not negotiated with another power, as in the case of Mother Britain and Australia, Canada, and New Zealand. Iceland also negotiated with Denmark for independence. The United States Patriots rejected the Loyalists' position and fought for independence and created the Constitution from scratch.

The purpose of the ensuing Constitution was to limit the government's power over its citizens but also to have sufficient strength to defend themselves from outside forces, instead of other countries that had rule by law that only applied to a small portion of the population.[348] The Founding Fathers consolidated the democracy so that the power of the state was constrained, giving most residents access to the rule of law.[349]

James Madison stated that, "Power is of an encroaching nature, and that it ought to be effectually restrained from passing the limits assigned to it."[350]

15: All elected and appointed officials and their spouse (or partner) at the national level will receive a financial audit each year of income and assets and the results reported to the respective Provate and/or Ameristralian agency. It will become a matter of public record and posted on a government website. The audit will be paid for by the Federal government.

Any conflicts of interest, suspicious or illegal activity will be identified, made public, and forwarded to the appropriate office. No organization or candidate may weaponize this public information unless the person is convicted of a crime as a result of the audit.

Any Congressional specified organization doing the audit may not prepare them for the same person more than three years out of the last six. Congress will define acceptable behavior.

These audits follow under the Accountability Principle discussed earlier in Chapter 8 of Book One. Elected federal officials need to be audited to make sure that all sources of incomes and all expenses are tracked to uncover any illicit activity. At the very least, it should significantly discourage illegal activity.

Elected and appointed officials will have to keep calendars of where they have been so that expenses can be tracked for each day and event. Records should be kept for who paid for the airfare, ground transportation, hotel room, meals, etc. Congress may prescribe the appropriate financial behavior for officials.

The elected or appointed person must also rotate who is doing their audits—fresh eyes are always good in an audit.

16: At the beginning of each new decade, prior to October 1, the House of Representatives will determine the reallocation of seats based on population from IDs in the Census and Identity Theft Agency database. No Provate may be given more seats than a Provate with a larger population.

After three years has passed, reallocation will also occur after a new country joins the Union.

The respective Provates will establish the Districts for each Representative along existing contiguous county and city boundaries. In extraordinary situations, in no more than one county, those boundaries may be along natural geographic separation (creeks, rivers or major highways).

Gerrymandering is the act of drawing districts with certain political demographics in mind. The intent is to guarantee that one party will always get a majority of votes, or, as in some cases, where a certain religion or certain ethnic group is guaranteed a representative getting elected.

Certain parts of Australia were notorious for gerrymandering the districts to keep a particular party in power.[351] Joh Bjelke-Petersen remained in power as the premier of Queensland from 1968 to 1987 while never receiving more than 39% of the vote through gerrymandering.[352] Gerrymandering was also active in Theodore Roosevelt's time and still very alive today in America and has become a science.[353]

Australia has a practice of using independent electoral boundaries commissions, which Manitoba copied and was later copied by other Canadian provinces and the Parliament followed suit.[354] Taking away the ability to divide districts into very narrow swaths a couple of blocks wide (which current data and technology make possible) will go a long way to making the districts represent all of the people, not just one ethnic group, party, or religion, thus largely eliminating Gerrymandering.

17: The Secretary of State for each Provate will be the sole authority in declaring the winners in their Provate and Federal races, and after each election, will produce a report indicating any deficiencies found and if wait times were too long

In Florida, after every primary and general election, the Secretary of State is required to produce a public report on the performance of the equipment and any noted errors or problems in the voting process.[355] Every Provate should do the same.

There was a disputed race in Louisiana in 1872 where the Republican candidate, William Kellogg, and Conservative candidate, John McEnery, both claimed victory. Each candidate held an inaugural ceremony and assumed the office of governor.[356] It must be constitutionally clear which responsible office determines the winner.

18: No eligible citizen will face any punishment for not voting.

In Australia, there is a fine for not voting. Citizens should have the right to not take part in the political process without being punished.

Section 3, LISAs,

1: Each citizen (whether working or receiving benefits) will have a Long-Term Individual Security Account (LISA) for retirement, special needs, and unemployment. The employer and government will put eleven percent of an individuals' pretax pay and benefits for up to $200,000 into an account until the month after their 65th birthday. The individual will select a third-party fund administrator that will place half of the funds in a "Retirement Account" that cannot be touched until retirement, or terminally ill, and the

other half into a "Special Needs" account that can be pulled out for approved special needs (unemployment, pay for college classes, exceptional medical expenses, marriage, funeral, down payment on a house, to start a business, etc.). Neither of these accounts may be accessed by courts, or by contract, for the payment of debts or fines. If the employee is married (or has a partner), then half the funds go to the spouse's Long-Term Individual Security Account (LISA). The employer and government must provide at least 5 different third-party administrators, each with at least 5 different investment options from which the employee (and spouse or partner) may choose.

A) In the former United States, at the time of transition to this system, the employer will give their 6% contribution under the old system to the employee as a pay raise. Individuals with income over $200,000 (not that portion under) will pay a 6% extra income tax for 30 years and then 3% for the next 20, to help fund the old social security system, 50 years in total. The former United States Social Security system will be frozen (except cost-of-living adjustments) and cease to exist after 50 years and unemployment benefits will be frozen and administered at the federal level and will cease to exist in 10 years.

B) The employee and employer may also make extra pre-tax contributions to these accounts up to a maximum of 100% of pay, up to the first $200,000 each year. Defined Retirement Programs that allow for the delayed funding of promised benefits down the road are no longer permitted and will be phased out. All existing Defined Retirement Programs monies set aside will be distributed to their employees' LISA. Existing retirees, or those within 20 years of retirement under these Defined Retirement Programs, and the monies set aside, will remain in place for their retirement or the employee may choose to take their money out of the Defined Retirement Program and put it into their LISA and exit the Defined Retirement Program.

C) **The LISA does away with pension funds controlled by employers, unions, or government entities and now gives everything to the employee and their spouse (or partner) each month. By definition then, the government will not guarantee any pension funds.**

D) **Upon death, all LISA accounts go tax-free to the current spouse's (or partner) LISA. LISA funds are taxed once they are withdrawn and used.**

Sometimes bad things happen to good people or businesses. LISAs will allow people to take care of themselves (being self-reliant) in times of unemployment, emergencies, and retirement. Also, in the current environment, if the company responsible for your retirement goes under, what are you going to do? The government gets out of the way and gives individuals authority over their lives and allows them to find solutions that work for them. In the transition to the new Union, the government will still be involved in unemployment, emergencies, and retirement until LISAs can replace current systems in place. At which time, the government may still be there as a backup in extreme situations.

To repeat what Nathan Nguyen said of the American Dream, "If achieving the American Dream is at least somewhat related to money, then understanding how to create, maintain, and grow wealth are the timeless keys to unlock it. What makes the rich different from the broke...is having the skills to turn income into assets, that can increase in value and generate more income."[357] LISAs will provide people with assets that will increase in value to take care of themselves.

Putting retirement funds in the hands of citizens takes it away from the control and sometimes corruption of employers, unions, and the government who currently control them. It also gives employees "skin in the game" to make sure businesses do well. Under the current scheme, you only hope the government does well.

According to the Government Accountability Office (GAO), public pensions are becoming a large burden on state and local governments and confronting the burden of pension obligations will necessitate taking painful steps.[358] LISA provides a framework to a better system.

While the above statements address the various welfare and safety net programs that emerged in the twentieth century, self-reliance has taken on even greater significance in the twenty-first century. The gig economy has given rise to a new wave of entrepreneurs whether it is rideshare, dog walking, a food truck, writing blog copy, or coding. Individuals working for themselves can only depend on themselves for their future savings.

Margaret Thatcher thought that socialism was only a less developed form of communism.[359] She said, "The unspoken objective of socialism…was to increase dependency. Poverty was not just the breeding ground of socialism: it was the deliberately engineered effect of it."[360] So in 2022, when the American government takes the equivalent of 12% of your pay every month with the promise of helping you down the road when you need it, fits into this category of creating dependency. With the LISA, I am proposing the individual keeps the money and accumulates it for their needs when they want it instead of depending on incompetent government systems to help them out. With LISAs in place, individuals on the financial edge of society would not have to go to payday lenders or pawn shops to fund a temporary financial emergency. LISAs would provide immediate access for help from their own resources.

As a side note, the difference between a spouse and a partner is simple. A spouse is a contractual relationship between two people - i.e., marriage license and other official filings. A partner is a voluntary relationship between two people with no formal commitment in the relationship and with no contractual obligations. The 50% contributions to a spouse's LISA are required, partners only receive the 50% if the other partner identifies their partner and designates them on the appropriate form.

There would be nothing to prevent an employer from making after-tax contributions into an employee's retirement account—one set up outside of LISA.

Long-Term Individual Security Account (LISA) - In Detail

In 1937, the US introduced a 1% Social Security tax on the first $3,000 of wages.

Currently in the United States, the employee pays a 6% payroll tax of their pay and the employer pays 6% into the Federal Insurance Contributions Act (FICA), with all 12% going straight to general revenues, *not set aside but spent in the current year.* In 2022, the Social Security payroll tax was actually 12.4% (I have rounded the number to 12% for simplicity) with half coming from the employee and half from the employer and applies only to wages of up to $142,800.[361] These monies get spent however politicians want in the current year and comes with a future politician's promises that funds will be there down the road when needed.

Australia has a "Superannuation" system already in place—an individual retirement fund. So LISA is not just an idea but a solution based on another country's actual experience. Currently in Australia, the employer contribution rate is 9.5% but is going up to 12% in 2025. The Australian system makes the individual responsible for their own retirement without having to rely on the government for administration or distribution of funds. In Australia, this removes government bureaucracy and reduces the size of the government. The current United States Social Security system has 2,728 primary rules governing the receipt of its 12 benefits, plus tens of thousands of secondary rules and employs about 60,000 employees.[362]

LISA redirects the money into accounts controlled by the individual rather than employers, unions, or the government. The following examples use round numbers to aid in the simplicity of the examples.

Current Situation in the United States			
	Spouse A Primary Earner		**Spouse B** The Caregiver
One spouse makes	$100,000/year	and the other	$50,000
Employee pays 6%	6,000/year		3,000/year
Net Take Home Pay	94,000/year		47,000/year
Employer 6% - an expense	6,000/year		3,000/year
Amount in investments	0		0

The government keeps all the money and spends it in the current year and promises to give you part of it back at some point in time. It's the government. You can trust them, right?

LISA Example - Proposed in Ameristralia		
	Spouse A Primary Earner	**Spouse B** The Caregiver
Everyone gets a 6% raise	$106,000/year	$53,000/year
Employee pays 11% to LISA	$11,660	$5,830
Net Take Home Pay	$94,340	$47,170
Both get a slight pay raise from before. Because they are married half of the 11% LISA contribution goes to the spouse.		
LISA self-contribution now	$5,830	$2,915
LISA spouse contribution	$2,915	$5,830
Total LISA Contribution	$8,745	$8,745

The employer does not pay 6% tax on payroll as before but instead gives it to the employee as a 6% raise. *The employer's contribution/expense remains exactly the same,* they just now give the money to the employee.

Both spouses share equally in the fruits of their combined labors. Half of this number goes into a Retirement Account and half goes into Special Needs Account.

In this proposed scenario, at the end of the first year, both spouses have $4,372.50 in a Retirement Account they control individually and $4,372.50 in a Special Needs Account they control individually. Without any appreciation in the value of the investments in their accounts or any pay increases, after 40 years each spouse would have $174,900 for Retirement and also $174,900 for Special Needs, for a total of $699,600 for joint use.

With these same assumptions, if you increase income by 2% each year and the return on investment rate is 6% annually, then the couple after 40 years would have $3,853,052 for retirement funds (Retirement and Special Needs) available for their joint use. Probably more than ample for their retirement.

Also, in this scenario, if something comes up that requires some cash (i.e., sudden unemployment, additional education, down payment for purchasing a home, and subsequently creating equity in an investment that will appreciate), people will have the money to take care of themselves. And without the voluntary additional contribution discussed in the next paragraph, *it hasn't cost the employee a dime* to get to this point. The employee is just keeping the money that would have gone to the government and keeping it for their own use. These are owned assets and will grow tax-free over time.

Now add in the equivalent of 401(k) contributions made today where the employee might set aside 6% of their income for retirement and the employer matches 4%, for 10% a total. In this example, an annual combined salary of $159,000 at 10% equals $15,900/year contribution. Take that $15,900, multiplied times 40 years and you get $646,000 for their joint use. Again, this number assumes that there is no return on investment and that there are no pay increases over 40 years. The total sum under this scenario is $699,600 in LISA plus $646,000 voluntary pre-tax contribution by the employee and their employer, for a total of $1,345,600. The $1,345,600 would be shared equally between both spouses. Again, with the magic of compounding return on investment of 6% and pay increases of 2%, the couple would have at the end of 40 years $6,421,754 for retirement. Total pre-tax savings/investment rate is 21%, with the 4% employer match. In Japan, the average person saves 20%, so this is not an unrealistic suggestion.

The proposal allows for up to 89% pretax contribution on top of the required 11% contribution, for a total of 100% is possible. For careers such as fire fighters, police officers, military service, professional athletes, or politicians, this allows the employing agency, or business, to superfund needed careers that are dangerous and currently offer retirement benefits after shorter than normal work cycles, and yes, that may include politicians too.

In this example, one spouse makes more money than the other, which is probably the typical situation. One spouse may take a job that frees that person up to take care of children after school or an aging parent in need of assistance. In this situation, the parenting team shares equally in the joint efforts of the couple. True partners in life.

Under the LISA proposal, the individuals and couple have money that can be accessed at a moment's notice by contacting the administrator of their LISA. The administrator will be obligated to ask the purpose of the withdrawal of Special Needs Account. The only time this information would be used is if the person withdrawing the funds uses up all the monies in that account and now needs assistance to get back on their feet. If still married, the other spouse could also help out. The funds could be used for things such as unemployment, starting a business, getting additional education or technical training, paying part of a child's college education, or in case of separation/divorce, instant access to funds that can be used as a safety net to allow the smooth and hassle-free departure from the other spouse.

If you control your own funds, you don't have to apply and wait for the government to qualify you and/or take action. And if you don't qualify, what do you do? Or what if the number of weeks of eligibility has expired? With LISA, you just do what is right for you and you should be able to get access to your money within one business day. If you lose your job, you have the right to those funds to keep yourself afloat. In today's environment, if you no longer qualify for unemployment benefits, you could end up unable to make regular mortgage or rent payments. LISA funds can be used to keep you afloat until you regain employment.

Also, in today's environment in the United States, you may be afraid to take an interim lower paying job for fear your benefits may go away. Now you can take an interim job to help yourself out without fear of being penalized by the government-run program. Taking this action would also help you keep as much money in your LISA as possible for your use down the road.

For those in Australia, the switch is fairly straightforward. In 2025, when their employer puts 12% into the employees' Superannuation accounts, the employer could simply give all employees a 12% raise and then distribute the 11% pre-tax money into their LISA, resulting in *no increased expense for the employer* and the employee gets a slight raise as in the US example.

For a brief explanation: if you give the employee the 12%, to get the equivalent 12% into the LISA you only need to put in 11% because of the higher pay. Let's do the math. Someone making $100 who gets a 12% raise (now $112) only needs to contribute 11% of the $112 ($12.32) to achieve the same contribution as 12% of $100 ($12.00). The employee gets a slight raise and a little more goes into LISA, $12.32 vs $12.00.

When your LISA Emergency Fund is Empty

If unforeseen circumstances cause LISA funds to be depleted, then the government may provide assistance if the individual has not been reckless with their LISA.

Another option would be assistance provided by NGOs (non-governmental organizations) with expertise in job training, healthcare, and housing. Ideally, NGOs will be funded through philanthropy, charitable contributions, and fundraising. Utilizing NGOs rather than government for safety-net programs lessens the bureaucracy and limits the size of government. In the twentieth century, local nonstate voluntary social welfare associations were deliberately crowded out in favor of impersonal political institutions.[363] We need to gravitate back to community rather than government-based support.

An excellent example of this approach is Mobile Loaves and Fishes. Founded by Alan Graham in 1998, the Austin-based non-profit provides housing, job training, and employment. The NGO coordinates with volunteers, other non-profits, and corporations to help find solutions for the chronically unemployed.

Other examples would be the Doe Fund's Ready, Willing & Able program in New York City and the Cincinnati Works program in Cincinnati, Ohio.[364] Both agencies are worth a closer look.

Philanthropy and charitable giving can be nimble and creative. It allows givers to codify their contributions. Private giving is quicker than government action and tends to adapt effectively to changing conditions.[365]

Current Issues and Problems in the US

Current unemployment systems are fraught with fraudulent activity. In Texas, the local CBS station in Dallas, in June of 2021, reported that Texas stopped $9 billion in fraudulent unemployment claims but they suspected that $893 million in fraudulent claims were still made. In January of 2021, a California state auditor estimated that $10.4 billion of roughly $11 billion paid out between March and December of 2020 was potentially lost to fraud. The auditor pointed out that 1,700 unemployment claims came from a single address.[366] On the national FOX news on, June 10, 2021, they stated that, of the almost $1 trillion in unemployment benefits paid, the consensus was that about $400 billion was fraudulent. And of those fraudulent dollars about 70% went overseas. The government needs to be taken out of this process due to poorly written mandates, mismanagement, corruption, and waste in the current system.

At the Provate level in the US, mismanagement is rampant because the Provates have no *incentive* to manage benefit programs correctly. A lot of the monies the Provates are passing out are someone else's money—the federal government's money—not their own taxpayer money.

Section 4,

1: Any dollar figures mentioned in this constitution will be adjusted based on inflation, unless otherwise noted. Any references to internet, web sites, databases, or other technology may evolve into other named technology, and still be valid.

Any dollar figure given in the document should be updated each year for inflation and published for easy access.

2: Executive branch regulations and codes, proposed by the respective government agencies, must first be passed by the appropriate Congressional bodies for comment, tweaked as necessary, and then resubmitted to Congress and the President for approval prior to going into effect.

Currently, there are very few *checks and balances* in the system that prevent each new administration from producing new regulations generated by unelected bureaucrats, often contrary to the previous administration. The rulemaking must be controlled, and Congress must do their job.

Compliance with constitutional rulemaking requirements have been inconsistent, undermining both democratic accountability and because improperly issued rules are subject to legal challenge, agencies' own agendas. This errant rulemaking is no small problem. The *Wall Street Journal* broke the news that hundreds of Food and Drug Administration rules were illegal because they had been issued by career staff. Subsequent Pacific Legal Foundation research on the Health and Human Services Department's rulemaking practices from 2001 to 2017 revealed that 1,860 FDA final rules (98% of the total) had been issued illegally and that other HHS agencies had similar problems.[367]

3: No individual, organization, or business may block free access to sidewalks, streets, highways, railroads, parks, or other public rights of way unless the City/County has authorized a permit for a parade or special event. No one can create a campground in any public areas, unless approved as a campground.

Every citizen and business needs to use these areas for everyday purposes and anyone blocking them needs to be removed. Protesters cannot block rights-of-way.

This item does not prevent a local government from licensing the activity of certain organizations to march past an individual's house or a business, but they may not stay and block entrances. It also allows for the permitting of businesses to use some of the space for temporary activity, such as a food truck.

In February, 2019, there was a blockade to help anti-pipeline protests 120 miles east of Toronto in an indigenous community. The blockage affected the main east-west corridor operated by Canadian National Railway. As a result, there were 50 ships on the Pacific Coast waiting to pick up grain. Anti-pipeline protesters later launched additional temporary rail blockades across the country affecting, among others, commuter-rail traffic servicing the suburbs of Toronto.[368]   Because protestors were blocking the rail line in Canada in February of 2020, Via Rail, Canada's passenger rail operator, issued temporary layoff notices for 1,000 workers, a day after Canadian National Railway said it would temporarily layoff 450 workers of its own.[369] Protestors can't block rail traffic in order to close or target businesses for their cause. People have a right to work, which is covered in more detail later.

4: All governmental and industrial bodies should provide for exceptions to their rules to allow for innovation in any industry. Reduced regulations should also be encouraged for brand new businesses.

For example, current regulations may say that a hard copy of an insurance policy must be provided to new customers, but a new entrant into the industry wants to try and keep costs down and provide a .pdf to customers instead. The company should be allowed to try it out and see how it works.

5: No department within the Federal government may have their own court system outside of the standard Federal court system, except the armed forces.

When a Federal department of the government has their own appointed judges, their loyalty is to the department they work for rather than the individual and their rights. This also does not make the judiciary a separate check on the executive branch. The *checks and balances* are missing.

6: Anyone elected or appointed to any Federal position will be reimbursed for their reasonable moving expenses to the location of their new position. For elected Federal officials who are temporarily residents to the new capital, they will be reimbursed for travel to and from their home and constituents. Elected officials returning home after their tenure has been completed will also have their reasonable moving expenses paid to get back to their place of retirement from the Government.

Earlier, we stipulated the maximum compensation for elected officials. However, this does not prevent them from receiving proper reimbursement for other necessary expenses, such as travel and moving.

The first and third sentence use the word "reasonable" and the second sentence when discussing air travel does not. For anyone who travels on a regular basis, flying Coach is a burden, particularly when traveling long distances.

7: In Ameristralia, all Territories, Commonwealths, Reservations, and Protectorates will be incorporated into the appropriate Provate and all residents will become equal citizens of Ameristralia.

Having separate levels of citizenship with different rights is against the core philosophy expressed in this document.

Prior to the Second World War, the United States had colonies and territories: Alaska, Puerto Rico, the Philippines, Guam, American Samoa, Hawaii, and Wake Island. After the war, the Philippines were given their independence while Alaska and Hawaii became states. Puerto Rico, Guam, American Samoa, and Wake Island are now considered territories or a commonwealth under the control of the United States.[370]

Furthermore, Puerto Ricans became US citizens in 1917, US Virgin Islanders in 1927, and Guamanians in 1950. Because their citizenship is statutory, it can be revoked at any time. Since 1900, American Samoans have been classified as American, but they are legally only US nationals.[371] There are approximately four million people living in these unincorporated territories and they have no representatives in Congress and cannot vote for President.[372] The Fourteenth Amendment's guarantee for citizenship to anyone born in the United States doesn't apply to the unincorporated territories.[373] The thirty thousand people of the Northern Marianas became a commonwealth to the United States just like Puerto Rico, and in 1986, its residents became US citizens.[374] Congress conferred citizenship for all Native Americans on reservations in June of 1924.[375]

Midway Island and Johnston Island were originally part of Hawaii but the US military took control and still holds them.[376] These islands, plus places like Guantanamo Bay in Cuba, would all become part of a Provate with full citizenship.

All of these territories, commonwealths, or reservations are too small to take care of themselves as a sovereign power and most of the citizens are already citizens in varying degrees of their protector country, the United States. The new Ameristralian Constitution will bring them officially into the fold as true, fully-privileged citizens.

As the July 2020 Supreme Court ruling in McGirt vs Oklahoma revealed, there are old issues about land rights and sovereignty because Congress never enacted a law explicitly reneging on the treaty with the Creeks when Oklahoma became a state in 1907.[377] [378]

Australia, Canada, and New Zealand are having similar issues regarding indigenous citizens in their countries.

The proposed Ameristralian Constitution has the Channel Islands, Gibraltar, and the British portion of Cypress becoming a Provate.

The grouping of territories such as the Northern Territory in Australia and, in Canada, the Northwest Territories, Nanavut, and Yukon are Federal Protectorates.[379] The status of these land areas, whether to become a Provate or merge with another Provate, will be discussed and decided at some point during the Constitutional

Convention. I am recommending that the District of Columbia will go back to being part of Maryland and the Territory of Canberra will go back to being part of New South Wales. (For a complete listing of Provates, please refer to Appendix B.)

I am also recommending that reservation ownership of the land will pass to the respective clan/tribe and/or at least some land be passed to individual members of those nations. If some of the land is not passed along to individuals in the clan/tribe, it makes it very difficult for them to finance a home. Ben Eisen addresses the problems of home ownership on tribal land in his article in the *Wall Street Journal.*[380]

All people living within Ameristralia will have equal rights and will no longer be second-class citizens by residing in a territory, commonwealth, protectorate, or reservation. Indigenous peoples will no longer be a sovereign nation unto themselves and their nation will be folded in with all the other nations joining the Union. The Union merely brings everyone into the fold as part of the larger family of Ameristralia, all equal citizens with equal rights and responsibilities.

8: In the Province of Quebec and the island of Puerto Rico, the citizens will be given twelve months after the Union takes effect to hold a separate referendum to determine whether they will be part of Ameristralia, or their own independent country. If the Province of Quebec or the island of Puerto Rico does not have a referendum in the prescribed time period and select independence, they will be incorporated into Ameristralia as a Provate.

In the Constitution of the United States, there was no special treatment for language or religion. All who voluntarily came to the United States were encouraged to assimilate together as one. The assimilation process does not mean that certain religions, people speaking other languages or having different spiritual beliefs were not discriminated against along the way. Assimilation can be messy in the short term.

Quebec

The British did a great disservice to Quebec in 1763 by giving special religious and language rights to the French-speaking Catholics versus the English-speaking Protestants. Quebec has voted several times to separate itself from Canada and has failed every time, sometimes very narrowly. The second Quebec referendum on separation narrowly lost in 1995.[381] So the question of Quebec keeping its special rights regarding language has been a long time coming. If Canada enters the proposed Union, that will force Quebec to finally decide whether it wants to assimilate with rest of North America or go its separate way.

Puerto Rico

Despite a 1902 English only language law, and later on February 4, 1952, Resolution 22, which made English official in Puerto Rico, those living there are still primarily Spanish speaking with a population of about three million people. In 1993, the populace approved the commonwealth status over statehood. However, on November 3, 2020, 52% of the population said they wanted statehood.[382] Because of the mandated language change, I think they should be given the opportunity to confirm their desires one way or the other.

There are always aggrieved people and regions of countries. In Scotland, First Minister Nicola Sturgeon said she would campaign for a mandate to hold a vote on independence between 2021 and 2025.[383] So whether it's Scotland, Quebec, Western Australia, or Hawaii, there will always be those folks who believe they are being wronged.

9: If Iceland and Greenland both join the Union as one Provate, then Greenland will get one Senator and Iceland will have one Senator. If only one joins, then that one will have the two Senators. If the other joins later, they will each get to select one of the two Senators.

A) If Greenland joins (with or without Iceland), it will get financial assistance, due to its unique

situation, of at least $650 million annually in financial assistance above and beyond normal allocated benefits and programs.

B) Hawaii will grow as a Provate and will consist of all the Pacific and Indian Ocean islands (Diego Garcia). It will also receive an additional $650 million annually above and beyond normal allocated benefits. The new Provates of Caribbean and Atlantic Islands will also get an additional $650 million annually above and beyond normal allocated benefits. The Channel Islands, Gibraltar, and Cypress (Akrotiri & Dhekelia) will also form a new Provate and get $100 million annually in the same scenario. The Channel Islands will be allocated one Senator, and Gibraltar and Cypress (Akrotiri & Dhekelia) will be allocated one Senator. The Channel Islands, Gibraltar, and Cypress (Akrotiri & Dhekelia) may also be merged into another country from the European continent if the appropriate opportunity arises and both parties approve.

The funds are designed to compensate for the unusual climate, travel, and logistical demands needed to maintain the infrastructure of the Provate in these remote areas. Greenland receives a subsidy from Denmark of about 4.3 billion Danish Krone,[384] which equates to $591 million US dollars—60% of their budget.[385] Greenland, because of its huge land mass, very small population and the extreme weather conditions needs special assistance. The same logic would apply to Hawaii, Caribbean and Atlantic Islands, and the new Provate consisting of the Channel Islands, Gibraltar, and Cypress (Akrotiri & Dhekelia).

Again, this is a proposal designed to start a discussion at the Constitutional Convention and the delegates will make the final decision.

Section 5,

1: Current laws stay in effect in each locale until new laws are written that override the old laws or declared unconstitutional. Businesses, organizations, local, and federal governments will have a five-year grace period to make any necessary changes for compliance with the new Constitution.

2: The new federal government will assume all of the debts of the previous countries, but not the Provates.

Greenland/Iceland and New Zealand may be an exception since the prior country and the new Provate will be one in the same.

3: A Federal Reserve Bank will be established with all the requisite powers to control the monetary system and alleviate any financial crisis.

The Federal Reserve Bank was not in the original US Constitution and caused issues early on in the United States that needed to be resolved. The Federal Reserve Bank is a necessary institution that needs to be in the constitution.

4: Any place where law enforcement may legally have an officer present, that law enforcement agency has the option of using any electronic devices in that location to replace the officer.

Deciding where to use surveillance rather than a physical presence may make law enforcement more efficient and thus augment the force in a cost-effective manner.

In small towns, law enforcement knows most of the people in its jurisdiction, also called "community policing." It is almost impossible to hide because everyone knows you. For example, Greely County, Kansas, where my mom was born and grew up, as of 2022, has a Sheriff, four fulltime deputies, two parttime deputies for a population of 1,247, equating to 178 resident per police officer. Their stated goal is "to be proactive, not reactive when serving the citizens" of the county. With that ratio, law enforcement knows all the citizens in the county. Also, when everyone attends the only high school in the county, the police officers probably went to school with everybody else's kids. No one can hide, making the community a safe place to live and raise a family.

On the flip side, Dallas County, Texas, has 3,100 officers and a population of 1.3 million, which equated to 419 residents per police officer. In this environment, law enforcement can only react to situations in the community. Law enforcement can be sitting at an intersection for an hour and 1,000 cars could pass by in which the officer in the patrol car doesn't know anyone in the cars and as a result, doesn't know when something doesn't look right. In this environment you can either hire more police officers or use more technology to help the officers out. Or a combination of the two.

In larger towns and cities law enforcement can't know and build a relationship with its citizens as in a small town, so people can hide among the masses. The installation of electronic equipment will allow law enforcement to bridge that gap. Giving law enforcement access to any and all technology just provides tools that can assist them in serving, protecting, and apprehending perpetrators within their jurisdiction. Law breakers do not have the right to hide in the crowds.

Many jurisdictions prevent law enforcement from using things such as facial recognition software to try and find perpetrators. Also, the use of cameras on police cars that can scan license plates of passing cars to identify a stolen vehicle is often discouraged. The government also requires scanners at airports to be less clear so a person's body shape is not overly precise. Technology is advancing, and just as with fingerprints and DNA, new tools and processes should be introduced to law enforcement once it is proven reasonably reliable.

Government needs to take the "handcuffs" off law enforcement.

5: Where allowed by technology, climate, and pertinent circumstances, all domestic law enforcement officers will wear a body camera that records audio and video while they

are outside of their vehicles. Law enforcement vehicles will also have a video camera that records views outside and inside the vehicle. None of this applies to undercover agents, but does apply to plains clothes officers.

a) All interrogations done by law enforcement inside their offices and buildings will also have recorded audio and visual of the entire event.

b) The Miranda type rights will be modified to include a notification that they are being recorded and anything they do or say, previously or in the future, can be used against them in a court of law. Recordings prior to the Miranda rights being given are admissible in court.

c) For a common recognition by the public, all law enforcement will have "Police" predominate on uniforms and vehicles. Specialized agencies then may have the City, Provate, FBI, ATF, etc., below in smaller letters.

d) Drug and Alcohol testing of suspected individuals is permitted by law enforcement after an accident or crime.

With current technology where it is today, having these recording devices will help in documenting and getting convictions of criminals and identifying improper policing activities. For a jury to see and hear the suspect from the beginning of their encounters with law enforcement should be invaluable in determining guilt or innocence. As shown in the Kyle Rittenhouse trial in Kenosha, Wisconsin, in November of 2021, having audio/video evidence of the three shootings from several angles was critical in determining the innocence of the accused. It takes it out of the realm of he said, she said.

We all trust our law enforcement officers and believe them when they tell us something. However, no profession is perfect and there will always be someone in law enforcement who shouldn't be, and the recording devices will help coach them to be better law enforcement officers where possible and, when not, to allow for the documentation to terminate their employment. Inspectors and code enforcement personnel may also fall into this category.

The waiving of the need to Mirandize someone prior to anything being admissible is no different than a bystander filming the event with their cell phone. Recorded history is recorded history regardless of who records the incident.

6: Anyone born after the date of the signing of this Constitution will only be taught classes in English. However, students under the age of 18 may take a non-English language class in school so long as it does not exceed five hours per week. There is no restriction for anyone taking non-English classes after high school.

> **A) Students will become proficient in reading, writing, math, science, history, the structure of our government and how it works. Money management, negotiations, critical thinking skills, the family unit, and physical fitness will also be part of the curriculum.**

> **B) Once a year, all school age children under the age of eighteen (or a Junior in High School) will be given a standardized Federal test to see how their academic performance compares with that of their peers. The testing will apply to children born after the acceptance of this new constitution.**

The proposed constitution will ensure that all children are educated in the English language so that everyone can speak with everyone else. Since the requirement is only for those born after the signing of the constitution, it creates a reasonable transition period for the school systems to get prepared for the change. All of this will help create a homogenous society. It also allows students the option to learn to read and speak in a language that may be the region's original native language or to prepare them to study or do business in a country where English is not the primary language. Learning a non-English language assumes that there are trained teachers or parent volunteers and a school budget that allows for the extra classes.

Approximately five years after ratification of the new constitution, when all children born after ratification start school in the first grade, those students will be taught in English, with the option of a class teaching another language—five hours per week maximum. Then the next year, all first and second grade students will be taught in English. The educational evolution continues for 10 years until all grades are taught in English, again with the option of learning another language under the constraints mentioned above. The educational evolution will provide a *framework* for a gradual and predictable assimilation for the educational system and society within Ameristralia.

Our children must learn that in the long run, a strong work ethic pays off in life. Work hard and work smart. As Larry Bradley says, "If our society through our government provides every opportunity to learn and to prepare for a life of satisfying work and prosperity, then that society owes no debt to those students who refuse to take advantage of those opportunities. This is a message that deserves to be communicated early and often throughout the period of time an individual is a student."[386]

People are chosen because of the skills they possess, the potential for growth that they show, and willingness to work hard. Therefore, in school, everyone needs to acquire knowledge and skills for a lifetime. When someone gets their first job they need to continue perfecting their skills so they can grow with the company and advance their career. If a particular company does not appreciate their skills, then they have the opportunity to move to another company that may appreciate them.

7: Right to a free education up to a senior in high school prior to their nineteenth birthday. Free is defined as the dollar figure the government (Federal, Provate, and Local) is willing to spend on its public schools. Federal monies will be the same throughout Ameristralia. Provate monies will be the same throughout the Provate. County/City/School District monies will be the same throughout the County/City/School District. Both Federal, Provate, and Local monies will be distributed on a per pupil basis by grade level

to public, charter, private schools, and for home schooled students.

> **A) Congress and the Provates may establish achieve-ment goals for each grade but may not dictate the policy and procedures to achieve those goals.**

> **B) Free English proficiency classes will be provided to individuals over the age of 19.**

If someone opts for something such as vocational training rather than finishing traditional high school that would be covered also, up to their nineteenth birthday or the completion of their senior year, whichever comes first. For example, if the teen wanted to go to high school for half a day and do vocational training for half a day, that would be allowed. The school should ensure that the students have all required classes finished in order to still receive a high school diploma.

Similarly, classes prior to grade school that teach course material such as Kindergarten and Pre-K may receive a per pupil stipend from the government. Different grade levels may be more expensive than others and the amount paid may differ as a result. The government also may not be willing to pay as much for certain grades either, Kindergarten and Pre-K for example.

Free English classes will be provided to any immigrant wishing to the learn the language so they may assimilate into society faster.

8. No politician may be in a public service announcement or government sponsored advertisement. Also, no politician still alive may be honored with their name on a government building or other asset.

Elected or appointed government officials may not be in advertisements or public service announcements whether paid for with government funds or other resources. In July, 2021, Kansas had a public service announcement discussing the status of Covid-19 vaccinations. The Democratic governor and a Democratic US House Member from Kansas were the only two featured politicians in the public service announcement. No Republican was in the television spot, only Democrats. They were using Kansas funds and/or resources to highlight two Democrats in a state that is typically a Republican stronghold.

As another example, at Love Field in Dallas in 2022, the mayor had two back-to-back public service announcements where he announces to everyone who he is and welcome to Dallas. Also great for name recognition in future elections.

No government asset (bridge, highway, building, ship, etc.) may be given the name of a living elected politician. For example, in Kansas City, Missouri, there is an Emanuel Cleaver II Boulevard, in honor of the former mayor. Mr. Cleaver, in 2022, is also a member of the US House of Representatives. Every time Mr. Cleaver runs for reelection, the voters have a constant reminder—for the purpose of name recognition and marketing—which is paid for by the local government.

The last example is where a politician gets funding for a pet project, for example, the erection of a building in their home Provate. Then the Provate names the building after the politician as a reward—an obvious conflict of interest.

9. No foreign organization or government may hold a citizen from Ameristralia as hostage without reasonable proof the individual has committed a crime, been charged and receiving a fair trial in public, with counsel, in a timely manner. If the organization or government continues to hold the hostage, then Ameristralia may also hold assets or citizens from the foreign organization or government until the Ameristralian citizen is released.

Some countries have a common practice and typical behavior of wrongfully detaining our citizens as a bargaining chip or ransom. Ameristralia is allowed to legally play the same game until our citizen is released.

Article 6 - Bill of Rights for Individuals,

1: Congress shall make no law respecting an establishment of religion, or prohibiting the free exercise thereof; or abridging the freedom of speech, or of the press; or the right of the people to **peaceable** (delete "to") **assemble, and to petition the Government for a redress of grievances.**

(Amendment 1 of the Original Bill of Rights - Freedom of Speech, ratified 12/15/1791).

a) No government entity has the power to make a list of unacceptable books, magazines, or newspapers.

b) Freedom of speech does not mean the freedom to threaten physical or financial harm to a person, family, business, organization, or government, or encourage others to do so.

c) Organizations who purport to present News to the public must be held to a higher standard. Congress will establish licensing requirements and standards of conduct for News Journalist, News Photo-journalist, News Copyright Editors, and News Producers. These will include reporting the news honestly, not just factually. Congress will establish a Bipartisan Commission for Elections and Media to review complaints and take disciplinary action when necessary.

d) Several examples of what News will not be; 1) reporting on information from unidentified sources, 2) using emotional or slanted language to distort the truth or move the audience in one direction, 3) using judgmental words to pass judgement in a report, 4) election polls or surveys, 5) weather forecast, 6) paraphrasing, 7) Deepfakes. Those licenses may be revoked or suspended for repeated violations.

e) Any network that presents current events, editorials, etc., must present at least 8 minutes of News during prime time, and it will be labeled as "News." Similarly, print media will also have a section labeled "News." If not News then articles will be labeled Current Events, Commentary, Editorial, Not-News, etc.

f) Audio and video clips must identify the date, time, and location of the clip and must be visible to the viewer or reader. Context should be identified.

These requirements do not stop anyone from having stories about current events, editorials, etc., any name they want to put with it, they just can't label them as News. TV Magazine shows such as *Special Report* or *The Situation Room* are all valid non-news names. These shows should have an eight-minute segment labeled "News," if news is actually being covered, otherwise, it is analysis and opinion. Weather forecasts, upcoming sporting events, political survey and polls, editorials, current events, and commentary can be in the other time segments available during the show. Other networks could change their nightly news names to something like ABC/CBS/NBC Nightly News and Current Events, as an example. But calling a whole program "News" when only a portion is actually news would be misleading.

The Radio Act of 1927 and the Fairness Doctrine of 1949 provided licensing requirements for radio and then television stations with regards to news broadcasts. These acts mandated that licensees should provide the public with matters of interest and do so in a fair manner. Programs on politics were required to include opposing views on any given issue presented by people best qualified to represent those views.

The Fairness Doctrine received a number of legal challenges over the years. In 1969, the Supreme Court ruled 9-0 (Red Lion Broadcasting Co. vs FCC) that while broadcasters had rights to free speech, the airwaves and licenses were owned by the federal government and, as lease owners, had the right to regulate news content.

By the mid-1980s, deregulation had become a central focus of the Reagan Administration. Reagan believed that the marketplace, not the government, should be the arbiter of competing viewpoints. Deregulation, along with new technologies, resulted in the abolishment of the Fairness Doctrine in 1987.[387] Media programming, AM radio especially, moved from primarily music stations to a rise in talk radio.

The press/media has been biased since the invention of the printing press. Let's look at some examples:

1) Thomas Jefferson encouraged setting up a Republican news-paper because he was "convinced that there was no real opposition press in the nation to tell the truth about his rival."[388] So began the venomous newspaper war of 1792-93.

2) In 1876, after the Presidential election, the *New York Times* engaged in mischief by publishing a headline: "The Battle Won. A Republican Victory in the Nation—Gov. Hayes Elected President…" and the *New York Sun's* declaration was: "Tilden is Elected."[389] Both reports were without any basis of truth. Then there is the more current incident where the *Chicago Daily Tribune* proclaimed, "Dewey Beats Truman," when Truman actually won.

Harry Truman

3) In Iceland, daily papers such as *The Time* were controlled by the Progressive Party. *The Morning Paper* by the Independence Party and the Labour Party also had their own paper.[390]

4) In the United Kingdom during Winston Churchill's time, *The Daily Herald,* a Labour newspaper, was subsidized by Russian money.[391]

5) In the late 1990s, multi-millionaire Conrad Black acquired much of Canada's daily press and created a new national daily, the *National Post,* to promote a "unite the right" agenda.[392]

6) On January 18, 2019, Nicholas Sandmann was a student at Covington Catholic High School and went to Washington, DC, for the annual March for Life rally. He was confronted by Nathan Phillips who was beating a hand-held drum and was singing. Sandmann tried to defuse the situation by remaining calm and motionless. Various news networks presented a small clip of the situation and said that Mr. Sandmann had approached, confronted, and mocked Mr. Phillips, a native American elder, in an aggressive manner. Mr. Phillips also said Mr. Sandmann had blocked his escape. Not the case. CNN, NBC, and the *Washington Post* settled lawsuits for libel out of court. The Associated Press and other news outlets were also sued and the results are still pending at the time of this book.

So yes, there is intentional bias both ways and has been around for centuries.

Without knowing the full context of the event, it is difficult to judge the event correctly. If someone provides only a small slice of a video to the media in lieu of the whole video, it will not be accepted. However, if the whole clip is provided to the news organization then they can make the judgement and show enough to give an honest accounting of the incident. After the media has aired a clip, the entire video must be available on the news organizations website for others to see everything that happened before and after.

A Gallup-Knight Foundation survey in 2018 found that 69 percent of Americans had lost trust in the news media. For Republicans, the figure was 94 percent.[393] Trust must be reestablished.

There have been too many instances over the centuries where the press/media has intentionally misrepresented the facts in order to emotionally whip up the populace so they can sell more papers, magazines, or television ads. The Spanish-American War (1898) was partly brought on by the Yellow Journalism that went on at the time. As an example, the Hearst's newspaper was not patient when it presented an artist's rendering of the burned-out hulk and diagrams to show exactly where and how the "Infernal Machine" (implying it was a torpedo, but later determined to be a mine) had struck and sunk the US battleship Maine in Havana Harbor. It appeared on its pages even before it had scarcely cooled, or they had all the facts. [394]

Theodore Roosevelt condemned the muckrakers of using "hysteria and sensationalism." The double tendency of subjective journalism, he felt, was toward "suppression of truth" and "assertion or implication of the false."[395]

News is not an anonymous source, that is a rumor. News is someone who is willing to go on the record and present something as fact. A senior Administration official, or a senior Justice Official, or an FBI source—these "leaks" are typically done for political reasons.

Factual reporting is not the same thing as honest reporting. An outlet may report that company ABC made billions of dollars of profit as factual. But that claim is not the whole story. They should also report that this profit is not only X% percentage of company ABC's revenue but also, for companies in ABC's industry, what the average profit margin is on revenues for their category. Everything must be put into context. Just because a company's profits are in the billions, versus millions, hundreds of thousands, or tens of thousands does not make a company bad.

Let me also say that honesty in reporting applies to lawyers and government officials as well. My friend Howard Pate suggested the following anecdote in dealing with truth.

I always watched the Perry Mason show with my parents and, in those days, they used the saying, "Do you swear to tell the truth, the whole truth and nothing but the truth?" As a teenager I never really dwelled on it but, in my business years I really tried to define what it meant. Well, "the truth" is simple. It is true or it is a lie. "The whole truth" . . . do you conveniently leave something out of the story that would have an impact on someone's complete understanding?

(The media, government officials and lawyers excel at this.) Finally, "Nothing but the truth" . . . i.e., do you tell the truth in such a way that my own mind stretches the truth into the mists of my probable distortions. When I was turning around companies, I never had the luxury of time to chase down information and clarify distortions of the truth. So, I would bring in the executive team and explain my Perry Mason story. And, I would tell them that the first downsizing would be the people who did not live by my truth philosophy. It worked always. There is no place for politicking with the truth.

As an example of putting things into proper context: a 2016 *Wall Street Journal* article investigated the income disparities between the men and women in a union shop. In this case, all promotions were based on seniority and there was a pretty equal blend of men and women at all levels of seniority. Still, researchers found that the women were significantly under earning when compared to the men even though they had enough seniority to get the better paying jobs.[396]

The researchers found that women, who are typically the Caregivers in the family, were less likely to take the higher paying jobs because of the overtime required or the additional stress involved with those jobs. These Caregivers were responsible for taking care of their children when they came home from school or taking care of aging parents.[397] Divorced Caregivers to whom the court awarded custody of the children (historically the women, but not always), have significantly reduced ability to work overtime. On the other hand, the spouse who didn't get custody (historically the man) can work all the overtime they want in order to pay the child support for their children and have enough left over for fun. This article did a great job of putting the data in proper context. Looking at only the raw numbers, without looking at the underlying drivers, leads to the superficial factual statistical claim that men still make significantly more than women—because of discrimination in the workplace. But in reality, the choice by

Caregivers (historically the woman, but not always) to put the family unit at a higher priority than work puts the Caregivers at a financial disadvantage. In this specific example, the financial disadvantage is not the result of sexual discrimination. It also provides an example of how individuals and politicians pushing specific narratives can use the raw factual data and say it shows discrimination when in reality it does not.

But thank God for all the Caregivers in our lives.

TRUTH:
An old axiom states:
"Liars can figure, and figures can lie."

"The numbers don't lie, but we can fix that."

There will always be an individual, a boss, or a company who does not treat people fairly because of their gender, ethnic background, skin color, or religion. There have been laws on the books for the last 50 years to provide a remedy for people in these situations, but bosses and businesses are not perfect and never have been. Humanity can only try to do better with each passing generation.

Label News as News. License journalists, just as individuals are licensed or certified to be lawyers, accountants, and even librarians. The news media must be held accountable for their work product. Social media outlets that allow for the distribution of current events and news must properly label the content so the reader understands what they are watching or reading.

After three decades of hyper-polarized media and news programs, the time has come to consider new licensing require-ments and standards of conduct for news, photojournalists, copyright editors, and news producers. Perhaps news should be defined as precisely as the condiment ketchup. A reasonable first step in our evolution is to define News.

The licensing requirement is simply to have eight minutes (somewhere between 5-7 p.m.) during a 24-hour day be "news." The other 23 hours and 52 minutes can be whatever the network wants to air.

To summarize, Americans today are increasingly concerned by the volume of news and frustrated by divisiveness, bias, and misinformation they see covered on television, newspapers, and online. Press bias has been a constant issue in society since the founding of America. It's time to evolve to a higher plane of discourse.

The prohibition of "deepfakes," computer generated audio and/or video of events that never happened, should be self-explanatory. News must show the time, date, and location for any audio and/or videos aired. Once the public knows the time, date, and location, if there is other evidence that the person was not there or acted differently, then the veracity of the clip can be challenged. If it can be reasonably shown that the audio and/or video is a "deepfake" then the news organization must release the identity of the individual or organization that provided the video to law enforcement, or the Bipartisan Commission for Elections and Media, when requested. If a media outlet knows from past experience that a source has been dubious, then members of the press should not trust that source going forward.

A secondary type of deepfake is a staged incident. In December of 2021, Jussie Smollett was convicted of lying to the Chicago police and claiming to be a victim of a hate crime in 2019. In essence, creating a hoax with two accomplices, then calling the police and trying to make it a real event that would be a matter of record.

Similarly, was the incident of five individuals from an anti-Youngkin group that stood in front of Youngkin's campaign bus with tiki torches dressed as Unite the Right protestors. The photo was spread across social media with some asserting it was a group of racist Youngkin supporters. The Lincoln Project eventually took credit for the hoax. Another common trick is to produce fake leaflets that disparage a political candidate with false information. All of these activities should be deplored and made illegal and fall under libel laws.

We teach our children that lying is a bad thing, so it must not be tolerated in adults.

2: A well-regulated Militia, being necessary to the security of a free Nation, the right of the people to keep and bear Arms, shall not be infringed.

(Amendment 2 - Original Right to Bear Arms. Ratified 12/15/1791)

a) **However, this does not prevent an individual's home Provate, or Ameristralia, from requiring Safety Training for those individuals who wish to carry a weapon in public places and acquire the necessary safety permit. Training may not last longer than eight hours over two days and may not exceed $100. No entity may restrict this right based on someone's need or lack of need, or** require insurance. The safety permit information will be included on the federally issued ID card.

b) A person's federal ID will be used for screening gun purchases and can be done on the spot with no waiting period. The federal ID will have a chip (or linked to the internet) indicating whether the person has a conviction for a crime or mental instability that would prevent the purchase. The government will not store the serial number, or weapon type purchased, unless greater than .45 caliber.

c) A felon convicted of a violent crime involving weapons may be denied a safety permit and not allowed to procure or possess weapons. These permits may be suspended or revoked by the individual's home Provate, or Ameristralia, for sufficient cause.

d) Individuals will not be required to register their Arms unless the size of the shell used is greater than .45 caliber. Civilians may not own a machine gun or magazines holding more than 13 rounds.

One of the first unwritten rules for colonial powers was to never let the indigenous population ever have weapons to defend themselves. However, citizens must have the right to protect themselves against any oppressive government.

Manufacturers and users of any utilitarian device have an obligation to ensure the public safety. Accidents happen and contingencies should be made to mitigate those accidents. For example, automobiles kill around 40,000 people per year, about the same as guns.[398] We require drivers to pass a test, obtain a license, and carry insurance. These measures are not to prevent vehicle ownership, but to promote responsibility and accountability and for the protection of other citizens.

3: No Soldier shall, in time of peace be quartered in any house, without the consent of the Owner, nor in time of war, but in a manner to be prescribed by law.

(Amendment 3, Original Bill of Rights, ratified 12/15/1791)

4: The right of the people to be secure in their persons, houses, papers, and effects, against unreasonable searches and seizures, shall not be violated, and no Warrants shall issue, but upon probable cause, supported by Oath or affirmation, and particularly describing the place to be searched, and the persons or things to be seized.

(Amendment 4, Originally Bill of Rights, ratified 12/15/1791)

5: No person shall be held to answer for a capital, or otherwise infamous crime, unless on a presentment or indictment of a grand jury, except in cases arising in the military forces, or in the Militia, when in actual service in time of War, or policing action, or public danger; nor shall any person be subject for the same offen[s]e to be twice put in jeopardy of life[,] limb, or financially; nor shall be compelled in any criminal or civil case to be a witness against himself, nor be deprived of life, liberty, or property, without due process of law; nor shall private property be taken for public use, without just compensation.

(Amendment 5, Original Bill of Rights, ratified 12/15/1791)

A) There will be one Penal Code at the Federal level for all citizens, organizations, and businesses. An individual, organization, or business has a right to only be tried in one court for all criminal and civil charges from any one incident. If not guilty of a criminal crime, then the citizen, organization, or business cannot be tried for the same offense in a civil case.

B) No spouse or attorney may be compelled to bear witness against their spouse or client.

Currently in the US, someone can be tried at the Provate level and then later at the Federal level for the same crime. For example, you can be charged and go to court for criminal crimes (murder) and then for civil crimes (deny someone of their civil rights because they were murdered), all for the same incident. Such practice is a waste of time and money for the government and the accused. While the government may be able to afford this waste, the average citizen, organization, or business cannot. Separate civil and criminal suits act as a form of double jeopardy.

Current US law makes marijuana illegal, but many Provates, and/or cities, have legalized the substance. So there is a conflict and one authority can prosecute while another will not. Is that fair to the citizen? What should they do? Equal justice under the law should be maintained wherever a citizen is in Ameristralia. Having one penal code would solve the problem of different rules in different places.

6: In all criminal and civil prosecutions, the accused (individuals, organizations, or businesses) shall enjoy the right to a speedy and public trial, by an impartial jury of the Provate and district wherein the crime shall have been committed, which district shall have been previously ascertained by law, and to be informed of the nature and cause of the accusation; to be confronted with the evidence and witnesses against them; to have compulsory process for obtaining witnesses in their favor, and to have the Assistance of Counsel for their defense.

(Amendment 6, Original Bill of Rights, ratified 12/15/1791)

"His" is replaced by "them" and "their."

Currently, only individuals can receive free legal help. Small or new businesses should also have access to help with litigation expenses. In my lifetime, I've seen a couple of examples reported in the press where large competitors used lawsuits and the excessively large legal bills as a way of financially hobbling or killing off a new competitor—usually dealing with patent issues. Not providing legal assistance is not fair to the small company trying to enter a market with a larger established player.

7: In Suits at common law, where the value in controversy shall exceed ten thousand dollars, the right of trial by jury shall be preserved, and no fact tried by a jury shall be

otherwise reexamined in any Court of Ameristralia, than according to the rules of the common law.

(Amendment 7, Original Bill of Rights, ratified 12/15/1791)

The old standard used to be $20, I have raised it to $10,000 here, hence, demonstrating an example of why we index all dollars figures in the Constitution.

In Texas, the Small Claims Court, which has no jury, will settle claims under $10,000.

8: For individuals [e]xcessive bail shall not be required, nor excessive fines imposed, nor cruel and unusual punishment inflicted while incarcerated.

A Business may not be fined by way of lawsuit and/or government (Federal, Provate or local) action that takes away more than half of its average profit for the last three years, in any given year.

(Amendment 8, Original Bill of Rights, ratified 12/15/1791)

Many government agencies and Provates have outlandish penalties for anyone violating a given regulation. For example, fining a telemarketer $1,000 for each infraction of the No Call List. The government uses these outlandish fines as a way to bully companies into submission and/or fine them into non-existence.

During the Covid-19 pandemic, a fine of $250,000 and a year in jail per incident was imposed by the Centers for Disease Control (CDC) for landlords evicting non-paying renters.[399] So a landlord of a $100,000 house that they rent out could be fined two and a half times the value of the property for improperly evicting a tenant and get jailed for a year. Or if it is a $50,000 apartment, the penalty is even worse. Over a year later, the courts ruled the CDC didn't have the authority to issue these rules.

I visited a radio station in St. Joseph, Missouri, and watched a broadcast on Ranked Choice Voting. After the show was over the host explained to us about the three second delay in the broadcast and the $250,000 fine if a "bad" word got on the air. He told us the $250,000 would bankrupt the station. The fine equates to the Death Penalty for a business.

9: The enumeration in the Constitution, of certain rights, shall not be construed to deny or disparage others retained by the people.

(Amendment 9, Original Bill of Rights, ratified 12/15/1791)

Justice Robert H. Jackson admitted that the Ninth Amendment was a "mystery" to him. Since that time, however, the Ninth Amendment has been used as a secondary source of liberties and has emerged as important in the extension of the rights of privacy. The amendment is kind of a catch-all for other rights.

The Ninth Amendment worked alongside the Tenth Amendment to suggest that nothing in the Bill of Rights should be read as conferring additional government power and any rights that are to be enforced in the name of the Ninth Amendment must genuinely be rights of "the people."[400]

10: The powers not delegated to Ameristralia by the Constitution, nor prohibited by it to the Provates, are reserved to the Provates respectively, or to the people.

(Amendment 10, Original Bill of Rights, ratified 12/15/1791)

This clause goes hand-in-hand with #9. Also, as in Item 6 under the Business Bill of Rights (covered later on in this book), individuals should be able to do just about anything that does not hurt others or society.

11: All persons born or naturalized in Ameristralia, and subject to the jurisdiction thereof, are citizens of Ameristralia and of the Provate wherein they reside. No Provate shall make or enforce any law which shall abridge the privileges or immunities of citizens of Ameristralia; nor shall any Provate deprive any person of life, liberty, or property, without due process of law; nor deny to any person within its jurisdiction the equal protection of the laws.

(Amendment 14, ratified July 9, 1868.)

Deleted sections 2 (talks about the selection of Representatives), 3 (also discusses the selection of people in Congress), 4 (discusses debt obligations), and 5 (discusses how Congress has the power to pass laws to enforce this amendment) are all covered in other areas and are updated.

The amendment was passed so the Civil Rights Act of 1866 (passed by northern Republicans) protected the rights of former slaves after the Civil War. The constitutional amendment would give teeth to the Act so any subsequent acts by Congress could not be overridden—once the Southern states were again admitted into the Union.

There are two key elements of this amendment as originally conceived. The first part applies to "citizens" of the US and the second applies to "persons" within the US. When originally presented in 1866, there were several classes of citizenship (for example, women were not allowed to vote yet and indigenous people were not consider citizens) and some questions of whether former slaves were now citizens of the country. The amendment broadly gives protection ("due process of law") to everyone within the confines of the country.

12: No organization, business, or governmental body may ask and/or then maintain data on a person's gender (except for birth certificates, Federal ID, schools, and health care institutions), ethnic background, skin color, or religion (except churches).

Voluntary cultural associations and genealogy groups may collect this data for the personal use of its members interested in genealogy. These voluntary cultural associations may not give or sell this information to any other organization or the government.

Obviously, schools that provide living accommodation for students would need to ask a student's gender to ensure that students get a roommate of the same gender, if requested.

Health care institutions would also need to maintain gender data because there is a biological difference between men and women and, as a result, different medical problems and issues for men and women.

If there is ever a question on gender, then a birth certificate or Federal ID can provide confirmation.

13: No retail storefront business may refuse service to any individual for any reason other than a) nonpayment of products and services, b) the individual has stayed past the normal time for the service they requested, c) they are creating a scene and disturbing the peace of the establishment, d) not following posted safety standards or dress codes, or e) has a history of, or is abusive to staff. Any custom requests or orders will be at the sole discretion of the business.

Individuals do not have the right to come into a retail business and just occupy space without purchasing a product or service from the business. The individual does not have the right to make a nuisance of themselves to the discomfort of other patrons or staff. It does allow a business to refuse service and admittance to individuals not following the stated safety procedures, such as wearing a mask in a pandemic.

14: All mortgage companies must offer fifteen and thirty-year fixed rate mortgages, as well as products with other maturities.

In Canada, the standard mortgage is five years, amortized over twenty-five years, which requires borrowers to refinance and requalify for a new mortgage every five years.[401] The practice is great for banks but terrible for the consumer. In the United States, fifteen and thirty-year fix rate mortgages are commonplace and should not be a problem for other Provates of the Union. Owning a home is one of the keys to maintaining the family unit and for a family to create wealth. A 30-year mortgage allows this to happen because a 30-year mortgage makes buying a home a lot easier than a five-, ten-, or fifteen-year note.

A realtor once told me to never buy a property with a balloon payment due 5 or 10 years down the road. Why, because you have no idea of what kind of financial situation you will be in when the term ends and you may not qualify for a loan with someone else. So in the Canadian scenario, if you have a temporary hardship, you may not qualify for a renewal of your loan, even if you have enough money in your LISA to cover you through any hardship.

Also, if interest rates go up in the interim, it may preclude the person from qualifying for a loan at the higher rate.

15: Right to protect oneself from bodily invasion or harm whether from another person or a manmade object. Terminally ill individuals have the right to die at a time of their own choosing, and without pain, if possible. Women have the right to make decisions about their bodies.

Individuals have a right not to have foreign matter put into their bodies. Whether that is a product of a rape, vaccination, food, or medicines. They also have a right to protect themselves from bodily harm and get advice from medical persons and/or clergy (not the government) about how to respond to any medical condition be it pregnancy, cancer, or any terminal illness.

If a parent does not want their children to receive a vaccination because their school requires it, then they have the option of going to a different school that doesn't require it. If all schools require the vaccination, then the other option is to home-school your children, or get them the vaccinated. The same applies if an employer requires a certain vaccination in order to work, then the option of changing jobs to an employer who does not mandate the vaccine is an option, as well as, starting your own business, or getting vaccinated.

Personal freedom means the government has no say in personal decisions regarding a person's body. Medical procedures and treatment are between a person, their doctors, their religion, and their personal beliefs. Parents (not the government) have the right to determine what is best for their minor children. Similarly, schools and clubs can determine if teams will be gender based or co-ed. The best way to ensure successful co-existence is to allow the people to negotiate what will best serve their community without government intrusion.

Individuals will have the religious and cultural freedoms to follow their personal beliefs.

16: Citizens have the right to join, or not join, a political party, union, or worker committee, but may not be allowed to strike more than five days in the last five years. Employees, or contractors, of the government or government agencies may not strike.

> **a) Unions will be re-certified by a secret vote of eligible employees once every 6 years at each work site.**

> **b) Employers will not provide payroll deduction for political parties, unions, or worker committees.**

At one point in their evolution, unions provided an opportunity for the oppressed worker to stand up and be treated with the respect and dignity they deserve. We thank all those union efforts in the evolution of all our countries for lifting us all up during the Industrial Revolution and providing us a better foundation for life. Political parties and unions have given us the 40-hour work week, the end of child labor, paid overtime, health insurance, and other benefits to society.

The workplace of the twenty-first century is a different place than of the nineteenth and twentieth centuries. Agriculture evolved into the Industrial Revolution and now has evolved into the Technology Revolution. Technology impacts everything from how plants are harvested, how products are manufactured, and how board meetings are conducted. Self-driving cars and delivery drones will make a difference in how commerce is conducted. Decades of working at the same company has been replaced by career changes, contractors, gig workers, and entrepreneurs.

Blue-collar and pink-collar jobs are being replaced by robotics. Coders are in greater demand than assembly line workers. Jobs, historically done in offices or cubicles, can now be done from home or even coffee shops. Automobile mechanics are being augmented by computer programs for identifying issues with our vehicles.

Worker compensation, worker benefits, and worker rights are complex and there is not a one size fits all situation. Workers should reasonably expect a fair wage, a safe environment, and to be treated with respect. The purpose of the Constitution is to promote life, liberty, and the pursuit of happiness. As part of that process, Ameristralia strives to create a level playing field in which to find that job that will provide an opportunity for a living wage for all citizens. You can only expect to earn a living wage if you work hard and acquire skills that make you valuable to your employer, or other employers.

An office environment should not be toxic and employees should be treated with respect. The three things people want are survival, belonging, and personal growth. As explained in an *Inc. Magazine* article, survival, the need for food, water, and shelter are all things a living wage should provide. In addition, belonging is the need to be accepted since so many hours a day are spent at work—belonging matters. It provides a sense of personal growth, not being stagnant.[402]

Government Employees

President Franklin D. Roosevelt (FDR) opposed unions for public workers.[403]

In 1962, President Kennedy signed Executive Order 10988 that authorized collective bargaining for federal employees as payback to the unions for getting him elected but deprived them of the right to strike. States and cities then followed the lead.[404] In 1966, Canadian postal workers, along with almost all federal civil servants in Canada, also gained the right to strike. They all started to take full advantage of it.[405]

1981

In the United States, the Professional Air Traffic Controller Organization (PATCO) controlled all planes taking off, inflight, and landing in the United States and had supported Ronald

Reagan during the 1980 Presidential election. Previously, Reagan was a Vice President in the Screen Actors Guild—a union. PATCO had previously had a three-day sick-out and "slowdowns."[406] In 1981, shortly after Ronald Reagan's election as President, PATCO went on strike and demanded a $600 million raise compared to the $105 million the government was offering which equated to a 11.4% increase over 3 years—twice what was offered to other federal employees. PATCO also demanded a 32-hour work week with the pay increase. Reagan told everyone, "If they do not report for work within 48 hours, they have forfeited their jobs and will be terminated."[407] More than 11,000 ignored the warning and Reagan fired them all. It took several years for the air traffic systems to get back up to normal operations. In striking, the union violated federal law which prohibits strikes by federal government employees. As a result, PATCO was later decertified by the Federal Labor Relations Authority on October 22, 1981. Reagan's comment after he fired the PATCO strikers was "Dammit, the law is the law."[408]

Government Contractors

There are two levels of government contractors. First are those dedicated 100% at a given location to perform specific tasks. Individuals could be putting up a government building or a contract employee working for an agency. No strikes are allowed.

Second is where the work is peripheral to other duties— for example, an airline that transports mail or packages for the government or an agency. In this scenario, the airline might have less than five percent of their revenue come from the delivery of mail or packages and would not fall under the no strike parameter.

Union and Worker Committee Elections

Elected politicians get reelected every two, four, or six years. What sense does it make that a group of employees elect to join a union and they are in that one union for life? There should be a recertification election every 6 years to confirm the employees still want that particular union to represent them. In a *Wall Street Journal* editorial, there were examples of individuals or groups who wanted to get rid of the Teamsters, but the union rules and National Labor Relations Board rules were structured in such a way that it was basically impossible.[409] Competition makes us all better, even the union.

Reform

In 1961, Walter Reuther, the President of the United Auto-workers Union said, "Power is the ability of a labor union like the UAW to make the most powerful corporation in the world, General Motors, say, 'Yes' when it wants to say 'No'. That's power."[410] But is there any wonder why most car production is now outside of the United States?

Martin Luther King said, "There is nothing wrong with power if power is used correctly."[411] The right kind of power should be more like in Germany where labor and management work together for the betterment of the company.

In 2020, in New York, New York, construction jobs were dwindling because of the pandemic. The union leadership was smart enough to lower the wages of its members by about a third in order to keep everyone employed.[412] A surprisingly smart move by the union leadership and other unions should learn from their example.

17: Employees have a right to work and earn an income in order to support themselves and their family.

   a) Political Parties, Unions, Worker Committees, other organizations, or any individual may not hinder or intimidate an employee from going to their place of work or doing their job. Also, an employer may not temporarily lock out employees.

   b) With very few exceptions (failure to appear, producing "deepfakes", repeat offenders, making fake IDs, etc.), the government will not incarcerate anyone whose crime was of a non-violent nature,

has a job, and is paying their income taxes.

c) The federal government will maintain a database of all convicted criminals and employers may ask an applicant if they have ever been convicted of a crime and verify it against that database. Some crimes may disqualify individuals from some jobs.

Below are examples of where individuals or organizations tried to keep someone from working and trying to support their family.

Violence in Missouri, 1970

In September of 1970, the Teamsters Local 823 had gone on strike against Tri-State Motors, a Joplin, Missouri based trucking company. Tri-State Motors continued to operate in spite of the strike. On September 30, 1970, 48-year-old truck driver John Galt (not Ayn Rand's John Galt) was driving a Tri-State Motors truck, hauling a load of more than 20 tons of dynamite along Interstate-44 en route to a mining area in southeastern Missouri. Galt had a right to work in order to support his family. Shots were fired by striking teamsters at Galt's truck, triggering a massive explosion that shattered windows 12 miles away in Springfield, Missouri. A crater that was 50 feet wide and 30 feet deep was left on Interstate-44. Galt died instantly in the explosion. Galt was a father of four. No one else was seriously hurt or killed.

A witness later reported seeing shots fired from a car and gave police the license plate number. Police were able to track down the car and found a .30-30-caliber rifle as well as a spent shell. Two Tri-State company drivers and Teamster members, Bobby Shuler and Gerald Bowden, both 29 at the time, were charged with second-degree murder.

Shuler later said that he had also fired at a flatbed Tri-State Motors truck traveling in front of Galt's semi but that he wasn't able to disable it. He argued that he didn't intend to hurt anyone.[413]

What kind of mindset exists within a union that would allow this kind of thought process and behavior to take place? Attacking your fellow employee? John Galt had a right to work.

Violence in Great Britain, 1981

In Great Britain in March of 1981, Margaret Thatcher observed the union activities in the coal fields, "Over the following two weeks the brutal weight of the militants' shock troops descended on the coal field and for a moment it seemed as if rationality and decency would go under."[414] and "Working miners were not the only targets: their wives and children were also at risk. The sheer viciousness of what was done provides a useful antidote to some of the more romantic talk about the spirt of the mining community."[415] Thatcher said the working coal miners explained to her how small shops in the coalfields were being blackmailed into supplying food and goods for striking miners and withholding them from working miners.[416] Thatcher said that the unions had priced many of their members out of jobs by demanding excessive wages for insufficient output, thus making British goods uncompetitive.[417]

A McClure's article by Ray Baker published in January of 1902 entitled, "The Right to Work," consisted of interviews with nonunion miners who had braved bullets and beatings to continue working. One was quoted as saying, "I believe that a man should have a right, no matter what his reasons are, to work when and where he pleases." Baker reported that this miner had been set upon by union vigilantes and blinded with a rock."[418] Unions were known to beat up fellow employees crossing the picket line.

Bad Company Behavior

Three examples:

1) In 1890, in Australia, the workers of coal, silver, and lead were locked out by the companies.[419]
2) In Britain, in 1921, a mine lockout was followed by more competition from Germany which lead to wage cuts.[420]
3) In Britain, on May 1, 1926, management again cut the coal miners pay, they protested and management locked them out again. Consequently, a nationwide general strike then followed.[421]

These examples demonstrate that both unions and companies have acted poorly in the past against workers who just want to work.

If an individual works and pays taxes and is arrested, charged, and then convicted of a nonviolent crime, the punishment should not prevent the individual from continuing to work, support their family, and continue to provide a positive impact on society. However, the job/career may no longer be in the former field or as lucrative due to the nature of the crime. In humanities' history, governments used to throw people into debtors' prison for their inability to pay their debts. But society evolved and now we allow people who get overextended to file for bankruptcy so they may start over again. Throwing someone in jail for their inability to pay their debts was not the answer. So, we must evolve again, here with non-violent crimes.

Here are a couple of examples to consider. If an individual is arrested for recreational drug use or possession and later convicted, that conviction should not prevent the individual from continuing to work. On the other hand, if an individual is an illegal drug dealer without a regular job and is arrested, charged, and convicted of drug use or possession, then that individual can be thrown in jail. A gang member who does not work at a regular job, is not paying taxes or contributing to a LISA account, is a menace to society and that person should be jailed for a nonviolent crime.

Let's say an accountant embezzles $200,000 from their employer. The accountant was fired from their job, but they have been working and paying taxes and supporting their family. In this example the accountant will now be a convicted felon and doesn't go to prison but now has to support their family with this felony conviction on their record and may never again have a job as an accountant. The accountant may end up working in a lower paying job—that is their punishment. But the accountant's family is still together and the accountant is still providing support for their family. The family unit is maintained. It does not prevent the government from trying to extract the ill-gotten gains from the individual and their family—i.e., Bernie Madoff.

People have a right to know before they hire an individual who has a bad history and is convicted of a crime. Actions have consequences. Again, people should not be able to hide among their fellow citizens.

18: Employees shall be granted the right to at least ten days paid time off that can be used for sick days or vacation days. Fifteen days if there is a dependent child at home.

Guaranteed Maternity and Paternity leave of at least 15 days minimum upon the arrival of a new child into the family.

Every employee deserves paid time off to take care of personal or family business, or for vacation. It contributes to their well-being. Whether they are full-time or part-time, it doesn't make any difference.

These paid times off are a minimum requirement, private employers and corporations may set the paid time-off benefits at higher levels, if they so desire.

When I worked for a truckline in 2009, they only provided one week of vacation a year. In driving a flatbed truck, we were typically home 3 out of 4 weekends in a given month. Home for the weekend sometimes meant just one night. So it was a very demanding job. Another driver at the company got sick on the road and had to be hospitalized. The company used his one week of vacation for his illness and the individual ended up missing the wedding of his daughter that year because he had no vacation left.

19: Any organization, government entity or business with customers in Ameristralia will have posted their full legal name, physical and mailing address of their headquarters (if different than the physical address), and a phone number on their website, letterhead, forms, and any other forms of hard or electronic communications.

All government bodies will have an easily found published phone number and during normal business hours, 80 percent of phone calls will be answered within 10 minutes. Web inquiries and letters will be answered within seven business days.

I started working for a warranty company in Madison, Wisconsin, in 1998. I was in temporary housing and my wife and family were still in Kansas shortly after starting. My wife tried to call me but didn't have my office number there, this was before everyone had a cell phone. She called the information line at the phone company to get the office number, this was before the internet was widely available. My wife was told by the phone company that there was no phone number available because it was an unlisted number. So even though the company had several thousand customers in multiple states, it didn't want the customers to be able to find them to place any warranty claims, unless they had their welcome packet information that had the toll-free phone number on it. Concealed or clandestine behavior by a business is morally wrong.

Commerce is predicated on competition but there is only one government so citizens don't have a choice of going someplace else. A government has to be responsive to its citizens and responsive to any messes it has created. Not answering the phone or answering correspondence in an untimely manner is not an option.

Companies, and governments, like individuals, don't have a right to hide.

20: Businesses must provide health insurance for all its permanent employees (full-time and part-time) and their minor children if the business meets the Rule of 10. The Rule of 10 is the combination of the number of years the business has been operating and the number of employees. If the combination of these two numbers equals 10 or more, and the business has been in operation for at least 5 years, then the business must provide health insurance. The Company paid health insurance (medical, vision, dental) must provide protection for at least 80% the projected expenses (which would include 100% of normal expenses for prenatal and delivery of children) of the average employee with a cap for each employee of one million dollars over the life of the employee and each of the employee's dependents. Businesses not meeting the Rule of 10 will be given a stipend of 95% of the average national

cost of health insurance from the Federal government for the company to provide the health care insurance for each employee and their dependent children.

A) The business will allow an employee to add their spouse if the business is reimbursed by the employee for the additional expense. The businesses' health care provider will allow departed employees to keep their insurance for 18 months, if the employee pays for the coverage.

B) For working, injured military veterans, health insurance companies will bill the Federal Government for normal out-of-pocket expenses above their policy limits to a total outlay of $5,000,000. For those injured military veterans unable to work who select an insurance company from an approved list, the Federal Government will pay all normal out-of-pocket expenses up to a total outlay of $10,000,000. In either situation these monies may also help acquire reasonable housing.

It is important to help new businesses get started. The Federal Government will provide a stipend to those employers so they can provide health insurance to its employees. As with any government stipend, the money will be treated as revenue to the company and taxed appropriately on their profits. For example, let's assume a new business had revenues of $100,000 in a given year and received a stipend from the government of $24,000 in that year for health insurance. Total revenue would be $124,000 that year. If the business lost money, there would be no tax on the monies received for the stipend. If the business made a profit of over $24,000 for the year, then in essence the entire stipend would be taxed at the appropriate rate. Again, the government per-person stipend is the same for all new businesses. Then based on the financial viability of the company, it may or may not pay taxes on the stipend.

According to the Bureau of Labor Statistics, approximately 20 percent of small businesses fail within the first year. By the end of the second year, 30 percent of businesses will have failed. By the end of the fifth year, about half will have failed. And by the end of the decade, only 30 percent of businesses will remain—a 70 percent failure rate.[422] Therefore, it is imperative that the government help these new companies get started for a limited time while they provide health insurance to their employees.

Health insurance is a costly benefit, which is why the proposed Ameristralia Constitution has a cap placed on taxes so that companies can afford to offer and pay for healthcare. Rather than over-tax businesses (take money away from them) and then turn around and have the government provide for health insurance, let companies keep the money and pay for it themselves. Currently, many businesses don't provide health insurance to their employees because their competitors don't provide health insurance. Providing health insurance would put them at a financial disadvantage. But by requiring all businesses to offer health insurance, it levels the playing field for all businesses.

Military injuries will be a life-long obligation of the government when wounded war veterans return home. If a wounded veteran is unable to work, then the Government will pay 100% of all their reasonable health insurance up to ten million dollars. If working, the government will pay any unpaid insurance bills between what was covered under the business plan and five million dollars. Reasonable housing may also be covered, including rent, purchase, or pay off a mortgage within the median range of housing costs in a city or Provate.

The US Congress has mandated that US COBRA (Consolidated Omnibus Budget Reconciliation Act) type benefits be made available to individuals. US COBRA allows individuals to keep their health insurance for up to 18 months after leaving a company, if the employee reimbursed the company for the premiums. I have added the continuation of health benefits for the employee if the former employee pays for the protection. LISA monies could be used to pay these premiums.

Most of the proposed countries included in Ameristralia have universal healthcare already in place. One of the key philosophies presented here is that competition creates accountability. Competition also creates better systems. A government-run system is potentially full of fraud or waste and is not accountable to anyone. Government should not have a monopoly on healthcare. Government programs should be able to compete with private sector programs. When competition exists, individuals have greater choices and an overall better healthcare system is created.

Having employers provide health insurance also provides an *incentive* to work.

21: Contracts must be "reasonable and fair" to both parties and this right cannot be waived in the contract.

Whether there is one provider or six in a given market, and they all have similar contract language, that does not give the consumer any real choices. Too often, contracts or terms and conditions are written in legalese, a tiny font, and multiple pages that are difficult to decipher. What really matters is the interpretation or application of those terms and alternatives should be offered or negotiated. If no alternatives are offered, then consumers have no choice but to accept the contract on the company's terms. The provision gives consumers a fighting chance.

22: Insurance companies providing protection for the physical structure of a home or place of business will not have exclusion for acts of God and will provide for replacement value in the policy.

   a) All owners of a home or a place of business must carry insurance on the physical structure that includes replacement value.

   b) Renters will have insurance to cover situations where their home or business building is no longer available for their use and the loss of their contents.

Homeowners carry insurance on their home and they expect their home to be protected. When a natural disaster hits, such as tornados, hurricanes, floods, or earthquakes, they are often categorized as "Acts of God." Depending on the policy and the insurer, Acts of God may or may not be covered. The government should not act as the insurer of last resort for people who have lost their home or business. Their insurance company should cover natural disasters and adjust their rates accordingly, especially when folks choose to rebuild in the same spot where disasters are prevalent such as floods, hurricanes, and forest fires.

Landlords have an obligation to carry insurance and at the same time renters should also have renters' insurance for their personal property. In either scenario, the penalty for not having the required insurance should not be a fine or imprisonment. The penalty is the loss incurred without the government stepping in to help out.

The government can still help with temporary food and housing in the immediate aftermath of any disaster.

Article 7 - Bill of Rights for Businesses

1: An individual business should not have to receive a license to operate in their home Provate except in professions or industries where the results of poor quality/workmanship could reasonably result in the possible death or serious injury (physically or financially) to others, such as a doctor or electrician. Para professionals such as barbers, beauticians, massage therapist, or home repair servicers should be encouraged to receive training and certification but not require a license, insurance, or a bond to operate.

Each Provate's Attorney General will maintain a website for complaints and reviews also validating the claims in the process. When practical, assist citizens in their Provate to find remedies with a company with whom they have a dispute.

The website should be categorized by industry.

The information of the complaints, the resolutions, and the reviews will all be posted on the Provate website so that citizens can research the company prior to employing their services. Many public or company review sites have screening criteria that restrict bad reviews from being displayed and people need a reliable alternative.

In 2020, in Kansas City, Missouri, restaurant wait staff, sellers of alcohol in the grocery store, and some lawn maintenance workers had to be licensed. If the individuals were not licensed, the business itself had to be licensed, for example, to sell alcoholic beverages. To buy a bottle of wine in a Kansas City, Missouri, grocery store and the cashier is under 21, that person must step aside while someone over 21 and licensed comes over and scans the bottle of wine. Totally unnecessary.

In France, my wife and I learned that tour guides were required to be licensed and it's about a two-year process to get necessary training and pass the exams. I can understand that training is necessary, but licensing is extreme. While I was on active duty at Fort Leonard Wood, Missouri, I gave VIP tours to educators—no license or two years of training required.

If you can buy insurance (car, home, or life insurance) through a web site, what sense does it make to have sales people licensed to sell those same products?

2: If a business is allowed or licensed to do business in its home Provate, then it may do business in any other Provate without having to pass any other regulatory hurdles, except to be properly registered with the Secretary of State in that Provate. Businesses do not have to register to do business at any level below the Provate level, i.e., county or city.

Businesses without a physical presence in a Provate will collect the necessary Provate sales tax, but not any lower level, like county or city. Businesses will also pay the appropriate income tax in each Provate it operates.

Many Provates use this licensing process to keep new companies from coming into their market, sometimes at the request of existing businesses.

Many Provates require businesses to register at the county level and pay sales tax as well as at the Provate level, which is an unnecessary burden on businesses operating nationwide. In colonial times, businesses operated in a very small geographical footprint. Today, the smallest of businesses can have customers across county lines and/or Provate lines.

3: The Federal Government, or any government entity, may not own part or all of any business or nationalize any industry.

    a) Courts that are supervising the bankruptcy of a business may take temporary control but not take ownership in a business.

    b) There may be rare instances where there is no current provider or there is a lack of competition in the market. In these rare situations, regulations and/or subsidies would be the preferred option over ownership of a business.

Some Provates may own railroads (Australia and Canada until 1995) or airlines (Greenland and New Zealand) as part of their public transportation systems. These types of public transportation systems may be necessary moving forward to ensure the ability for goods and people to move freely around the country.

In 2019 a CBS report from Baldwin City, Florida, revealed that the only grocery store had closed, so the city started its own grocery store for the convenience of the citizens. The alternative was for them to drive 20-30 miles to another city for their groceries. Instead of starting its own store, the city might have been better served to give incentives to a proven operator to open a store in Baldwin City.

Margaret Thatcher noted that in Britain, the previous government had nationalized industries, either directly by taking ownership, or indirectly by using its powers of regulation to contain the decisions of private management in the direction the Government wanted. Arthur Shenfield said, "The difference between the public and private sectors was that the private sector was controlled by government, and the public sector wasn't controlled by anyone."[423]

Fannie Mae and Freddie Mac, large players in the mortgage market, were put under government control during the 2008-09 financial crisis through a process known as conservatorship. In January of 2021, the Treasury Department decided not to restructure the taxpayers' stake in Fannie Mae and Freddie Mac. The administration at the time tried to return both to private hands.[424] As part of this process, Congress was skimming off profits and putting these profits to use in other places.[425] The Fannie Mae and Freddie Mac example again confirms the principle that the Government should not take control of a business.

Prior to the 1980s, US railroad rates and service were set by the Government and carriers were often forced to provide service on lines lacking commercial viability. Railroads were forced to post rates for specific commodities independent of market conditions. The impact on railroads was predictable and disastrous. At one point, one in five rail miles was serviced by bankrupt railroads. Partial deregulation was chosen over nationalization, which would have cost taxpayers billions of dollars. The Staggers Rail Act of 1980 put American freight transportation back on track. By allowing large railroads to shed inefficient, low-density, or unprofitable lines in order to focus on core businesses, the Staggers Act not only improved service along the mainline network but also helped give birth to a short-line rail industry that today operates 50,000 miles of the 140,000-mile network that spans across the United States.[426]

The US government did nationalize passenger rail travel (Amtrak) in 1970 and in 50 years of ownership has never shown a profit.[427] In 2021, Amtrak received a $66 billion aid package to help it out.

4: No government body may shut a business down or tell it to temporarily close its doors without sufficient due process and multiple opportunities to fix any problems or establish necessary safety standards.

Businesses must be given sufficient time to adapt to any new regulatory or safety issues. Whether it is the next pandemic, or some recently announced regulatory hurdles, businesses must be given time to adjust. Just shutting businesses down is not an acceptable answer. Let businesses see the studies that have been done and how the new measures are derived from that data. Then allow the businesses sufficient time to make accommodations to meet the new standards. Being a small business owner myself, my heart bled for all businesses that had to shut down during the pandemic because they did not match someone's definition of an essential business, especially when some larger competitors were allowed to stay open.

The Government must not be allowed to arbitrarily shut down, or temporarily close, the doors of certain industries.

5: No mergers will be allowed when it will leave less than five providers in a given industry and/or market. No business with over 20% of market share may acquire a competitor.

6: Businesses may form associations, trade groups, and

cartels that promote their products in the market but may not do anything that restricts competition in the areas of production, distribution, methods of production, or pricing. When possible, these groups should agree on voluntary standards for their industry, but they will also not restrict innovation and will have rules allowing experimentation.

In many parts of the world, cartels and governments place major restrictions on how businesses compete. These constraints make for a stable environment for businesses, and people to live, but it restricts competition and innovation.

For example, in the US there are industry groups that promote milk and cotton. Their goal is to promote their products for the general good of their industry, which has numerous small players that individually can't afford to promote their industry. The milk and cotton industries provide a good example of a trade group.

7: Product liability cases are limited to products or services that have been produced in the last twenty years.

Defining the window for lawsuits prohibits class action lawsuits that go back many decades for such things as the asbestos suits that date back to when the Navy and private industries used asbestos during the Second World War. The courts and the law should not reasonably use present-day technology and scientific knowledge to punish companies for what was unknown decades ago. Winston Churchill said, "The past should not be judged by the standards of the present."[428]

The General Aviation Revitalization Act of 1994 shielded most aircraft manufacturers (carrying fewer than 20 passengers) from liability for most accidents involving products manufactured more than 18 years ago. The average cost of manufacturer's liability insurance for each airplane manufactured in the US had risen from approximately $50 per plane in 1962 to $100,000 per plane in 1988, according to a report cited by the Bureau of Labor Statistics, a 2,000-fold increase in 24 years.[429]

8. Allow virtually all kinds of currently illegal businesses to

operate in the open, including such activity as prostitution and drug use. Laws and regulation will be passed to make them reasonably safe and then pay their taxes.

No essential service (banks, utilities, credit card processers, etc.) may "black ball" an industry, political group or politicians and not provide necessary services for their survival.

Article 4 of the French Constitution says that liberty consists of being able to do anything which does not harm others. Article 5 of the French Constitution also says that the law can forbid only acts that are harmful to society, and that anything which is not forbidden by law is permitted.[430] In this regard, the French are very smart people. As Thomas Jefferson said, "The government is best which governs least."[431]

Society makes many things illegal, which drives a lot of activity underground, just like the 18th Amendment for the abolition of alcohol in the United States, which was later reversed by the 21st Amendment. People still found a way to make and consume alcohol, and created a large underground economy that organized crime used to fund their operations.

Once the folly of the experiment was realized, the experiment stopped. Gambling used to be illegal in many parts of the country, but now it isn't. If prostitution and drug use were legal and safe, it would deprive organized crime of a large share of their revenue streams. Hopefully, it would significantly reduce sex trafficking, but it could also increase the tax base at the same time. Some states such as Nevada in the US have legalized prostitution as have many foreign countries such as Austria, France, Germany, Greece, Switzerland, and New Zealand.[432]

Legalizing drugs should also greatly reduce crime because drug addicts will now be able to buy their pharmacy grade drugs cheaply, in controlled recreational amounts, as opposed to mystery drugs obtained on the street. Providing this option would greatly diminish the need to break into someone's house to steal something or rob someone on the street so addicts can turn around and buy drugs.

If it doesn't hurt society or another individual, and can be responsibly controlled, then legalize it and make it safe. Just because something is legalized does not mean an individual has to partake. Each individual has the right to make decisions based upon their own religious or moral beliefs and have every right to abstain. Citizens should not pressure the Government to make laws that restrict others from making their own decisions. For example, the consumption of alcohol, if done responsibly is okay, if not, people may get hurt. All actions have consequences.

In November of 2020, Oregon became the first Provate to decriminalize the possession of small amounts of heroin, cocaine, methamphetamine, and LSD. The move was inspired by a 2001 law in Portugal that removed incarceration as a penalty for drug possession. In his book *Drug Use for Grown-Ups,* Carl Hart claims that most heroin users show that addiction affects only 10% to 30% of those who regularly use heroin and methamphetamine, among other drugs.[433]

Oregon voters have agreed to end nearly all criminal penalties for drug possession. In 2017, an Oregon law reduced drug-possession charges to a misdemeanor from a felony. As a result, most addicts don't go to jail now unless they have committed other crimes or have been arrested multiple times for possession of large amounts of drugs.[434] Measure 110, which went into effect February 1, 2021, allows a maximum fine of $100 for possession of drugs including heroin, cocaine, and methamphetamines along with a mandatory health assessment. The first statewide law of its kind passed with support of 58% of voters. The law also mandates new recovery centers, paid for by marijuana taxes and savings from less incarceration.

If we can get 1/4, 1/3, 1/2, or 2/3 of drug users to get recreational sized doses over the counter from a pharmacy that are prescription quality (without hazardous fillers), this would be a benefit to all of society. First, it would reduce overdoses and people getting sick from a bad product. In a *Wall Street Journal* article, in 2021, they claim over 100,000 people died in 2020 from overdose.[435] Second, it would put a major hole in organized crimes' revenue stream and make them much weaker financially.

On the flip side, illegal drug use is a major reason kids go into foster care. In 2019, parental substance abuse was listed as a cause for a child's removal to foster care 38% of the time. Experts suggest that the percentage has risen steadily in the past decade. Experts also believe this is an underestimate and the real number may be up to 80%.[436] There will always be some parents who abuse alcohol or drugs. Again, the question is whether a cleaner product and doses that are recreationally safe would do less harm to society, parents, and their children than the current situation?

9. The Government may not require that businesses report activity that is outside their core business or do the Government's job.

In 2020, the US Drug Enforcement Agency brought charges against a drug wholesaler (RDC) for not monitoring the volume of drugs particular retail pharmacies had requested. But isn't it the government's job to do this? The wholesaler's job is to deliver products to licensed pharmacies who order the product. The primary job of the pharmacy is to fill legal prescriptions from doctors. The wholesaler does not know what the retail pharmacy is doing or not doing and doesn't know anything about the doctors in their area and what they are doing or not doing.

As another example, a federal agency directed Bank of America, which issued unemployment benefit payments on debit cards, to freeze any suspicious accounts. Yet when unemployed workers with legitimate claims were unable to access their benefits, the department blamed the bank.[437] It is not the bank's job to monitor the benefits going through the bank's debit cards for a government-run program and take action. The Government is responsible for oversight. The Government is trying to pass blame for mismanagement in the system on to the bank rather than the way the program was set up and monitored.

10: Businesses have a right to choose their customers.

Over the years I have read that many consulting firms who advise businesses who are doing poorly often recommend getting rid of bad customers as a first step. That's because the cost of having a relationship with a bad customer does not provide a net benefit to the company. For example, if you have a retail customer who keeps staff on the phone for hours complaining about a service or product, the small profit margin on that service or product may not justify the time it takes to service that customer. Removing the customer and concentrating on the good customers will help make money and continue the growth of the business.

For a specific example, I know of a company that provides opening, maintenance, and closing services of pools in Kansas City. The managers in the field sometime give their cell phone numbers to customers as a way to contact them in an emergency. The company had a lady that abused the privilege and called two or three times a week on the slightest thing going wrong. The company finally told the lady she needed to find another pool company—they were done with dealing with her.

11: No business or government entity may discriminate based on the ethnic background, skin color, religion, gender, or whether a good or service is being provided by individuals who are organized by a union/political party or not.

> **A) Where possible, monies from government programs will be uniformly distributed on a per person, per pupil, per mile, or per acre basis, and competition for the delivery of that service will be encouraged.**

> **B) Government financial benefits/stipends, and an employee's pay, will be distributed via direct deposit into a citizen's bank account. The LISA contribution of 11% will also be made electronically out of these monies.**

> **C) LISA third party administrators and Banks will make available accounts for anyone with a Federal ID card for an appropriate fee.**

> **D) Individuals will be allowed to purchase additional services above the minimum standard set by the government.**

If a government entity is providing money for schooling programs, the citizen should be allowed to choose between a government-run program and a program provided by a private entity. If the Federal government, Provate, or Local government provides a benefit of say $6,000/pupil per year, then the public school, charter school, private schools, or home schooling should get the same dollar figure. The minimum standards for the end product would be the same whether public schools, charter schools, private schools, or home-schooled children.

The per person subsidy for all programs should be the same nationwide and the individual should be able to float between public and private programs. The Government may determine the definition of the minimum end product for consistency and to protect the consumer, which allows for an apples-to-apples comparison. However, the individual will be allowed to purchase extra services above the minimum standard if they wish. Federal standards will not conflict with standard religious beliefs.

12: Insurance companies providing structural Property and Casualty insurance may have two sets of rates in each County/Provate based on the risk. Those demarcation lines will be logically based, for example, so many miles from a coastline and/or for land residing in a designated flood plane.

Currently, the government offers flood insurance because private insurance companies do not. Private companies typically have restrictions on damage caused by water.

Homeowners in high-risk areas should pay more appropriate amounts to insure their homes when living in a flood plane, on a cliff, or near a beach. Again, the government should not be put into a position of being the insurer of last resort in these situations. The homeowner must pay for the higher risk themselves based on where the home is located, not other taxpayers. Again, actions/choices have consequences.

13. An employer has the right to expect its employees to come to work each day and be productive members of its team.

Sick outs (organized people taking turns calling in sick in order to disrupt business) or work slowdowns (showing up for work but not working at the normal pace) are not permitted.

Workers coming to work "high" creates dangerous situations for fellow employees, particularly if they operate heavy equipment.

14. An individual may incorporate their sole proprietorship.

Typically, to incorporate a business it needs to have at least two people so there is a division of responsibilities. The requirement of at least two owners does not give sole proprietorships the opportunity to enjoy the same protection from liability than that of an incorporated business. The provision here levels the playing field and also allows for an easier separation of business and personal activity for a sole proprietor.

15. No person, government employee, organization, or business may ask for a bribe or ransom. No person, organization, business, or government may pay a bribe or ransom.

If no one paid a bribe or ransom, then no one would ask for one and expect to get it. People in power should not expect special treatment (a bribe) for doing their job. We have to raise our moral standards to a higher plane. Yes, there will be casualties along the way, but in the long-term there will be less pain.

Paying a commission to a person or company is not a bribe and will be reported to the appropriate taxing authority as a course of normal business. For commissions paid to foreign individuals, organizations, or businesses, those payments will be reported to the appropriate foreign government.

Article 8 - Mode of Amendment

The Congress, whenever two thirds of both Houses shall deem it necessary, shall propose Amendments to this Constitution or call for a Constitution Convention, or, on the Application of the Legislatures of two thirds of the several Provates, shall call a Convention for proposing Amendments, which, in either Case, shall be valid to all Intents and Purposes, as Part of this Constitution, when ratified by the Legislatures of three-fourths thereof, as the several Provates, or by Conventions in threefourths thereof, as the one or the other Mode of Ratification may be proposed by the Congress (and then strike, "Provided that no Amendment that may be made prior to the Year One thousand eight hundred and eight shall in any Manner affect the first and fourth Clauses in the Ninth Section of the first Article." The references clauses dealt with the importation of slaves.); and that no Provate, without its Consent, shall be deprived of its equal Suffrage in the Senate.

Article 9 - Ratification

The Ratification by the US and one other country, shall be sufficient for the Establishment of this Constitution between the two or more countries so ratifying the same.

Done in Convention by the Unanimous Consent of the Countries present the (insert the appropriate day and month here) in the Year of our Lord (insert the appropriate year here) and of the Creation of the Union of Ameristralia the witnesses were of We have hereunto subscribed our Names.

Summary of Book Two

If you have gotten this far, I commend you. There is a tremendous amount of material in Book Two with a lot of new ideas and concepts to solve a lot of issues and problems. Again, I would be shocked if all the ideas presented here were to be adopted. But it gives you, the reader, a lot to think about.

As stated earlier, there are many items that are open for revision and update in our constitution. As of 2018, Robert Natelson tells us that at least 27 state legislatures have valid applications outstanding for a convention to propose a balanced budget amendment, which is just seven shy of the number required. He also states that six states have an application for an open-ended amendments convention.[438] These are all signs that the populace wants issues to be addressed. But no one appears to be listening.

Again, some of the highlights of the proposed changes to the US Constitution are:

- Assimilating and evolving into speaking a single language: English

- Equal rights for all

- Term limits for all elected officials

- Financial audits of federally elected and appointed officials

- End gerrymandering

- Uniform election laws

- Congress cannot overturn elections

- Fix the Electoral College

- Congress must approve all federal agency rules

- Benefit of doubt goes to the citizens or businesses over the Government

- Government is no longer the insurer of last resort for natural disasters

- Universal Identification Card, (no voter registration necessary and no census)

- Immigration reform
- Right to die for the terminally ill
- Right to work
- Control over your own retirement monies
- Guaranteed vacation and maternity leave
- All employers will provide medical insurance
- Reestablish trust in the media
- Equal rights and responsibilities for individuals living in territories, commonwealth, protectorates, or reservations
- Require a balanced budget
- School choice

Maintaining the status quo and resisting change seems basic to human nature. The primary reason is that change is difficult and it is easier to go along with the "way it has been." Not all of the Colonists supported the Revolution and rebelling against a lawful government. Even among the participants of the Constitutional Convention of 1787, there were differences of opinions and many compromises needed to be made to move the new nation forward. The same will be true here.

Conclusion

No one who reads this book will agree with everything that has been proposed and may even have different ideas on how to accomplish the goals presented. Discussion, negotiation, and compromise will be required by all parties and the Constitutional Convention will provide the framework to accomplish these goals. Change and reform is about turning the best ideas into practical action. By taking action to solve relevant problems and finding new ways to improve our society, we can continue to prosper well into the future.

Change is necessary not only to grow and advance a society, but also to preserve our core values enumerated in Book One and maintain our personal and economic freedoms, as well as our independence. The world in the twenty-first century is much different than in the eighteenth, nineteenth, and twentieth centuries. We can control our destinies by a willingness to adapt to well thought out change. More importantly, in these troubled times is the need for the English-speaking countries to come together as one. Not like in the Second World War where Britain and the US led and Australia, Canada, India, and New Zealand who willingly followed. Instead, we all need to be together under the same tent and have all our voices heard in the decision-making process, making the sacrifices equally among all. We must not allow our enemies to divide us. Their goal is to divide and conquer, one by one.

The old adage of "strength in numbers" has never become more important. Combining military forces in both hemispheres, and space, creates the power of might to keep rogue nations in check while protecting everyone under our tent. Also, while we create a level playing field for all businesses and individuals to compete, we will all prosper together as one.

The cycle of history is repeating itself. We now have a new Hitler—Russia's Putin. As I am finishing this book, Putin has invaded Ukraine and has expressed his intention of returning Russia back to the glory of the old Soviet Union. He has every intent to continue his advances into other former Soviet lands over time. Not unlike Hitler, wanting to return land to Germany he believed stolen through the Treaty of Versailles, Putin believes that all of the different parts that broke away (like Estonia, Lithuania, Georgia, Kazakhstan, Belarus, and Ukraine) from the Soviet Union in 1991 should not have happened. Putin is trying to swallow up the former parts of the Soviet Union who are now freedom loving and democratic countries.

China has a different approach than Russia. Because of their economic strength they are reaching out to the world through its Road and Bridges program, that allows them to get a foothold in many developing countries in Africa, and South and Central America. In Book One I gave the example of Greenland being approached by China in an effort to help build airports on their island. As part of this process China is also acquiring the access and rights to many strategic minerals, eventually being able to choke off access to those minerals from other large industrial countries like those in North America or Europe. One of the reasons Japan attacked the United States at Pearl Harbor was because the United States cut off Japan's access to our oil, a strategic resource it needed. China's Xi Jinping also has designs on Taiwan and is building islands in the south China Sea to grow their military presence in the region for an eventual invasion of Taiwan or to put China in a position where it can isolate Taiwan, cut off access to the island and bring them to their knees and surrender.

The collusion between China and Russia presents a major problem for peace-loving democratic countries. The threat is growing. A new world order is truly at hand and the United Nations is not the answer. The United Nations is supposed to be there to bring peace and prosperity to it member nations. The United Nations has no role because Russia vetoed and the Chinese abstained when voting on the resolution condemning its invasion of the Ukraine and it cannot take action for the same reason—a Russian veto, or a Chinese veto, or abstention. Combining freedom-loving countries into one nation to combat the threat is increasingly becoming the answer to our economic prosperity and to our safety as a people. We must be able to speak with one voice.

Peace-loving democracies are being threatened again. And, like in the Second World War, the English-speaking countries need to come together again and say NO! Otherwise, like in the Second World War where 70 million people died, the outcome could be similar. The current world order said that, with nuclear weapons on both sides, another war wouldn't happen. But Putin has shown that assumption is no longer valid with his invasion of Ukraine. A war with conventional weapons is a very real possibility.

Our political leaders must step up and put us into a position to better resist and lead against the Chinese and Russian collusion that threatens our existence. The success of Democracy cannot be taken granted. We must evolve and Ameristralia is the solution.

For Ameristralia to happen, the United States government needs to provide a framework so the issues and ideas presented in Books One and Two can be looked at and addressed. A Constitutional Convention will also provide the framework so that other countries are given an opportunity to participate in the process and find solutions good for all parties. More importantly, from Book One, the United States government also needs to start the process of exploring Ameristralia with the proposed countries in Book One and with any other country that expresses an interest in joining.

It is time to act. The English-speaking nations must come together as one. Here I have presented a vision of the future and a framework (plan) necessary to complete the vision. Let's do this now!

Appendix A

The Constitution of Ameristralia

We the People of Ameristralia, in Order to form a more perfect Union, establish Justice, ensure domestic Tranquility, provide for the common Defense, promote the general Welfare, and secure the Blessings of Liberty to ourselves and our Posterity, do ordain and establish this Constitution for Ameristralia.

We the people believe a common language is essential for a cohesive society. Therefore, English is the official language, and all organizations, businesses, and governmental bodies will use only English and the English alphabet of 26 letters for all advertising, ballots, contracts, documents, forms, websites, and other official written communications when interacting with the public.

We the people believe in the family unit and the government should do nothing that disincentivizes a family unit from forming and staying together. Part of the common culture is the realization that we are free individuals and responsible for our own actions. Therefore, we must be self-reliant, and we all have a responsibility to work hard in order to provide for our family with the goal of each generation getting a little further ahead.

We the people believe that we treat all men and women equally under the law without regard to ethnic background, skin color, or religion. While men and women are equal, they are biologically different and as such deserve their own separate bathrooms, locker rooms, and living arrangements if they so desire.

The government will consist of three separate but equal branches of government: Legislative, Executive, and Judicial.

Article 1 - Legislative Branch

Section 1,

All legislative Powers herein granted shall be vested in the Congress of Ameristralia, which shall consist of a Senate and House of Representatives.

Section 2,

1: The House of Representatives shall be composed of Members chosen every second Year by the people of the several Provates, and the Electors in each Provate shall have the Qualifications requisite for Electors of the most numerous Branch of the Provate Legislature.

2: No person shall be a Representative who shall not have attained the age of thirty Years, and been seven Years a Citizen of Ameristralia. They must also be an Inhabitant of the Provate and Congressional District from which they will be chosen.

3: Representatives shall be apportioned among the several Provates which may be included within this Union, according to their respective Numbers, which shall be determined by counting all Ameristralia citizens having been issued a federal identification card. The actual Enumeration shall be made within three years after the first Meeting of the Congress of Ameristralia. The Number of Representatives in the House shall be three times the number in the Senate and the proportion shall be so regulated by Congress based on population, but each Provate shall have at Least one Representative; and until such enumeration shall be made, the Provates will be allocated as shown in Appendix B. Each Representative will have one vote.

4: When vacancies happen in the Representation from any Provate, the Provate will schedule a special election for a replacement if there is sufficient time prior to the next scheduled round of elections for that position.

5: The House of Representatives shall choose their Speaker and other Officers; and shall have the sole Power of Impeachment.

Section 3,

1: The Senate of Ameristralia shall be composed of two Senators from each Provate, elected by a vote of the People in the Provate, for six Years; and each Senator shall have one vote.

2: Immediately after they shall be assembled in Consequence of the first Election, they shall be divided as equally as may be into three Classes. The Seats of the Senators of the first Class shall be vacated at the Expiration of the second year, or the second Class at the Expiration of the fourth Year, and the third Class at the Expiration of the sixth Year, so that one third may be chosen every second year. At the time of Union, if the Provate already has two Senators with six-year terms then they will assume the positions with the established time frame as long as it conforms to the goal of having one-third of the members being elected every two years.

3: No Person shall be a Senator who shall not have attained to the Age of thirty Years, and have been nine Years a Citizen of Ameristralia. They must also be an Inhabitant of the Provate in which they will be chosen.

4: The Senate shall choose their Speaker and other Officers.

5: The Senate shall have the sole Power to try all Impeachments. When sitting for that Purpose, there shall be an Oath or Affirmation. When the President of Ameristralia is tried, the Chief Justice shall preside: And no Person shall be convicted without the Concurrence of two-thirds of the Members present.

6: Judgment in Cases of impeachment shall not extend further than removal from Office, and disqualification to hold and enjoy any Office of honor, Trust or Profit under the Union of Ameristralia: but the Party convicted shall nevertheless be liable and subject to Indictment, Trial, Judgment and Punishment, according to Law.

Section 4,

1: The terms of Senators and Representatives shall end at noon on the 3rd day of January, of the years in which such terms would have ended if this article had not been ratified; and the terms of their successor shall then begin.

2: The Congress shall assemble at least once in every year, and such meeting shall begin at noon on the 3rd day of January, unless they shall by law appoint a different day.

Section 5,

1: A Majority of each House shall constitute a Quorum to do Business; but a smaller Number may adjourn from day to day, and may be authorized to compel the Attendance of absent Members, in such Manner, and under such Penalties as each House may provide.

2: Each House may determine the Rules of its Proceedings, punish its Members for disorderly Behavior, and, with the Concurrence of two thirds, expel a Member.

3: Each House shall keep a Journal of its Proceedings, and from time to time publish the same, excepting such Parts as may in their Judgment require Secrecy; and the Yeas and Nays of the Members of either House on any question shall, at the Desire of one fifth of those Present, be entered on the Journal.

4: Neither House, during the Session of Congress, shall, without the Consent of the other, adjourn for more than three days, nor to any other Place than that in which the two Houses shall be sitting.

Section 6,

1: The Senators and Representatives shall receive a Compensation for their services, to be ascertained by Law but at no time more than six times the average per capita income of the average citizen, and paid out of the Treasury of Ameristralia. No law varying the compensation of the services of the Senators and Representative shall take effect until an election of Representatives shall have intervened. They shall in all Cases, except Treason, Felony and Breach of the Peace, be privileged from Arrest during their Attendance at the Session of their respective Houses, and in going to and returning from the same.

Housing or a stipend may be provided for members of Congress.

2: No Senator or Representative shall, during the Time for which they were elected, be appointed to any civil Office under the Authority of Ameristralia, which shall have been created, or the Emoluments whereof shall have been increased during such time; and no Person holding any Office under the Union of Ameristralia, shall be a Member of either House during his Continuance in Office.

3: Elected officials in Congress are not exempt from the laws and regulations they pass.

Section 7

1: Every Bill which shall have passed the House of Representatives and the Senate, shall, before it becomes a Law, be presented to the President of Ameristralia; If the President approves, the President shall sign it. If not signed, it will be returned with Objections to the chamber where it was originated to be recorded and considered. After reconsideration, two thirds of that chamber shall agree to pass the Bill, it shall be sent, together with the Objections, to the other legislative chamber, by which it shall likewise be reconsidered. If approved by two thirds of that chamber, it shall become a Law. But in all such Cases the Votes of both Houses shall be determined by Yeas and Nays, and the names of the persons voting for and against the Bill shall be entered on the Journal of each House respectively. If any Bill shall not be returned by the President within ten Days (Sundays excepted) after it shall have been presented to the President, the same shall be a Law, in like Manner as if had been signed, unless the Congress by their Adjournment prevent its return, in which case it shall not be a Law.

2: Every Order, Resolution, or Vote to which the Concurrence of the Senate and House of Representatives may be necessary (except on a question of Adjournment) shall be presented to the President of Ameristralia; and before the Same shall take Effect, shall be approved by the President, or being disapproved by the President, shall be repassed by two thirds of the Senate and House of Representatives, according to the Rules and Limitations prescribed in the Case of a Bill.

3: No bill or legislation may exceed 1,000 pages, must address a single issue, and legislatures in each House must be given seven days for consideration prior to voting.

Section 8

1: The Congress shall have Power To Lay and Collect Taxes, Duties, Imposts and Excises, to pay the Debts and provide for the common Defense and general Welfare of Ameristralia; but all Duties, Imposts and Excises shall be uniform throughout Ameristralia. After a second country joins Ameristralia and until new laws are passed setting a common standard, the President may set these policies;

2: The Congress shall have Power to borrow Money on the credit of Ameristralia. Passing bonds for special projects or purposes is permissible – but not more than one year in three, unless in times of war.

3: To regulate Commerce with foreign Nations, and among the several Provates, the federal government shall have primary regulatory and criminal authority over any business, or crimes committed, that involves multiple Provate jurisdictions. The federal authorities also have primary jurisdiction over bank robberies, kidnappings, digital software, social platforms, pipelines, electrical transmission lines, rivers, lakes, waterways, ports, harbors, and international airports.

With a two-thirds vote of Congress and approval of the President, this list may be expanded, so that the federal government takes primary jurisdiction over more items.

4: To establish a uniform Rule of Naturalization and uniform Laws on the subject of Bankruptcies throughout Ameristralia.

> a) Existing 1) citizens, 2) inhabitants of territories, common-wealths, reservations, protectorates 3) or any family (spouse and siblings) living, working, and paying income taxes inside Ameristralia is automatically considered a citizen with full privileges at the time of adoption.

> b) Congress will set a number for immigrants (or refugees) wishing to enter the country each year and Congress and the President will ensure there are physical barriers where needed on land borders and sufficient Coast Guard assets to prevent illegal immigration from the water. All immigrants and refugees must apply for entrance into Ameristralia from outside Ameristralia. Each year the President may approve 25 individuals to stay in the country and apply for asylum from within Ameristralia.

> c) After a second country joins Ameristralia, and until new laws are passed, setting a common standard/policy resides with the President;

5: To coin and print Money, regulate the Value thereof, and of foreign Currency and use the Metric System for the Standard of Weights and Measures. No currency other than the Ameristralian dollar may be used in Ameristralia's commerce.

6: To provide for the Punishment of counterfeiting the Securities and current Coin and Currency of Ameristralia;

7: Establish Post Offices and post Roads;

8: To promote the Progress of Science and useful Arts, by securing for limited Times to Authors and Inventors the exclusive Right to their respective Writings and Discoveries;

9: To constitute Tribunals inferior to the Supreme Court; subordinate Tribunals will have no more than 5 judges each and the Supreme Court will have 9 judges;

10: To define and punish Piracies and Felonies committed on the high Seas, and Offenses against the Law of Nations;

11: To declare War, grant Letters of Marque and Reprisal, and make Rules concerning Captures on Land and Water;

12: To raise, provide and maintain military forces.

13: To make Rules for the Government and Regulation of military forces;

14: To provide for calling forth the Militia to execute the Laws of the Union, suppress Insurrections and repel Invasions;

15: To provide for organizing, arming, and disciplining, the Militia, and for governing such Part of them as may be employed in the Service of Ameristralia, reserving to the Provates respectively, the Appointment of the Officers, and the Authority of training the Militia according to the discipline prescribed by Congress;

16: To exercise exclusive Legislation in all Cases whatsoever, over such District/City (not exceeding ten square miles) as may, by Cession of particular Provate, and the Acceptance of Congress, becomes the Seat of the Government of Ameristralia, and to exercise like Authority over all Places purchased through eminent domain by the Consent of the Legislature of the Provate in which the Same shall be, for the Erection of Forts, Magazines, Arsenals, dock-Yard, rights-of-way for transportation and utility service, and other needful Buildings; And also natural gas pipelines, electric transmission lines, electrical generation, mass transit corridors, etc., for the establishment of the new Capital city.

17: To make all Laws which shall be necessary and proper for carrying into Execution the foregoing Powers, and all other Powers vested by this Constitution in the Government of Ameristralia, or in any Department or Officer thereof.

Section 9,
1: The Privilege of the Writ of Habeas Corpus shall not be suspended, unless when in Cases of Rebellion or Invasion the public Safety may require it.

2: No Bill of Attainder or ex post facto Law shall be passed.

3: In any given year, every organization, business or individuals' income will pay a minimum of 1% and a maximum of 20% in income tax to the federal government, unless in time of war. Income for organizations and businesses is defined as revenues minus expenses. Religious, Charitable and non-government educational institutions will be subject to a 1% federal income tax.

    a) The federal government may only raise revenue through a tax on income (wages earned, governments benefits received, inheritance/gifts/lottery/gambling proceeds, interest, dividends, capital gains), nominal one-time usage fees, duties, tariffs, bonds issued, mineral royalties on federal land, and fines.

    b) Provates and local governments, together, may not charge individuals, organizations, or businesses more than 5% on income. Provates and local governments may only raise revenue by a tax on income (wages earned, government benefits received, inheritances/gifts/lottery/gambling proceeds, interest, dividends, capital gains), sales taxes, real and personal property taxes, nominal one-time usage fees, bonds issued, fines, and mineral royalties within the Provate. Property tax rates may not be higher for commercial properties than residential properties.

    c) Inheritance, gifts, lottery and gambling proceeds will be taxfree on the first one million dollars when the money goes into a person's LISA. The first million not going into a LISA will be taxed at the normal Federal and Provate rate and any monies received over that amount will be taxed 60% at the Federal level and 15% at the Provate level.

    d) Everyone over the age of 18, and all organizations and businesses, must file an income tax return each year.

4: No Tax or Duty shall be laid on Articles exported from any Provate. However, Congress has the authority to deny exports of specific products and services to particular countries.

5: No Preference shall be given by any Regulation of Commerce or Revenue to the Ports of one Provate over those of another: nor shall Vessels bound to, or from, one Provate, be obliged to enter, clear, or pay Duties in another.

6: No Money shall be drawn from the Treasury, but in Consequence of Appropriations made by Law; however, if Congress fails to pass a budget for the coming fiscal year in the appropriate time, then the President will have the power to pay the country's bills. The President may not exceed expenditures from the previous year's budget for each department and has the latitude to spend less than the amount for the previous year.

The exception would be defense spending where the President can increase defense spending by the amount that is cut from other domestic programs; and a regular Statement and Account of the Receipts and Expenditures of all public Money shall be published from time to time.

Each department will receive a financial audit each year, looking for fraud, monies not spent, and lack of controls in the systems. The exception would be defense/security spending for non-traditional purposes.

7: All budgets passed will be balanced, i.e. projected revenues and projected expenses will be equal. In the event of a projected overage or shortage at the end of the fiscal year, the amount of overage or shortage will be rolled over into the next budget.

Congress has five years to implement.

8: No Title of Nobility shall be granted by Ameristralia: and no Person holding any Office of Profit or Trust under them, shall, without the Consent of the Congress, accept any present, Emolument, Office, or Title, of any kind whatever, from any King, Queen, Prince, or foreign State.

Section 10,

1: No Provate shall enter into any Treaty, Alliance, or Confederation; grant Letters of Marque and Reprisal; coin or print Money; emit Bills of Credit; pass any Bill of Attainder, ex post facto Law, or Law impairing the Obligation of Contracts, or grant any Title of Nobility.

2: No Provate shall, without the Consent of the Congress, lay any Imposts or Duties on Imports or Exports, except what may be absolutely necessary for executing its inspection Laws: and the net Produce of all Duties and Imposts, laid by any Provate on Imports or Exports, shall be for the Use of the Treasury of Ameristralia; and all such Laws shall be subject to the Revision and Control of the Congress.

3: No Provate shall, without the Consent of Congress, lay any Duty of Tonnage, or Ships of War in time of Peace, enter into any Agreement or Compact with another Provate, or with a foreign Power, or engage in War, unless actually invaded, or in such imminent Danger as will not admit of delay.

Article 2 - Executive Branch

Section 1,

1: The executive Power shall be vested in a President of Ameristralia. The President shall hold Office during the Term of four Years, and, together with the Vice President, chosen for the same Term, be elected, as follows.

2: The Electoral College system will be used for the election of the President and Vice President. The voting for the Electoral College will be done in the Senate and the Senior Senator of each Provate's delegation will cast all votes, one for each Senator and one for each Representative of the Provate, for the winning candidate based on their Provate's election for the office. If the Senior Senator is absent, then the Junior Senator will cast the appropriate votes. If no representatives are present from a given Provate then the Speaker may cast the votes for the Provate.

All of a Provate's votes will go for just one candidate. If there isn't a winner after the first ballot, then Rank Choice voting comes into play for each Provate. In case of a tie, a coin toss will determine the winner.

3: The terms of the President and Vice President shall end at noon on the 20th day of January.

If, at the time fixed for the beginning of the term of President, the President elect shall have died, the Vice President elect shall become President. If a President shall not have been chosen before the time fixed for the beginning of their term, or if the President elect shall have failed to qualify, then the Vice President elect shall act as President until a President shall have qualified; if neither the President elect or Vice President elect shall have qualified by the day prior to taking office, then the senior Senator in leadership from their party shall appoint a successor President.

4: If neither the President or Vice President shall have qualified to hold office, then the senior Senator in leadership from their party shall appoint a successor President.

5: The Electors shall meet in the Senate Chamber on Tuesday six weeks after the election at 1:00 p.m. for casting the votes for President.

6: No Person except a natural born Citizen, or a Citizen of Ameristralia, at the time of the Adoption of this Constitution, shall be eligible to the Office of President; neither shall any Person be eligible to that Office who shall not have attained to the Age of thirty-five Years, and been fourteen Years a Resident within the Union of Ameristralia.

7: No person shall be elected to the office of the President more than twice, and no person who has held the office of President, or acted as President, for more than two years of a term to which some other person was elected President shall be elected to the office of the President more than once.

8: In Case of the removal of the President from Office or their Death or Resignation the Vice President shall become President.

9: Whenever there is a vacancy in the office of the Vice President, the President shall nominate a Vice President who shall take office upon confirmation by a majority vote of both Houses of Congress.

10: Whenever the President transmits to the Speaker of the Senate and the Speaker of the House of Representatives their written declaration that they are unable to discharge the power and duties of his office, and until they transmit to them a written declaration to the contrary, such power and duties shall be discharged by the Vice President as Acting President.

11: Whenever the Vice President and a majority of either the principal officers of the executive departments or of such other body as Congress may by law provide, transmit to the Speaker of the Senate and the Speaker of the House of Representatives their written declaration that the President is unable to discharge the powers and duties of their office, the Vice President shall Immediately assume the powers and duties of the office as Acting President.

Thereafter, when the President transmits to the Speaker of the Senate and the Speaker of the House of Representatives their written declaration that no inability exists, they shall resume the power and duties of their office unless the Vice President and a majority of either the principal officers of the executive department or of such body as Congress may by law provide, transmit within four days to the Speaker of the Senate and the Speaker of the House of Representatives their written declaration that the President is unable to discharge the powers and duties of the office. Thereupon Congress shall decide the issue, assembling within forty-eight hours for that purpose if not in session. If the Congress, within twenty-one days after receipt of the latter written declaration, or, if Congress is required to assemble, determines by two-thirds vote of both Houses that the President is unable to discharge the powers and duties of the office, the Vice President shall continue to discharge the same as Acting President; otherwise, the President shall resume the powers and duties of their office.

12: The President shall, at stated Times, receive for their Services, a Compensation, which shall neither be increased nor diminished during the Period for which they shall have been elected, and shall not receive within that Period any other Emolument from Ameristralia, but said compensation will never exceed 14 times the average per capita income of the average citizen.

  a) Vice Presidents compensation will never exceed eight times the average per capita income of the average citizen.

  b) The government will provide a residence for the President and another residence for the Vice President and while in office the equivalent of their full pay will be put into their LISA, tax free.

  c) After leaving the office of President, the President will receive a salary, security staff and administrative staff for 12 years.

13: Before they enter on the Execution of their office, they shall take the following Oath or Affirmation: "I do solemnly swear (or affirm) that I will faithfully execute the Office of President of Ameristralia, and will to the best of my Ability, preserve, protect and defend the Constitution of Ameristralia."

Section 2,

1: The President shall be Commander in Chief of the Army, Air Force, Coast Guard, Marines, Navy, and Space Force of Ameristralia, and of the Militia of the several Provates, when called into the actual Service of Ameristralia; they may require the Opinion, in writing, of the principal Officer in each of the executive Departments, upon any Subject relating to the Duties of their respective Offices, and the President shall have Power to grant Reprieves and Pardons for Offenses against Ameristralia or any Provate, except in Cases of Impeachment.

2: The President shall have Power, by and with the Advice and Consent of the Senate, to make Treaties, provided two thirds of the Senators present concur; and shall nominate, and by and with the Advice and Consent of the Senate, shall appoint Ambassadors, other public Ministers and Consuls, Judges of the Supreme Court, and all other Officers of Ameristralia, whose Appointments are not herein otherwise provided for, and which shall be established by Law: but the Congress may by Law vest the Appointment of such inferior Officers, as they think proper, in the President alone, in the Courts of Law, or in the Heads of Departments.

3: The President shall have Power to fill all Vacancies that may happen during the Recess of the Senate, by granting Commissions which shall expire at the end of their next Session.

All presidential nominees must be voted on within 90 days of nomination. For the Secretaries of Defense and State, or a Vice Presidential nominee, they must be acted on within 30 days. If the President has nominated two people to fill a particular vacancy and both are rejected, then the President may nominate any new person to fill the position without the necessary approval.

4) All individuals appointed to board or commission positions will not have terms longer than six years. The President may not fire an existing board member or commissioner. No political party may occupy more than fifty percent of the seats on a board or commission.

Appointed Cabinet or Department heads may be fired at any time by the President.

5) The President, with the consent of Congress, may negotiate with other countries that express an interest in joining the Union. All countries will conform to Ameristralia's standards over an allotted time frame, and some may need financial assistance for the necessary transition.

6) If the President invokes powers in case of an emergency, that emergency power may not last longer than twelve months.

Section 3,
The President shall from time to time give to the Congress Information on the State of the Union, and recommend to their Consideration such Measures as the President shall judge necessary and expedient; the President may, on extraordinary Occasions, convene both Houses, or either of them, and in Case of Disagreement between them, with Respect to the Time of Adjournment, the President may adjourn them to such Time as the President shall think proper; the President shall receive Ambassadors and other public Ministers; the President shall take Care that the Laws be faithfully executed, and shall Commission all the Officers of Ameristralia.

Section 4,
The President, Vice President, and all civil Officers of Ameristralia, shall be removed from Office on Impeachment for, and Conviction of, Treason, Bribery, or other high Crimes and Misdemeanors.

Article 3 - Judicial Branch

Section 1,

1: The judicial Power of Ameristralia, shall be vested in one Supreme Court, and in such inferior Courts as the Congress may from time to time ordain and establish. The Judges, both of the Supreme and inferior Courts, shall hold their Offices during good Behavior until the age of 80, and shall, at stated Times, receive for their services, a Compensation, which for the Supreme Court will never exceed nine times the average per capita income of the average citizen and which shall not be diminished during their continuance in Office. A residence or stipend will be provided for each justice on the Supreme Court.

  a) Lower federal courts pay will never exceed six times the average per capita income of the average citizen.

  b) For the first 60 years the members of the Supreme Court, when possible, will be distributed as follows; 3 from North America, 3 from Australia/New Zealand and 3 from outside of those first two areas, if such areas exist.

  c) The justices on the respective courts will select a Chief Justice to lead their respective courts.

2: Judges will rule on the issues before them based on the Ameristralia Constitution and the laws as they were originally written and conceived. Being a judge requires the ability to decipher between the letter and "spirit" of the Constitution and laws passed by Congress.

  a) Judges may not impose solutions or accept plea deals by the government that allows the court or government to, in essence, legislate from the bench, but rather stop illegal activity. Sentencing should be based upon legal course of action, restitution, rehabilitation, and burden on the government.

  b) All acts and/or laws passed by Congress and any regulatory rules promulgated by regulatory agencies must always be logical, fair, and reasonable, and when based on science, thoroughly researched and the underlying data made available to the public.

3: In decisions between individuals or businesses and the government, the individual or businesses will receive the benefit of the doubt on the interpretation of regulations promulgated by the government.

Section 2,

1: The Judicial Power shall extend to all Cases, in Law and equity, arising under this Constitution, the Laws of Ameristralia, and Treaties made, or which shall be made, under their Authority;–to all Cases affecting Ambassadors, other public Ministers and Consuls;– to all Cases of admiralty and maritime Jurisdiction;–to Controversies to which Ameristralia shall be a Party;–to Controversies between two or more Provates;–between a Provate and Citizens of another Provate; –between Citizens of different Provates;—between Citizens of the same Provates claiming Lands under Grants of different Provates, and between a Provate, or the Citizens thereof, and foreign States, Citizens or Subjects.

If other parties to a treaty are not fulfilling their obligations, then Ameristralia will not be bound by the treaty.

2: In all Cases affecting Ambassadors, other public Ministers and Consuls, and those in which a Provate shall be Party, the Supreme Court shall have original Jurisdiction. In all the other Cases before mentioned, the Supreme Court shall have appellate Jurisdiction, both as to Law and Fact, with such Exceptions, and under such Regulations as the Congress shall make.

3: The Trial of all Crimes, except in Cases of Impeachment, shall be by Jury; and such Trial shall be held in the Provate where the said Crimes shall have been committed; but when not committed within any Provate, the Trial shall be at such Place or Places as the Congress may by Law have directed.

All courts and trials will be recorded.

Section 3,

1: Treason against Ameristralia, shall consist only in levying War against them, or in adhering to their Enemies, giving them Aid and Comfort. No Person shall be convicted of Treason unless on the testimony of two Witnesses to the same overt Act, or on Confession in open Court.

2: The Congress shall have Power to declare the Punishment of Treason, but no Attainder of Treason shall work Corruption of Blood, or Forfeiture except during the Life of the Person attainted.

3: Any elected, appointed, or staff person who has publicly or privately (with two witnesses) stated that they are going to go after a person, organization, or business based on their party affiliation, or a political cause they support, may not be allowed to harass that person or business through law enforcement or the courts, and they will forfeit their position.

4: The Judicial power of Ameristralia shall not be construed to extend to any suit in law or equity, commenced or prosecuted against one of the Provates by Citizens of another Provate, or by Citizens or Subjects of any Foreign State.

Article 4 - Provate Relations

Section 1,

1: Full Faith and Credit shall be given in each Provate to the public Acts, Records, and Judicial Proceedings of every other Provate. And the Congress may by general Laws prescribe the Manner in which such Acts, Records, and Proceedings shall be proved, and the Effect thereof.

2: The Provates' primary responsibilities are to provide and adequately maintain physical infrastructure (roads, bridges, park, etc.), safety (policing, fire protection and sanitation), schools and universities, voting systems, and lower courts and jails.

3: The Provates do not have authority to establish different standards than the federal government has already set.

Section 2,

1: The Citizens, Organizations or Businesses of each Provate shall be entitled to all Privileges and Immunities of Citizens, Organizations or Businesses in the other Provates.

2: A Person charged in any Provate with Treason, Felony, or other Crime, who shall flee from Justice, and be found in another Provate, shall on Demand of the executive Authority of the Provate from which they fled, be delivered up, to be removed to the Provate having Jurisdiction of the Crime.

Anyone fleeing the country to escape prosecution, gives up their citizenship and their ability to return.

3: Involuntary servitude, except as a punishment for crime whereof the party shall have been duly convicted, shall not exist within Ameristralia, or any place subject to their jurisdiction.

Section 3,

1: New Provates may be admitted by the Congress into this Union; but no new Provate shall be formed or erected within the Jurisdiction of any other Provate; nor any Provate be formed by the Junction of two or more Provates, or Parts of Provates, without the Consent of the Legislatures of the Provates concerned as well as of the Congress, except as otherwise noted in this document.

2: The Congress shall have Power to dispose of and make all needful Rules and Regulations respecting the territory or other Property belonging to the Ameristralia; and nothing in this Constitution shall be so construed as to Prejudice any Claims of Ameristralia, or of any particular Provate.

Section 4,

1: Ameristralia shall guarantee to every Provate in this Union a Republican Form of Government, with three separate branches of government; Executive with a Governor, Legislative and Judicial; and Ameristralia shall protect each of them against Invasion; and on Application of the Legislature, or of the Governor (when the Legislature cannot be convened) against domestic Violence.

2: Judges in the Provates, at any level, will not be elected, but rather appointed. However, Judges may be removed by a vote of the people.

3: Remote, isolated and inaccessible areas of a Provate may receive special consideration by the respective Provate

Article 5 - General

Section 1, Identification Cards

1: The federal government will provide all identification cards and/or drivers licenses for free as well as license plates for vehicles for a fee. Anyone a) already a citizen, b) inhabitant of a territory, commonwealth, reservation or protectorate, c) or any family (parent and siblings) living, working, and paying income taxes in Ameristralia will be considered a citizen at the time of the acceptance of this constitution and will be issued a government identification card.

A citizen must have a federal government identification card in order to work, attend a school, rent a room, rent property, rent a car, vote or receive any benefits.

A non-citizen must have a Green Card in order to work in Ameristralia. For foreign travelers who want to rent a car, hotel room, or a house short-term, a passport is sufficient. For foreign exchange students or those wishing to attend college, a passport is also sufficient.

2: At birth, a DNA sample will be taken from the child, as well as from the mother and father (if he is available). At age 16 (when applying for a Driver's License/ID card), and at death, another DNA sample will be taken to validate the identity of the person. The federal government will verify the consistency of the sample each time. New immigrants will also provide a DNA sample upon arrival.

Congress will setup and sufficiently fund a Census and Identity Theft Agency to track and monitor the DNA, fingerprints, physical and mailing address, where they work, criminal history, and appropriate licenses. Should inconsistencies arise, or identity theft take place, they will be investigated and resolved.

3: Individuals will be required to notify the federal government when they move. The Post Office will also notify the federal government of any address changes as a double check.

   a) The federal identification (ID) cards will allow anyone to move from Provate to Provate without having to get a new driver's license, license plate or register to vote.

   b) The federal government will notify the respective Provate when someone new has moved into or out of their jurisdiction.

4: Individuals will get replacement ID cards every 10 years, starting on their 20th birthday and an updated photo will be added. Every person over 16 is required to have their Identification Card/Driver's License on them or in close proximity. Under 16, then the parent is responsible for their children's identification cards. Visiting or working foreigners are required to have their passport in close proximity.

Starting at age 20, required taxes and LISA contributions must have been paid for all prior applicable years in order to receive the new/replacement ID card.

5: Every time someone's ID card has been read by a government entity (voting, traffic stop, applying for benefits, attending school, death certificates, etc.), or a business verifying the citizenship of a prospective employee, or landlords renting property, that information will be passed on to the federal government electronically on a real time basis, when possible. Provates and other federal departments will link, and share data, to the appropriate national databases.

6: An up-to-date federal ID is also required in order to receive a government benefit or stipend, the individual (or their spouse if they have dependent children) must be working if physically and mentally able.

Section 2, Elections
1: All elections will be held on the third Monday of April and the third Monday of October each year. Early voting will take place for the 9 consecutive days prior to the actual election day. Polling places will be open 7:00 a.m. to 7:00 p.m. on Election Day and 9:00 a.m. to 3:00 p.m. for the 9 days of early voting. All times are local time.

   a) Federal Primaries will be held in April and Federal General Elections in October of even number years.

   b) Provate, special, and local elections will typically be held in odd numbered years but may also be held in even number years.

   c) In case of a pandemic, or other declared emergency, the number of days for early voting will increase to 16 consecutive days prior to the actual election day.

   d) Congress will determine the dates for Presidential Primaries because they are the exception to the rule. Voting will be on one given day with no early voting, 7:00 a.m. to 7 p.m.

   e) Poll watchers from multiple parties will be allowed.

2: Provates, and their counties, will have primary responsibility for running all elections. All ballots will be cast in person without assistance in the voting booth after presenting their federal identification card and verifying the physical address is in their jurisdiction and that the identification card has not been used for voting elsewhere. Backup databases of voter rolls and who has voted will be updated daily in case of internet failure.

a) All cast ballots, whether made on paper or made via a terminal at the polling center, will result in a paper ballot the voter can read and verify for self-auditing purposes prior to being submitted/cast and also be machine readable for accurate and faster results.

b) All voting for any public office at any level of government must be done in secret.

c) Each polling center will have an accumulator(s) that reads the paper ballots as they are submitted/cast and accumulates the results. All ballots will be saved for at least eighteen months for audits.

d) Each day the accumulators at each polling center will print off a summary of the raw results on paper for auditing purposes, as well as, a raw electronic version sent to the 1) Provate Secretary of State, 2) appropriate county office, and 3) an acceptable news service office (selected by Congress) within an hour of the last vote being cast. Besides the number of first place votes cast for each candidate, it will show the split for the second and third choice votes of that candidate—as done in Ranked Choice Voting. After the election, the accumulators and ballots will be taken to a central facility for storage and possible auditing.

e) The respective County and Provate Secretary of State will then review the results for accuracy and accountability. After the appropriate local officials feel everything is correct, the Provate Secretary of State will certify the results of the election no later than three weeks after the election. After the results are certified by the Provate Secretary of State, any entity may audit the ballots under the supervision of local authorities.

f) No voting results (whether early voting, mail, or actual voting day) may be shared with the public or political parties until all polling stations are closed in each Provate on the last day of voting. Raw results may be shared at that time.

g) Neither Congress or Provate legislatures will have the authority to overturn the election results. A federal court may invalidate, correct, or require an audit after the results have been certified.

h) Provisional ballots for individuals with 1) an identification card without the proper physical address, or 2) if the identification card has already been used someplace else, or 3) if the internet is down and no back up database is onsite to verify 1 and 2 above, will be later researched to determine if valid.

i) No polling data will be provided to the public within four weeks of election day.

j) Releasing exit polling after the Provate has closed all polling stations is permissible.

k) Voting in a) remote, isolated, or inaccessible areas, and b) voting for the legally blind, or c) for individuals who are physically unable to mark a ballot on their own, all will be left to the discretion of the respective Provate to manage, as long as in all cases the results can be reported prior to the last polling station in the Provate closing.

3: An absentee ballot will be allowed for individuals stationed or working out of the country and their physical address in Ameristralia is for that voting location. Absentee voters may not request a ballot earlier than 90 days prior to the election. The county clerk will have verified the voter's signature on their ID, physical address in Ameristralia, foreign mailing address, and employer against the federal rolls prior to sending the ballot out.

Completed absentee ballots must be received by 5:00 p.m. on the Monday prior to election day (one week prior to election day) by mail or package service from a foreign country. Signatures will be manually verified upon receipt of the completed ballot. Voters will not be able to fix ballots that do not qualify.

4: Paid advertising, except non-electric billboards, for candidates are restricted to a period of 61 days prior to the Primary or General election, to the day before the election itself. Only one advertisement per 30-minute segment, per TV/Cable/Streaming channel is allowed.

a) Two out of three advertisements in a given day must be strictly about their candidate and their policy positions. All advertising for a candidate must identify the party affiliation of the candidate.

b) Attack advertisements about the opposition candidate must be factually based and honest. Candidates and organizations running attack ads for individuals running for a federal office may run them by the Bipartisan Commission for Elections and Media (with co-chairs from two opposing parties, and no party occupying more than 50% of the seats) set up by the federal government and must approve/disapprove them within two business days. If approved by the Bipartisan Commission for Elections and Media the candidate or organization running the ads may not be sued, but the Bipartisan Commission for Elections and Media can be sued on an expedited basis for judicial review. If the candidate or organization runs unapproved attack advertisements, then they may be sued if not factual and honest. All ads will predominately display whether the Commission has approved or not approved of the attack ad.

c) Attack ads may not contain information about donors or organizations that support the opposition candidate, and the ads must identify the party affiliation of the sponsoring organization.

d) Any advertisements to notify people about rallies or gatherings that do not contain any messaging about positions are always permitted. Bumper Stickers and Yard signs are always permitted.

e) No foreign money will be accepted by any candidate or organizations participating in the election process.

f) Individuals or organizations may not accept money from foreign sources and then turn around and funnel it to a candidate. No foreign individual, organization or business may directly pay for advertisements for any candidate or cause.

g) Producing Deepfakes will be a felony crime requiring time in prison.

5: Ads for a candidate or a cause must identify sponsorship. It must be clear which party they support (as opposed to a PAC, organization, or cause with very ambiguous names), as well as a website with details. Sponsorship must be in a font large enough to be easily read on the page or screen.

6: Each Provate will determine the age of majority at between 18 and 21 years old. The age of majority determines when a citizen has the maturity to exercise their full rights such as voting, drinking alcohol, purchasing a weapon, and taking legal drugs. Any Ameristralian citizen above the age of majority with a federal ID and not currently incarcerated is eligible to vote in the district and Provate they live.

7: A political party may be registered at the Provate level by paying a $10,000 annual fee to the Provate's Secretary of State, or at the Federal level by paying a $100,000 annual fee to the Secretary of State of Ameristralia. If the party has registered at the Provate or Federal level, then any individual running for an office in that Provate will be put on the ballot for the office they are running as a representative of that party in that Primary. Individuals with no party affiliation may run for any office and they will be under the Independent designation, no fees required.

8: Congress will establish the filing dates for Federal offices, except for the Vice President where the party selects the candidate. Presidential candidates only have to file once at the Federal level with the Secretary of State of Ameristralia in order to be on the ballot of all Provates for the Primary, and the party will notify the Secretary of State of Ameristralia of their candidate for the General election. When possible, the candidate selected for Vice President will be from a different continent than the Presidential candidate.

9: The Primary for the President will be held in a sequence of individual Provates because of the geographical challenges in a national campaign covering multiple continents. The first Primary will be in South Australia starting in January, followed by Alberta, Iowa, Scotland (then one of any new continents added later), and then Congress will dictate the sequence of regional Provates from that point on—giving preference for geographic neighbors and/or common media markets.

The tally from all these individual primaries will be passed on to the respective parties and the party will then decide who is going to represent them in the general election.

a) The Bipartisan Commission for Elections and Media will reimburse candidates and staff for airfare between continents up to $1,000,000 for the Primary and another $1,000,000 for the General election.

b) If more than one individual is running as an independent, then Ranked Choice Voting will also be used. The Bipartisan Commission for Elections and Media, which is set up to look at and approve political advertisement, will decide which

Independent will prevail. The Independent Candidate for President will announce who they have selected for their Vice President in a timely manner.

10: Every elected office in the country shall first have a primary election where the members of each party will have the opportunity to determine the consensus majority choice to run for the party in the general election. Individuals without a party affiliation will run as an Independent.

11: Upon arrival at the polling station for the Primary election, the Voters will notify the staff of the Party they intend to participate with for voting, or if they are independent.

12: Voters may identify their top three choices for an office and Ranked Choice Voting will be used in the primary election to determine the winner for each party. When two candidates are left with no one having the majority, the candidate with the most votes wins the party's nomination to the general election.

In the rare case of a tie, a coin flip will decide the winner.

13: Each party and the winning Independent will then present their candidate in the General election. Voters may identify their top three choices for each office and Ranked Choice Voting will also be used in the General election to determine the winner. If two candidates are left and a majority is not achieved, the candidate with the most votes wins the election for that position. In the rare case of a tie, a coin flip decides the winner.

14: No elected official in the Executive or the Legislative Branch of any Government may hold the same office for more than thirteen years or run for the same office again if reelection will put their tenure in that position over thirteen years, except for the President and Vice President of the Union who have stricter limits. The thirteen-year clock begins after the first election under the new constitution.

15: All elected and appointed officials and their spouse (or partner) at the national level will receive a financial audit each year of income and assets and the results reported to the respective Provate and/or Ameristralian agency. It will become a matter of public record and posted on a government website. The audit will be paid for by the Federal government.

Any conflicts of interest, suspicious or illegal activity will be identified, made public, and forwarded to the appropriate office. No organization or candidate may weaponize this public information unless the person is convicted of a crime as a result of the audit.

Any Congressional specified organization doing the audit may not prepare them for the same person more than three years out of the last six. Congress will define acceptable behavior.

16: At the beginning of each new decade, prior to Octobern 1, the House of Representatives will determine the reallocation of seats based on population from IDs in the Census and Identity Theft Agency database. No Provate may be given more seats than a Provate with a larger population.

After three years has passed, reallocation will also occur after a new country joins the Union.

The respective Provates will establish the Districts for each Representative along existing contiguous county and city boundaries. In extraordinary situations, in no more than one county, those boundaries may be along natural geographic separation (creeks, rivers or major highways).

17: The Secretary of State for each Provate will be the sole authority in declaring the winners in their Provate and Federal races and, after each election, will produce a report indicating any deficiencies found and if wait times were too long.

18: No eligible citizen will face any punishment for not voting.

Section 3, LISAs,

1: Each citizen (whether working or receiving benefits) will have a Long-Term Individual Security Account (LISA) for retirement, special needs, and unemployment. The employer and government will put eleven percent of an individuals' pretax pay and benefits for up to $200,000 into an account until the month after their 65th birthday. The individual will select a third-party fund administrator that will place half of the funds in a "Retirement Account" that cannot be touched until retirement, or terminally ill, and the other half into a "Special Needs" account that can be pulled out for approved special needs (unemployment, pay for college classes, exceptional medical expenses, marriage, funeral, down payment on a house, to start a business, etc.). Neither of these accounts may be accessed by courts, or by contract, for the payment of debts or fines. If the employee is married (or has a partner), then half the funds go to the spouse's Long-Term Individual Security Account (LISA). The employer and government must provide at least 5 different third-party administrators, each with at least 5 different investment options from which the employee (and spouse or partner) may choose.

a) In the former United States, at the time of transition to this system, the employer will give their 6% contribution under the old system to the employee as a pay raise. Individuals with income over $200,000 (not that portion under) will pay a 6% extra income tax for 30 years and then 3% for the next 20, to help fund the old social security system, 50 years in total. The former United States Social Security system will be frozen (except cost-of-living adjustments) and cease to exist after 50 years and unemployment benefits will be frozen and administered at the federal level and will cease to exist in 10 years.

b) The employee and employer may also make extra pre-tax contributions to these accounts up to a maximum of 100% of pay, up to the first $200,000 each year. Defined Retirement Programs that allow for the delayed funding of promised benefits down the road are no longer permitted and will be phased out. All existing Defined Retirement Programs monies set aside will be distributed to their employees' LISA. Existing retirees, or those within 20 years of retirement under these Defined Retirement Programs, and the monies set aside, will remain in place for their retirement or the employee may choose to take their money out of the Defined Retirement Program and put it into their LISA and exit the Defined Retirement Program.

c) The LISA does away with pension funds controlled by employers, unions, or government entities and now gives everything to the employee and their spouse (or partner) each month. By definition then, the government will not guarantee any pension funds.

d) Upon death, all LISA accounts go tax-free to the current spouse (or partner) LISA. They are taxed once funds are withdrawn and used.

Section 4,

1: Any dollar figures mentioned in this constitution will be adjusted based on inflation, unless otherwise noted. Any references to internet, web sites, databases, or other technology may evolve into other named technology, and still be valid.

2: Executive branch regulations and codes, proposed by the respective government agencies, must first be passed by the appropriate Congressional bodies for comment, tweaked as necessary, and then resubmitted to Congress and the President for approval prior to going into effect.

3: No individual, organization, or business may block free access to sidewalks, streets, highways, railroads, parks, or other public rights of way unless the City/County has authorized a permit for a parade or special event. No one can create a campground in any public areas, unless approved as a campground.

4: All governmental and industrial bodies should provide for exceptions to their rules to allow for innovation in any industry. Reduced regulations should also be encouraged for brand new businesses.

5: No department within the Federal government may have their own court system outside of the standard Federal court system, except the armed forces.

6: Anyone elected or appointed to any Federal position will be reimbursed for their reasonable moving expenses to the location of their new position. For elected Federal officials who are temporarily residents to the new capital, they will be reimbursed for travel to and from their home and constituents. Elected officials returning home after their tenure has been completed will also have their reasonable moving expenses paid to get back to their place of retirement from the Government.

7: In Ameristralia, all Territories, Commonwealths, Reservations, and Protectorates will be incorporated into the appropriate Provate and all residents will become equal citizens of Ameristralia.

8: In the Province of Quebec and the island of Puerto Rico, the citizens will be given twelve months after the Union takes effect to hold a separate referendum to determine whether they will be part of Ameristralia, or their own independent country. If the Province of Quebec or the island of Puerto Rico does not have a referendum in the prescribed time period and select independence, they will be incorporated into Ameristralia as a Provate.

9: If Iceland and Greenland both join the Union as one Provate, then Greenland will get one Senator and Iceland will have one Senator. If only one joins, then that one will have the two Senators. If the other joins later, they will each get to select one of the two Senators.

a) If Greenland joins (with or without Iceland), it will get financial assistance, due to its unique situation, of at least $650 million annually in financial assistance above and beyond normal allocated benefits and programs.

b) Hawaii will grow as a Provate and will consist of all the Pacific and Indian Ocean islands (Diego Garcia). It will also recieve an additional $650 million annually above and beyond normal allocated benefits. The new Provates of Caribbean and Atlantic Islands will also get an additional $650 million annually above and beyond normal allocated benefits. The Channel Islands, Gibraltar, and Cypress (Akrotiri & Dhekelia) and will also form a new Provate and get $100 million annually in the same scenario. The Channel Islands will be allocated one Senator, and Gibraltar and Cypress (Akrotiri & Dhekelia) will be allocated one Senator. The Channel Islands, Gibraltar, and Cypress (Akrotiri & Dhekelia) may also be merged into another country from the European continent if the appropriate opportunity arises and both parties approve.

Section 5,

1: Current laws stay in effect in each locale until new laws are written that override the old laws or declared unconstitutional. Businesses, organizations, local, and federal governments will have a five-year grace period to make any necessary changes for compliance with the new Constitution.

2: The new federal government will assume all of the debts of the previous countries, but not the Provates.

3: A Federal Reserve Bank will be established with all the requisite powers to control the monetary system and alleviate any financial crisis.

4: Any place where law enforcement may legally have an officer present, that law enforcement agency has the option of using any electronic devices in that location to replace the officer.

5: Where allowed by technology, climate, and pertinent circumstances, all domestic law enforcement officers will wear a body camera that records audio and video while they are outside of their vehicles. Law enforcement vehicles will also have a video camera that records views outside and inside the vehicle. None of this applies to undercover agents, but does apply to plain clothes officers.

a) All interrogations done by law enforcement inside their offices and buildings will also have recorded audio and visual of the entire event.

b) The Miranda type rights will be modified to include a notification that they are being recorded and anything they do or say, previously or in the future, can be used against them in a court of law. Recordings prior to the Miranda rights being given are admissible in court.

c) For a common recognition by the public, all law enforcement will have "Police" predominate on uniforms and vehicles. Specialized agencies then may have the City, Provate, FBI, ATF, etc., below in smaller letters.

d) Drug and Alcohol testing of suspected individuals is permitted by law enforcement after an accident or crime.

6: Anyone born after the date of the signing of this Constitution will only be taught classes in English. However, students under the age of 18 may take a non-English language class in school so long as it does not exceed five hours per week. There is no restriction for anyone taking non-English classes after high school.

a) Students will become proficient in reading, writing, math, science, history, the structure of our government and how it works. Money management, negotiations, critical thinking skills, the family unit, and physical fitness will also be part of the curriculum.

b) Once a year, all school age children under the age of eighteen (or a Junior in High School) will be given a standardized Federal test to see how their academic performance compares with that of their peers. The testing will apply to children born after the acceptance of this new constitution.

7: Right to a free education up to a senior in high school prior to their nineteenth birthday. Free is defined as the dollar figure the government (Federal, Provate, and Local) is willing to spend on its public schools. Federal monies will be the same throughout Ameristralia. Provate monies will be the same throughout the Provate. County/City/School District monies will be the same throughout the County/City/School District. Both Federal, Provate, and Local monies will be distributed on a per pupil basis by grade level to public, charter, private schools, and for home schooled students.

a) Congress and the Provates may establish achievement goals for each grade but may not dictate the policy and procedures to achieve those goals.

b) Free English proficiency classes will be provided to individuals over the age of 19.

8. No politician may be in a public service announcement or government sponsored advertisement. Also, no politician still alive may be honored with their name on a government building or other asset.

9. No foreign organization or government may hold a citizen from Ameristralia as hostage without reasonable proof the individual has committed a crime, been charged and receiving a fair trial in public, with counsel, in a timely manner. If the organization or government continues to hold the hostage, then Ameristralia may also hold assets or citizens from the foreign organization or government until the Ameristralian citizen is released.

Article 6 - Bill of Rights for Individuals

1: Congress shall make no law respecting an establishment of religion, or prohibiting the free exercise thereof; or abridging the freedom of speech, or of the press; or the right of the people to peaceable assemble, and to petition the Government for a redress of grievances.

   a) No government entity has the power to make a list of unacceptable books, magazines, or newspapers.

   b) Freedom of speech does not mean the freedom to threaten physical or financial harm to a person, family, business, organization, or government, or encourage others to do so.

   c) Organizations who purport to present News to the public must be held to a higher standard. Congress will establish licensing requirements and standards of conduct for News Journalist, News Photojournalist, News Copyright Editors, and News Producers. These will include reporting the news honestly, not just factually. Congress will establish a Bipartisan Commission for Elections and Media to review complaints and take disciplinary action when necessary.

   d) Several examples of what News will not be; 1) reporting on information from unidentified sources, 2) using emotional or slanted language to distort the truth or move the audience in one direction, 3) using judgmental words to pass judgement in a report, 4) election polls or surveys, 5) weather forecast, 6) paraphrasing, 7) Deepfakes. Those licenses may be revoked or suspended for repeated violations.

   e) Any network that presents current events, editorials, etc., must present at least 8 minutes of News during prime time, and it will be labeled as "News." Similarly, print media will also have a section labeled "News." If not News then articles will be labeled Current Events, Commentary, Editorial, Not-News, etc.

   f) Audio and video clips must identify the date, time, and location of the clip and must be visible to the viewer or reader. Context should be identified.

2: A well-regulated Militia, being necessary to the security of a free Nation, the right of the people to keep and bear Arms, shall not be infringed.

a) However, this does not prevent an individual's home Provate, or Ameristralia, from requiring Safety Training for those individuals who wish to carry a weapon in public places and acquire the necessary safety permit. Training may not last longer than eight hours over two days and may not exceed $100. No entity may restrict this right based on someone's need or lack of need, or require insurance. The safety permit information will be included on the federally issued ID card.

b) A person's federal ID will be used for screening gun purchases and can be done on the spot with no waiting period. The federal ID will have a chip (or linked to the internet) indicating whether the person has a conviction for a crime or mental instability that would prevent the purchase. The government will not store the serial number, or weapon type purchased, unless greater than .45 caliber.

c) A felon convicted of a violent crime involving weapons may be denied a safety permit and not allowed to procure or possess weapons. These permits may be suspended or revoked by the individual's home Provate, or Ameristralia, for sufficient cause.

d) Individuals will not be required to register their Arms unless the size of the shell used is greater than .45 caliber. Civilians may not own a machine gun or magazines holding more than 13 rounds.

3: No Soldier shall, in time of peace be quartered in any house, without the consent of the Owner, nor in time of war, but in a manner to be prescribed by law.

4: The right of the people to be secure in their persons, houses, papers, and effects, against unreasonable searches and seizures, shall not be violated, and no Warrants shall issue, but upon probable cause, supported by Oath or affirmation, and particularly describing the place to be searched, and the persons or things to be seized.

5: No person shall be held to answer for a capital, or otherwise infamous crime, unless on a presentment or indictment of a grand jury, except in cases arising in the military forces, or in the Militia, when in actual service in time of War, or policing action, or public danger; nor shall any person be subject for the same offense to be twice put in jeopardy of life, limb, or financially; nor shall be compelled in any criminal or civil case to be a witness against himself, nor be deprived of life, liberty, or property, without due process of law; nor shall private property be taken for public use, without just compensation.

a) There will be one Penal Code at the Federal level for all citizens, organizations, and businesses. An individual, organization, or business has a right to only be tried in one court for all criminal and civil charges from any one incident. If not guilty of a criminal crime, then the citizen, organization, or business cannot be not tried for the same offense in a civil case.

b) No spouse or attorney may be compelled to bear witness against their spouse or client.

6: In all criminal and civil prosecutions, the accused (individuals, organizations, or businesses) shall enjoy the right to a speedy and public trial, by an impartial jury of the Provate and district wherein the crime shall have been committed, which district shall have been previously ascertained by law, and to be informed of the nature and cause of the accusation; to be confronted with the evidence and witnesses against them; to have compulsory process for obtaining witnesses in their favor, and to have the Assistance of Counsel for their defense.

7: In Suits at common law, where the value in controversy shall exceed ten thousand dollars, the right of trial by jury shall be preserved, and no fact tried by a jury shall be otherwise reexamined in any Court of Ameristralia, than according to the rules of the common law.

8: For individuals excessive bail shall not be required, nor excessive fines imposed, nor cruel and unusual punishment inflicted while incarcerated.

A Business may not be fined by way of lawsuit and/or government (Federal, Provate or local) action that takes away more than half of its average profit for the last three years, in any given year.

9: The enumeration in the Constitution, of certain rights, shall not be construed to deny or disparage others retained by the people.

10: The powers not delegated to Ameristralia by the Constitution, nor prohibited by it to the Provates, are reserved to the Provates respectively, or to the people.

11: All persons born or naturalized in Ameristralia, and subject to the jurisdiction thereof, are citizens of Ameristralia and of the Provate wherein they reside. No Provate shall make or enforce any law which shall abridge the privileges or immunities of citizens of Ameristralia; nor shall any Provate deprive any person of life, liberty, or property, without due process of law; nor deny to any person within its jurisdiction the equal protection of the laws.

12: No organization, business, or governmental body may ask and/or then maintain data on a person's gender (except for birth certificates, Federal ID, schools, and health care institutions), ethnic background, skin color, or religion (except churches).

Voluntary cultural associations and genealogy groups may collect this data for the personal use of its members interested in genealogy. These voluntary cultural associations may not give or sell this information to any other organization or the government.

13: No retail storefront business may refuse service to any individual for any reason other than a) nonpayment of products and services, b) the individual has stayed past the normal time for the service they requested, c) they are creating a scene and disturbing the peace of the establishment, d) not following posted safety standards or dress codes, or e) has a history of, or is abusive to staff. Any custom requests or orders will be at the sole discretion of the business.

14: All mortgage companies must offer fifteen and thirty-year fixed rate mortgages, as well as products with other maturities.

15: Right to protect oneself from bodily invasion or harm whether from another person or a manmade object. Terminally ill individuals have the right to die at a time of their own choosing, and without pain, if possible. Women have the right to make decisions about their bodies.

16: Citizens have the right to join, or not join, a political party, union, or worker committee, but may not be allowed to strike more than five days in the last five years. Employees, or contractors, of the government or government agencies may not strike.

 a) Unions will be re-certified by a secret vote of eligible employees once every 6 years at each work site.

 b) Employers will not provide payroll deduction for political parties, unions, or worker committees.

17: Employees have a right to work and earn an income in order to support themselves and their family.

 a) Political Parties, Unions, Worker Committees, other organiza-tions, or any individual may not hinder or intimidate an employee from going to their place of work or doing their job. Also, an employer may not temporarily lock out employees.

b) With very few exceptions (failure to appear, producing "deepfakes", repeat offenders, making fake IDs, etc.), the government will not incarcerate anyone whose crime was of a non-violent nature, has a job, and is paying their income taxes.

c) The federal government will maintain a database of all convicted criminals and employers may ask an applicant if they have ever been convicted of a crime and verify it against that database. Some crimes may disqualify individuals from some jobs.

18: Employees shall be granted the right to at least ten days paid time off that can be used for sick days or vacation days. Fifteen days if there is a dependent child at home.

Guaranteed Maternity and Paternity leave of at least 15 days minimum upon the arrival of a new child into the family.

19: Any organization, government entity or business with customers in Ameristralia will have posted their full legal name, physical and mailing address of their headquarters (if different than the physical address), and a phone number on their website, letterhead, forms, and any other forms of hard or electronic communications.

All government bodies will have an easily found published phone number and during normal business hours, 80 percent of phone calls will be answered within 10 minutes. Web inquiries and letters will be answered within seven business days.

20: Businesses must provide health insurance for all its permanent employees (full-time and part-time) and their minor children if the business meets the Rule of 10. The Rule of 10 is the combination of the number of years the business has been operating and the number of employees. If the combination of these two numbers equals 10 or more, and the business has been in operation for at least 5 years, then the business must provide health insurance. The Company paid health insurance (medical, vision, dental) must provide protection for at least 80% the projected expenses (which would include 100% of normal expenses for prenatal and delivery of children) of the average employee with a cap for each employee of one million dollars over the life of the employee and each of the employee's dependents. Businesses not meeting the Rule of 10 will be given a stipend of 95% of the average national cost of health insurance from the Federal government for the company to provide the health care insurance for each employee and their dependent children.

a) The business will allow an employee to add their spouse if the business is reimbursed by the employee for the additional expense. The businesses' health care provider will allow departed employees to keep their insurance for 18 months, if the employee pays for the coverage.

b) For working, injured military veterans, health insurance companies will bill the Federal Government for normal out-of-pocket expenses above their policy limits to a total outlay of $5,000,000. For those injured military veterans unable to work who select an insurance company from an approved list, the Federal Government will pay all normal out-of-pocket expenses up to a total outlay of $10,000,000. In either situation these monies may also help acquire reasonable housing.

21: Contracts must be "reasonable and fair" to both parties and this right cannot be waived in the contract.

22: Insurance companies providing protection for the physical structure of a home or place of business will not have exclusion for acts of God and will provide for replacement value in the policy.

a) All owners of a home or a place of business must carry insurance on the physical structure that includes replacement value.

b) Renters will have insurance to cover situations where their home or business building is no longer available for their use and the loss of their contents.

Article 7 - Bill of Rights for Businesses

1: An individual business should not have to receive a license to operate in their home Provate except in professions or industries where the results of poor quality/workmanship could reasonably result in the possible death or serious injury (physically or financially) to others, such as a doctor or electrician. Para professionals such as barbers, beauticians, massage therapist, or home repair servicers should be encouraged to receive training and certification but not require a license, insurance, or a bond to operate.

Each Provate's Attorney General will maintain a website for complaints and reviews also validating the claims in the process. When practical, assist citizens in their Provate to find remedies with a company with whom they have a dispute.

The website should be categorized by industry.

2: If a business is allowed or licensed to do business in its home Provate, then it may do business in any other Provate without having to pass any other regulatory hurdles, except to be properly registered with the Secretary of State in that Provate. Businesses do not have to register to do business at any level below the Provate level, i.e., county or city.

Businesses without a physical presence in a Provate will collect the necessary Provate sales tax, but not any lower level, such as county or city. Businesses will also pay the appropriate income tax in each Provate it operates.

3: The Federal Government, or any government entity, may not own part or all of any business or nationalize any industry.
  a) Courts that are supervising the bankruptcy of a business may take temporary control but not take ownership in a business.
  b) There may be rare instances where there is no current provider or there is a lack of competition in the market. In these rare situations, regulations and/or subsidies would be the preferred option over ownership of a business.

4: No government body may shut a business down or tell it to temporarily close its doors without sufficient due process and multiple opportunities to fix any problems or establish necessary safety standards.

5: No mergers will be allowed when it will leave less than five providers in a given industry and/or market. No business with over 20% of market share may acquire a competitor.

6: Businesses may form associations, trade groups, and cartels that promote their products in the market but may not do anything that restricts competition in the areas of production, distribution, methods of production, or pricing. When possible, these groups should agree on voluntary standards for their industry, but they will also not restrict innovation and will have rules allowing experimentation.

7: Product liability cases are limited to products or services that have been produced in the last twenty years.

8. Allow virtually all kinds of currently illegal businesses to operate in the open, including such activity as prostitution and drug use. Laws and regulation will be passed to make them reasonably safe and then pay their taxes.

No essential service (banks, utilities, credit card processers, etc...) may "black ball" an industry, political group or politicians and not provide necessary services for their survival.

9. The Government may not require that businesses report activity that is outside their core business or do the Government's job.

10: Businesses have a right to choose their customers.

11: No business or government entity may discriminate based on the ethnic background, skin color, religion, gender, or whether a good or service is being provided by individuals who are organized by a union/ political party or not.

  a) Where possible, monies from government programs will be uniformly distributed on a per person, per pupil, per mile, or per acre basis, and competition for the delivery of that service will be encouraged.

  b) Government financial benefits/stipends, and an employee's pay, will be distributed via direct deposit into a citizen's bank account. The LISA contribution of 11% will also be made electronically out of these monies.

  c) LISA third party administrators and Banks will make available accounts for anyone with a Federal ID card for an appropriate fee.

  d) Individuals will be allowed to purchase additional services above the minimum standard set by the government.

12: Insurance companies providing structural Property and Casualty insurance may have two sets of rates in each County/Provate based on the risk. Those demarcation lines will be logically based, for example, so many miles from a coastline and/or for land residing in a designated flood plane.

13. An employer has the right to expect its employees to come to work each day and be productive members of its team.

14. An individual may incorporate their sole proprietorship.

15. No person, government employee, organization, or business may ask for a bribe or ransom. No person, organization, business, or government may pay a bribe or ransom.

Article 7 - Mode of Amendment

The Congress, whenever two thirds of both Houses shall deem it necessary, shall propose Amendments to this Constitution or call for a Constitution Convention, or, on the Application of the Legislatures of two thirds of the several Provates, shall call a Convention for proposing Amendments, which, in either Case, shall be valid to all Intents and Purposes, as Part of this Constitution, when ratified by the Legislatures of three-fourths thereof, as the several Provates, or by Conventions in three-fourths thereof, as the one or the other Mode of Ratification may be proposed by the Congress; and that no Provate, without its Consent, shall be deprived of its equal Suffrage in the Senate.

Article 9 - Ratification

The Ratification by the US and one other country, shall be sufficient for the Establishment of this Constitution between the two or more countries so ratifying the same.

Done in Convention by the Unanimous Consent of the Countries present the (insert the appropriate day and month here) in the Year of our Lord (insert the appropriate year here) and of the Creation of the Union of Ameristralia the witnesses were of We have hereunto subscribed our Names.

Appendix B

The distribution of Representatives will need to be decided at the Constitutional Convention. The chart is trying to depict the inclusive list of Provate resulting from the Union.

Number	Provate	Population	Number of Represent.
1	Alabama	4,903,185	?
2	Alaska	731,545	?
3	Alberta	4,421,876	?
4	Arizona	7,278,717	?
5	Arkansas	3,018,000	?
6	Atlantic Islands – Bermuda, Faulkland,	63,000	?
7	British Columbia	5,147,712	?
8	California	39,512,223	?
9	Caribbean Islands		?
10	Colorado	5,758,736	?
11	Connecticut	3,565,278	?
12	Delaware	973,764	?
13	England	55,980,000	?
14	Florida	21,477,737	?
15	Georgia	10,617,423	?
16	Gibraltar, Cyprus, Channel Islands	32,000 + 170,000	?
17	Hawaii	1,415,872	?
18	Iceland/Greenland	356,991 + 56,081	?
19	Idaho	1,787,065	?
20	Illinois	12,671,821	?
21	Indiana	8,732,219	?
22	Iowa	3,155,070	?
23	Kansas	2,913,314	?
24	Kentucky	4,467,673	?

25	Louisiana	4,648,794	?
26	Maine	1,344,212	?
27	Maryland and D.C.	6,046,000	?
28	Massachusetts	6,893,000	?
29	Michigan	9,987,000	?
30	Minnesota	5,640,000	?
31	Mississippi	2,976,000	?
32	Missouri	6,137,000	?
33	Manitoba	1,383,765	?
34	Montana	1,069,000	?
35	Nebraska	1,934,000	?
36	Nevada	3,080,000	?
37	Newfoundland and Labrador	520,553	?
38	New Brunswick	789,225	?
39	New Hampshire	1,360,000	?
40	New Jersey	8,882,000	?
41	New Mexico	2,097,000	?
42	New York	8,419,000	?
43	New Zealand	5,084,000	?
44	New South Wales, Territory of Canberra, Territory of Jervis Bay	8,176,368	?
45	Northern Ireland	1,885,000	?
46	North Carolina	10,490,000	?
47	North Dakota	762,062	?
48	Nova Scotia	992,055	?
49	Northern Territory, Australia	247,023	?
50	Northwest Territories, Canada	44,826	?
51	Nunavut	38,780	?

52	Ohio	11,690,000	?
53	Oklahoma	3,957,000	?
54	Ontario	14,826,276	?
55	Oregon	4,218,000	?
56	Pennsylvania	13,011,844	?
57	Prince Edward Island	164,318	?
58	Quebec	8,604,495	?
59	Queensland	5,206,400	?
60	Rhode Island	1,214,000	?
61	Saskatchewan	1,179,844	?
62	Scotland	5,454,000	?
63	South Australia	1,771,703	?
64	South Carolina	5,149,000	?
65	South Dakota	884,659	?
66	Tasmania	541,965	?
67	Tennessee	6,829,000	?
68	Texas	29,000,000	?
69	Utah	3,206,000	?
70	Vermont	623,989	?
71	Victoria	6,648,564	?
72	Virginia	8,536,000	?
73	Wales	1,136,000	?
74	Washington	7,615,000	?
75	Western Australia	2,675,797	?
76	West Virginia	1,792,000	?
77	Wisconsin	5,822,000	?
78	Wyoming	578,759	?
79	Yukon	40,000	?

End Notes

[1] *A Testament of Hope: The Essential Writings and Speeches,* "I Have A Dream", by Martin Luther King, Harper One Reprints, 2003 pg. 75.

[2] *The Sydney Morning Herald,* "Ameristralia? No thanks, Says Indifferent Public." May 20, 2013.

[3] *WSJ Central Edition* ISSN 1092-0935, pg. A11, 1/4-5/20 "Boris and Britain After Brexit" by Adam O'Neal.

[4] *A Concise History of Australia* by Stuart Macintyre, pg. 141.

[5] https://www.historyhit.com/key-quotes-by-winston-churchill-in-world-war-two/

[6] *The Australian Constitution as it is Actually Written* Graham L Paterson, pg. 5-7.

[7] https://ukma.org.uk/the-case-for-change/

[8] *How to Hide an Empire: a History of the Greater United States* by Daniel Immerwahr, pg. 299.

[9] *How to Hide an Empire: a History of the Greater United States* by Daniel Immerwahr, pg. 302.

[10] *Theodore Rex,* by Edmond Morris, pg. 460.

[11] *Theodore Rex,* by Edmond Morris, pg. 461.

[12] *How to Hide an Empire: a History of the Greater United States* by Daniel Immerwahr, pg. 303.

[13] *How to Hide an Empire: a History of the Greater United States* by Daniel Immerwahr, pg. 299.

[14] *The First Americans* by W.H. Brands, pg. 437

[15] *The Rise of Theodore Roosevelt,* by Edmund Morris pg. VXI.

[16] *Foreign Affairs* September/October 2021, pg. 70, "Winning Ugly" by Elliot Ackerman.

[17] *Foreign Affairs* September/October 2020, pg. 99, "The Tragedy of Vaccine Nationalism" by Thomas J. Bollyky and Chad P. Brown.

[18] *WSJ Central Edition* ISSN 1092-0935, pg. A1, 4/21/20 "Oil Takes Historic Dive Below $0" by Ryan Dezember.

[19] *A Shorty History of Canada* by Desmond Morton, pg. 213.

[20] *Borgen Magazine,* "The Positive Effects of Education" by Hannah Cleveland, August, 2014, https://www.borgenmagazine.com/positive-effects-education/

[21] *WSJ Central Edition* ISSN 1092-0935, pg. A15, 12/4/20 "Unemployment Bonus Proves It's Harm" by Casey B. Milligan and Stephen Moore.

[22] *WSJ Central Edition* ISSN 1092-0935, pg. A16, 8/3/20 "Economist vs. Common Sense" an editorial.

[23] *Foreign Affairs,* March/April 2020, "The Folly of Retrenchment," by Thomas Wright, pg. 14.

[24] https://factsanddetails.com/china/cat6/sub32/item228.html

[25] *WSJ Central Edition* ISSN 1092-0935, pg. C9, 1/23-24/21 "A Purely Domestic Conspiracy" by Michael Doran.

[26] Foreign Affairs, July/August 2021, "A Measure Short of War," by Jill Kastner and William C. Wohlforth, pg. 125.

[27] WSJ Central Edition ISSN 1092-0935, pg. A1 & 8, 1/6/21 "Russia's Neighbors Rebuild Defenses" by Michael M. Phillips and James Mason.

[28] *Sir Robert Borden* by Martin Thornton, pg. 125.

[29] https://www.iwm.org.uk/history/how-britain-hoped-to-avoid-war-with-germany-in-the-1930s

[30] *WSJ Central Edition* ISSN 1092-0935, pg. A15, 1/12/21 "Beijing Won't Bow to Bluster on Taiwan" by Walter Russell Mead.

[31] *WSJ Central Edition* ISSN 1092-0935, pg. A15, 1/12/21 "Beijing Won't Bow to Bluster on Taiwan" by Walter Russell Mead.

[32] *WSJ Central Edition* ISSN 1092-0935, pg. A15, 7/20-21/19 "America's Nationalist Awakening" by Christopher DeMuth.

[33] *WSJ Central Edition* ISSN 1092-0935, pg. A11, 7/6-7/19 "The Founders Who Opposed the Constitution" by Jason Wiliick.

[34] *WSJ Central Edition* ISSN 1092-0935, pg. A11, 7/6-7/19 "The Founders Who Opposed the Constitution" by Jason Wiliick.

[35] *WSJ Central Edition* ISSN 1092-0935, 2/18/20 "Europeans Try to Have It Both Ways" by Walter Russell Mead, pg. A15.

[36] *The First Americans* by H. W, Brands pg. 306

[37] *The History of Iceland* by Gunnar Karlsson, pg. 169.

[38] Footnote Churchillarchive.com/collection

[39] "Leaving the Enclave: Historical Evidence on Immigrant Mobility from the Industrial Removal Office," by Ran Abramitzky, SIEPR, Stanford University

[40] *A Testament of Hope: The Essential Writings and Speeches,* "I Have A Dream", by Martin Luther King, Harper One Reprints, 2003 pg. 75. "I Have A Dream", by Martin Luther King, pg. xx.

[41] *Australia, History for Dummies* by Alex McDermott pgs. 316-17.

[42] *How to Hide an Empire: a History of the Greater United States* by Daniel Immerwahr, pg. 230.

[43] *Australia, History for Dummies* by Alex McDermott pg. 358.

[44] S. A. McLeod, (2008) "Prejudice and discrimination," *Simply Psychology* https://www.simplypsychology.org/prejudice.html

[45] marketingworldchoise.wordpress.com/2013/08/08/why-english-has-become-the-universallanguage- of-the-world

[46] *The Federalist Papers* by Alexander Hamilton, John Jay and James Madison, pg. 16.

[47] *Foreign Affairs,* March/April 2020, "Learning to Live With Despots", by Stephen Krasner, pg. 50.

[48] *Foreign Affairs,* March/April 2020, "Learning to Live With Despots", by Stephen Krasner, pg. 53.

[49] *A Short History of Canada* by Desmond Morton, pg. 49.

[50] *A Short History of Canada* by Desmond Morton, pg. 3.

[51] *The Audacity of His Enterprise* by M. Max Hamon, pg. 142.

[52] *A Concise History of New Zealand* by Philippa Mein Smith, pg. 96.

[53] *A Concise History of New Zealand* by Philippa Mein Smith, pg. 117.

[54] *A Concise History of New Zealand* by Philippa Mein Smith, pg. 119.

[55] *A Concise History of New Zealand* by Philippa Mein Smith, pg. 268.

[56] *The Federalist Papers* by Alexander Hamilton, John Jay and James Madison, pg. 269.

[57] *WSJ Central Edition* ISSN 1092-0935, pg. A15, 9/29/20 "The EU Isn't Built to Lead" by Walter Russell Mead.

[58] *The Downing Street Years* by Margaret Thatcher, pg. 191.

[59] *WSJ Central Edition* ISSN 1092-0935, pg. A13, 7/29/20 "Free Markets and the Meaning in Life" by Clay Routledge and John Bitzan.

[60] *WSJ Central Edition* ISSN 1092-0935, pg. A15, 10/12/20 "To Serve the Public, Seek Profits" by Andy Kessler.

[61] Begley, Jason; Collis, Clive; Morris, David. "THE RUSSIAN AUTOMOTIVE INDUSTRY AND FOREIGN DIRECT INVESTMENT" (PDF). Applied Research Centre in Sustainable Regeneration. Archived from the original (PDF) on 2011-02-23. https://en.wikipedia.org/wiki/Automotive_industry_in_Russia

[62] *Dutch,* by Edmond Morris, pg. 518.

[63] *Theodore Rex,* by Edmond Morris, pg. 434.

[64] *WSJ Central Edition* ISSN 1092-0935, pg. A10A, 8/20/20 "Amtrak Blamed for Busting Station Budget" by Ted Mann.

[65] WSJ, "The $392,000 Lifeguard: Baywatch as a Union Shop," May 13, 2021, pg. A17

[66] *A Concise History of Australia* by Stuart Macintyre, pg.269.

[67] *Foreign Affairs*, January/February 2020, "The Clash of Capitalisms", by Branko Milanovic, pg.s10-12.

[68] *Foreign Affairs*, July/August 2020, "The Rise of Strategic Corruption", by Philip Zelikow, Eric Edelman, Kristofer Harrison, and Celeste Ward Gventer, pg. 107.

[69] *Foreign Affairs*, Jan./Feb. 2020, "The Clash of Capitalisms," by Branko Milanovic, pg. 20.

[70] *Foreign Affairs*, January/February 2020, "Unmerited", by Nicholas Lemmann, pg. 140.

[71] *Foreign Affairs*, September/October 2020, "The Pandemic Depression" by Carmen Reinhart and Vincent Reinhart, pg. 94.

[72] *Thomas Jefferson An Intimate History* by Fawn M. Brodie, pg. 251.

[73] *The Downing Street Years* by Margaret Thatcher, pg. 800.

[74] *Foreign Affairs*, "The Kremlin's Strange Victory," by Fiona Hill , page 47.

[75] *The Federalist Papers* by Alexander Hamilton, John Jay and James Madison, pg. 290.

[76] *A Concise History of New Zealand* by Philippa Mein Smith, pg. 184.

[77] *A Concise History of New Zealand* by Philippa Mein Smith, pg. 223, 224.

[78] *A Concise History of New Zealand* by Philippa Mein Smith, pg. 236.

[79] *Foreign Affairs,* September/October 2019, "The Transformer", by Paul Lendvai, pg. 50.

[80] "Germany Renounces Nuclear Power," BBC News Thursday, 15 June 2000.

[81] *WSJ Central Edition* ISSN 1092-0935, pg. A8, 12/12/19 "Israel to Hold Third Vote Amid Deadlock" an article.

[82] *The Downing Street Years* by Margaret Thatcher, pg. 288.

[83] *The Federalist Papers* by Alexander Hamilton, John Jay and James Madison, pg. 160.

[84] *The Economist,* "Why does Italy go through so many governments," Jan. 31, 2021 https://www.economist.com/the-economist-explains/2021/01/31/why-does-italy-go-through-somany- governments

[85] *A Concise History of Australia* by Stuart Macintyre, pg. 246.

[86] *A Concise History of Australia* by Stuart Macintyre, pg. 247.

[87] *A Short History of Canada* by Desmond Morton, pg. 139.

[88] *Sir Robert Borden* by Martin Thornton, pg. 127-8.

[89] *Just Watch Me: the Life of Pierre Elliott Trudeau* by John English, pg. 14-15.

[90] *WSJ Central Edition* ISSN 1092-0935, pg. A9, 10/30/19 "U.K. Set December Election," by Max Colchester.

[91] *The PM Years* by Kevin Rudd, pg. 310.

[92] *A Concise History of Australia* by Stuart Macintyre, pg. 235.

[93] *A Concise History of Australia* by Stuart Macintyre, pg. 312.

[94] *The PM Years* by Kevin Rudd, pg. 330.

[95] *The PM Years* by Kevin Rudd, pg. 357.

[96] http://www.nyf.hu/angol/sites/www.nyf.hu.angol/files/Westminster_system_of_government.pdf

[97] *WSJ Central Edition* ISSN 1092-0935, pg. A11, 9/7/19 "The High Court's Rocky Mountain Originalist" by Kyle Peterson.

[98] The Australian Constitution as it is Actually Written by Graham L. Patterson, pg. viii.

Endnotes

⁹⁹ *The Australian Constitution as it is Actually Written* by Graham L. Patterson, pg. viii-ix.

¹⁰⁰ *The PM Years* by Kevin Rudd, pg. 1.

¹⁰¹ *The Rise of Theodore Roosevelt,* by Edmond Morris, pg. 370.

¹⁰² *The PM Years* by Kevin Rudd, pg. 11.

¹⁰³ *A Concise History of Australia* by Stuart Macintyre, pg. 302.

¹⁰⁴ *Just Watch Me: the Life of Pierre Elliott Trudeau* by John English, pg. 462.

¹⁰⁵ *Foreign Affairs,* January/February 2020, "Paths to Power", by Anna Grzymal-Busse, pg. 175.

¹⁰⁶ *Foreign Affairs,* May/June 2020, "The Right Way to Fix the EU," by Matthias Matthijs, pg. 164.

¹⁰⁷ *Foreign Affairs,* Sept/Oct. 2019, "The Dictator's Last Stand", by Yascha Mounk, pg. 138.

¹⁰⁸ *The Downing Street Years* by Margaret Thatcher, pg. 22.

¹⁰⁹ *The Downing Street Years* by Margaret Thatcher, pg. 25.

¹¹⁰ *The Downing Street Years* by Margaret Thatcher, pg. 29.

¹¹¹ *Just Watch Me: the Life of Pierre Elliott Trudeau* by John English, pg. 358.

¹¹² *The Downing Street Years* by Margaret Thatcher, pg. 242.

¹¹³ *A Short History of Canada* by Desmond Morton, pg. 190.

¹¹⁴ *WSJ Central Edition* ISSN 1092-0935, pg. A6, 9/6/19 "Brexit Saunders Johnson Brothers" by Jason Douglas.

¹¹⁵ *America's Constitution* by Akhil Reed Amar, pg. 83.

¹¹⁶ *America's Constitution* by Akhil Reed Amar, pg. 75 and 147.

¹¹⁷ *The PM Years* by Kevin Rudd, pg. 15.

¹¹⁸ *History of Australia and New Zealand From 1606 to 1890* by Alexander and George Sutherland, pg. 13.

¹¹⁹ *A Short History of Canada* by Desmond Morton, pg. 50.

¹²⁰ *Australia, History for Dummies* by Alex McDermott, pg. 404.

¹²¹ *The Australian Constitution as it is Actually Written* by Graham L Patterson, pg. 6-7.

¹²² *A Concise History of Australia* by Stuart Macintyre, pg. 144.

¹²³ *A Concise History of Australia* by Stuart Macintyre, pg. 140.

¹²⁴ *History of Australia and New Zealand From 1606 to1890* by Alexander and George Sutherland, pg. 35.

[125] *The Australian Constitution as it is Actually Written* by Graham L Patterson, pg. 20.

[126] *The Last Lion: Winston Spencer Churchill* by William Manchester, pg. 662.

[127] *How to Hide an Empire: a History of the Greater United States* by Daniel Immerwahr, pg. 200.

[128] *Australia, History for Dummies* by Alex McDermott pg. 306.

[129] *History of Australia and New Zealand From 1606 to 1890* by Alexander and George Sutherland, pg. 41.

[130] *A Concise History of Australia* by Stuart Macintyre, pg. 185.

[131] *The Australian Constitution as it is Actually Written* by Graham L Patterson, pg. 199.

[132] *A Concise History of New Zealand* by Philippa Mein Smith, pg. 110.

[133] *Australia, History for Dummies* by Alex McDermott pg. 404.

[134] *The PM Years* by Kevin Rudd, pg. 9.

[135] *The PM Years* by Kevin Rudd, pg. 10.

[136] *The Australian Constitution as it is Actually Written* by Graham L Patterson, pg. 221.

[137] *Foreign Affairs,* March/April 2020, "Reality Check", by Jennifer Lind and Daryl Press, pg. 45.

[138] *Foreign Affairs,* September/October 2019, "Party Man", by Richard Mc Gregor, pg. 24.

[139] *Foreign Affairs,* September/October 2019, "Party Man", by Richard Mc Gregor, pg. 24.

[140] *Foreign Affairs,* July/August 2020, "The Rise of Strategic Corruption," by Philip Zelikow, Eric Edelman, Kristofer Harrison, and Celeste Ward Gventer, pg. 115.

[141] *The PM Years* by Kevin Rudd, pg. 446.

[142] *Foreign Affairs,* September/October 2019, "Party Man", by Richard Mc Gregor, pg. 25.

[143] *The PM Years* by Kevin Rudd, pg. XIV.

[144] Reuters, "Japan, Australia sign defense pact for closer cooperation," 1/6/2022, https://www.reuters.com/world/asia-pacific/japan-australia-sign-defence-cooperation-pact-2022-01-06/

[145] https://en.wikipedia.org/wiki/Superannuation_in_Australia

146 *The Downing Street Years* by Margaret Thatcher, pg.127.

147 https://www.australiansuper.com/superannuation/superannuation-articles/2020/08/howincreasing-super-guarantee-could-see-big-benefits

148 *The PM Years* by Kevin Rudd, pg. 57.

149 *The PM Years* by Kevin Rudd, pg. 167.

150 *Sir Robert Borden* by Martin Thornton, pg. 14.

151 *The Last Lion: Winston Spencer Churchill* by William Manchester, pg. 662.

152 *A Short History of Canada* by Desmond Morton, pg. 98.

153 *Federalism and the Constitution of Canada* by David E. Smith, pg. 12.

154 *The Federalist Papers* by Alexander Hamilton, John Jay and James Madison, pg. 198.

155 *The First American* by H. W. Brands, pg. 602,

156 *A Short History of Canada* by Desmond Morton, pg. 27.

157 *A Short History of Canada* by Desmond Morton, pg.39.

158 *A Short History of Canada* by Desmond Morton, pg. 97.

159 *A Short History of Canada* by Desmond Morton, pg. 107.

160 https://www.geographyrealm.com/interesting-geography-facts-about-the-us-canada-border/

161 *Federalism and the Constitution of Canada* by David E. Smith, pg. 136.

162 *Just Watch Me: the Life of Pierre Elliott Trudeau* by John English, pg. 243.

163 *Federalism and the Constitution of Canada* by David E. Smith, pg. 71.

164 *Federalism and the Constitution of Canada* by David E. Smith, pg. 71.

165 *Federalism and the Constitution of Canada* by David E. Smith, pg. 72.

166 *Federalism and the Constitution of Canada* by David E. Smith, pg. 73.

167 *A Short History of Canada* by Desmond Morton, pg. 132.

168 https://www.thecanadianencyclopedia.ca/en/article/wilfrid-laurier-let-them-become-canadians-1905

[169] *A Short History of Canada* by Desmond Morton, pg. 132.

[170] *A Short History of Canada* by Desmond Morton, pg. 133.

[171] *A Short History of Canada* by Desmond Morton, pg. 133.

[172] *A Short History of Canada* by Desmond Morton, pg. 133.

[173] *Just Watch Me: the Life of Pierre Elliott Trudeau* by John English, pg. 73.

[174] *Just Watch Me: the Life of Pierre Elliott Trudeau* by John English, pg. 8.

[175] *Just Watch Me: the Life of Pierre Elliott Trudeau* by John English, pg. 81.

[176] *A Short History of Canada* by Desmond Morton, pg. 308.

[177] *Just Watch Me: the Life of Pierre Elliott Trudeau* by John English, pg. 144.

[178] *Just Watch Me: the Life of Pierre Elliott Trudeau* by John English, pg. 129.

[179] *Just Watch Me: the Life of Pierre Elliott Trudeau* by John English, pg. 301-2.

[180] *Just Watch Me: the Life of Pierre Elliott Trudeau* by John English, pg. 545.

[181] *A Short History of Canada* by Desmond Morton, pg. 331.

[182] *Just Watch Me: the Life of Pierre Elliott Trudeau* by John English, pg. 480.

[183] *Just Watch Me: the Life of Pierre Elliott Trudeau* by John English, pg. 499.

[184] *Just Watch Me: the Life of Pierre Elliott Trudeau* by John English, pg. 503.

[185] *Just Watch Me: the Life of Pierre Elliott Trudeau* by John English, pg. 508.

[186] *Just Watch Me: the Life of Pierre Elliott Trudeau* by John English, pg. 527.

[187] *A Short History of Canada* by Desmond Morton, pg. 367.

[188] *A Short History of Canada* by Desmond Morton, pg. 383.

[189] *A Short History of Canada* by Desmond Morton, pg. 405.

[190] *Just Watch Me: the Life of Pierre Elliot Trudeau* by John English, pg. 330

[191] *Just Watch Me: the Life of Pierre Elliott Trudeau* by John English, pg. 330-1.

[192] *Just Watch Me: the Life of Pierre Elliott Trudeau* by John English, pg. 370.

[193] *The History of Iceland* by Gunnar Karlsson, pg. 103.

[194] *WSJ*, "Greenland Isn't for Sale, Island Tells Trump" by Vivian Salama, Andrew Restuccia, 8/17/2019. https://www.wsj.com/articles/greenland-tells-trump-were-open-for-business-not-forsale-11565960064

[195] *WSJ Central Edition* ISSN 1092-0935, pg. A3, 7/16/19 "Trump Eyes U.S. Buying Greenland" by Vivian Salama, Rebecca Ballhaus, Andrew Restuccia and Michael Bender.

[196] *WSJ Central Edition* ISSN 1092-0935, pg. A3, 7/16/19 "Trump Eyes U.S. Buying Greenland" by Vivian Salama, Rebecca Ballhaus, Andrew Restuccia and Michael Bender.

[197] *WSJ Central Edition* ISSN 1092-0935, pg. C3, 7/18-19/20 "The Key to Iceland's Long, Improbable Survival? Books" by A. Kendra Greene.

[198] *The History of Iceland* by Gunnar Karlsson, pg. 65.

[199] *The History of Iceland* by Gunnar Karlsson, pg. 258.

[200] *The History of Iceland* by Gunnar Karlsson, pg. 361.

[201] *The History of Iceland* by Gunnar Karlsson, pg. 166.

[202] *The History of Iceland* by Gunnar Karlsson, pg. 195-198.

[203] *The History of Iceland* by Gunnar Karlsson, pg. 216.

[204] *The History of Iceland* by Gunnar Karlsson, pg. 315.

[205] *The History of Iceland* by Gunnar Karlsson, pg. 318.

[206] *The History of Iceland* by Gunnar Karlsson, pg. 338.

[207] *The History of Iceland* by Gunnar Karlsson, pg. 362.

[208] *The History of Iceland* by Gunnar Karlsson, pg. 105.

[209] *The History of Iceland* by Gunnar Karlsson, pg. 200.

[210] *WSJ*, "A Digital Future for the Icelandic," May 22-23, 2020, pg. C3.

[211] *WSJ*, "No Longer a Homespun Nation," by Brad Leithauser, May 28, 2021D2-3.

[212] *A Concise History of New Zealand* by Philippa Mein Smith, pg. 45.

[213] *A Concise History of New Zealand* by Philippa Mein Smith, pg. 179.

[214] *A Concise History of New Zealand* by Philippa Mein Smith, pg. 4.

[215] *A Concise History of New Zealand* by Philippa Mein Smith, pg. 256-7.

[216] *WSJ Central Edition* ISSN 1092-0935, pg. A9, 6/10/20 "New Zealand Scraps Plan for Armed Police Units" by Stephen Wright.

[217] *A Concise History of New Zealand* by Philippa Mein Smith, pg. 228.

[218] *A Concise History of New Zealand* by Philippa Mein Smith, pg. 232.

[219] *Foreign Affairs*, May/June 2020, "The Right Way to Fix the EU", by Matthias Matthijs, pg. 160.

[220] *Foreign Affairs*, May/June 2020, "The Right Way to Fix the EU", by Matthias Matthijs, pg. 161.

[221] *The Downing Street Years* by Margaret Thatcher, pg. 691.

[222] *WSJ Central Edition* ISSN 1092-0935, pg. A7, 1/2-3/20 "U.K., EU Part Ways on Day 1 of Brexit" by Jason Douglas.

[223] *The Downing Street Years* by Margaret Thatcher, pg. 39.

[224] *The Downing Street Years* by Margaret Thatcher, pg. 159.

[225] *The Downing Street Years* by Margaret Thatcher, pg. 145.

[226] *The Downing Street Years* by Margaret Thatcher, pg. 146.

[227] *Foreign Affairs*, May/June 2020, "The Right Way to Fix the EU", by Matthias Matthijs, pg. 162.

[228] *Foreign Affairs*, Sept/Oct. 2019, "The Dictator's Last Stand," by Yascha Mounk, pg. 139.

[229] *Quartz*, "Three things that make British elections so different from American ones" by Jenny Anderson, November 7, 2019, https://qz.com/1743234/the-three-main-differences-between-usand- uk-elections/

[230] *WSJ Central Edition* ISSN 1092-0935, pg. A7, 9/1/20 "U.K. Presses Unity as Scotland's Calls for Independence Grown" by Max Colchester and James Hookway.

[231] *How to Hide an Empire: a History of the Greater United States* by Daniel Immerwahr, pg. 228.

232 *The First American,* by H. W. Brands, pg. 463.

233 *WSJ Central Edition* ISSN 1092-0935, pg. A10, 7/17/19 "The Race Card Has Gone Bust" by Jason L. Riley.

234 *WSJ Central Edition* ISSN 1092-0935, pg. A13, 11/13/20 "What Gentiles Can Learn From Lord Sacks" by Meir Soloveichik.

235 *The Rise of Theodore Roosevelt,* by Edmond Morris, pg. 470.

236 *The Best Investment a Nation Ever Made: a Tribute to Dwight D Eisenhower and the Interstate Defense Highways* by Wendell Cox and Jean Love, 1996 pg.

237 Pew Research Center: Social & Demographic Trends. Parenting in America December 17, 2015

238 *Babbel Magazine,* "How Many People Speak English and Where is it Spoken" by Dylan Lyons, May 10, 2021, https://www.babbel.com/en/magazine/how-many-people-speak-english-andwhere-is-it-spoken

239 *How to Hide an Empire: a History of the Greater United States* by Daniel Immerwahr, pg. 329.

240 *How to Hide an Empire: a History of the Greater United States* by Daniel Immerwahr, pg. 329.

241 https://www.gofluent.com/blog/why-english-will-remain-the-language-of-business/

242 *How to Hide an Empire* by Daniel Immerwahr, page 332.

243 *How to Hide an Empire* by Daniel Immerwahr, page 333.

244 *English as a Global Language* by David Crystal, second edition, pg. 2.

245 *You Can Do Anything: The Surprising Power of a "Useless" Liberal Arts Education* by George Anders, Little Brown and Co., 2017, pg. 113.

246 https://www.bosshunting.com.au/hustle/bill-gates-200-million-apple-investment/

247 *The PM Years* by Kevin Rudd, page XV.

248 *A Concise History of Australia* by Stuart Macintyre, pg. 313.

249 WSJ Central Edition ISSN 1092-0935, page A15, 1/5/21 "Why We're Ending the EPA's Reliance on Secret Science" by Andrew Wheeler.

250 *WSJ Central Edition* ISSN 1092-0935, page A14, 7/17/20 "Florida's Licensing Breakthrough" an editorial.

[251] https://www.brookings.edu/articles/how-home-schooling-will-change-public-education/

[252] https://nces.ed.gov/programs/schoolchoice/ind_08.asp

[253] *WSJ Central Edition* ISSN 1092-0935, editorial, pg. A16, 10/30/19 "Denver's Education Stakes."

[254] *WSJ Central Edition* ISSN 1092-0935, editorial pg. A16, 10/30/19 "Denver's Education Stakes."

[255] *Neither Liberal Nor Conservative Be* by Larry R. Bradley, p.86.

[256] How Does a Vesting Schedule Work by David Fisher 02/07/2021 https://www.thebalance.com/what-is-a-vesting-schedule-and-how-does-it-work-4047274

[257] The Role of Individual Personal Saving Accounts in Social Security Reform by Gary Burtless, 6/18/1998 https://www.brookings.edu/testimonies/the-role-of-individual-personal-savingaccounts-in-social-security-reform/

[258] *Neither Liberal Nor Conservative Be* by Larry R. Bradley, pg.6.

[259] *Miracle at Philadelphia: The Story of the Constitutional Convention,* May to September 1787 by Catherine Drinker Bowen, pg. 44.

[260] *Miracle at Philadelphia: The Story of the Constitutional Convention,* May to September 1787 by Catherine Drinker Bowen, pg. XXI.

[261] *How to Hide an Empire: a History of the Greater United States* by Daniel Immerwahr, pg. 225.

[262] *How to Hide an Empire: a History of the Greater United States* by Daniel Immerwahr, pg. 226.

[263] *Just Watch Me* by John English, pg. 472.

[264] *The Australian Constitution as it is Actually Written* by Graham L Patterson, pg. 23.

[265] *The Australian Constitution as it is Actually Written* by Graham L Patterson, pg. 24.

[266] *The Australian Constitution as it is Actually Written* by Graham L Patterson, pgs. 24-25.

[267] *Miracle at Philadelphia: The Story of the Constitutional Convention,* May to September 1787 by Catherine Drinker Bowen, pg. xxii.

[268] *WSJ Central Edition* ISSN 1092-0935, page A13, 11/9-10/21 "The Founders' Guide to 'Knock Down, Drag Out' Fighting" by Alexander Zubia.

[269] *Foreign Affairs*, "The Coming Democratic Revival: America's Opportunity to Lead the Fight Against Authoritarianism," by Madeline Albright, November/December 2021. https://www.foreignaffairs.com/articles/world/2021-10-19/madeleine-albright-coming-democratic-revival

[270]*A Testament of Hope: The Essential Writings and Speeches*, "I Have A Dream", by Martin Luther King, Harper One Reprints, 2003 pg. 75. "I Have A Dream", by Martin Luther King, pg. 75.

[271] *The Federalist Papers*, "The Structure of the Government Must Furnish the Proper Checks and Balances Between the Different Departments" by James Madison

[272] *White Guilt: How Blacks and Whites Together Destroyed the Promise of the Civil Rights Era* by Shelby Steele, pg. 9.

[273] *White Guilt: How Blacks and Whites Together Destroyed the Promise of the Civil Rights Era* by Shelby Steele, pg. 9.

[274] *Federalism and the Constitution of Canada* by David E. Smith, pg. 45.

[275] https://www.mygermanuniversity.com/articles/english-universities-in-germany

[276] https://educaloi.qc.ca/en/capsules/language-laws-and-doing-business-in-quebec/

[277] https://www.canada.ca/en/canadian-heritage/services/official-languagesbilingualism/publications/statistics.html

[278] *Federalism and the Constitution of Canada* by David E. Smith, pg. 9.

[279] *Federalism and the Constitution of Canada* by David E. Smith, pg. 10

[280] *How to Hide an Empire* by Daniel Immerwahr, pg. 317.

[281] *Epic of America* by James Truslow Adams, pg. xii.

[282] *WSJ Central Edition* ISSN 1092-0935, pg. A14, 2/14/20 "The American Dream is Real for My Family" by Nathan Nguyen.

[283] *WSJ Central Edition* ISSN 1092-0935, pg. A9, 6/13-14/20 "'Lucky Duck' Funded Schools for the Poor" an Obituary.

[284] *WSJ Central Edition* ISSN 1092-0935, pg. A11, 9/14-15/19 "Hair-Care Matriarch Knew When to Sell" by James R Hagerty.

[285] *WSJ Central Edition* ISSN 1092-0935, pg. A17, 10/10/19 "A Disney Story for Young Socialist" by Art Diamond.

[286] *The Force* by Saul David, pg. 35.

[287] *WSJ Central Edition* ISSN 1092-0935, pg. C1-2, 11/28-29/20 "The Predicament of Counting Americans by Race" by Janet Adamy and Paul Overberg.

[288] *Thomas Jefferson An Intimate History* by Fawn M. Brodie, pg. 434.

[289] *White Guilt: How Blacks and Whites Destroyed the Promise of the Civil Rights Era* by Shelby Steele, pg. 10.

[290] *WSJ Central Edition* ISSN 1092-0935, pg. A1, 8/14/20 "Yale Discriminates in Admissions, DOJ Says" by Melissa Korn.

[291] *WSJ Central Edition* ISSN 1092-0935, pg. A11, 1/16-17/21 "How the Left Hijacked Civil Rights" by Robert L. Woodson Sr. and Joshua Mitchell.

[292] *The Federalist Papers* by Alexander Hamilton, John Jay and James Madison, pg. 5.

[293] *WSJ Central Edition* ISSN 1092-0935, pg. A12, 11/28-29/20 "Who Is an American 'Person'?" by an editorial.

[294] *Federalism and the Constitution of Canada* by David E. Smith, pg. 11.

[295] *Federalism and the Constitution of Canada* by David E. Smith, pg. 17.

[296] *Federalism and the Constitution of Canada* by David E. Smith, pg. 19.

[297] *Federalism and the Constitution of Canada* by David E. Smith, pg. 26.

[298] *The Federalist Papers* by Alexander Hamilton, John Jay and James Madison, pg. 263.

[299] https://billofrightsinstitute.org/primary-sources/federalist-no-10

[300] *A Concise History of New Zealand* by Philippa Mein Smith, pg. 4.

[301] *How to Hide an Empire: a History of the Greater United States* by Daniel Immerwahr, pg. 314.

[302] www.supremecourt.gov>about>institutiion 1/23/21.

303 "Demographic and Social Characteristics of Poverty: 2018" by the Congressional Research Service pg. 2. https://sgp.fas. org/crs/misc/R46294.pdf

304 *WSJ Central Edition* ISSN 1092-0935, editorial page A16, 11/17/20 "State Tax Revenue Rebound."

305 *The French Revolution: From Enlightenment to Tyranny* by Ian Davidson, pg. 56.

306 *WSJ Central Edition* ISSN 1092-0935, pg. A2 12/6/19 "Tax Cuts Push U.S. Burden to Near World's Lowest" an article.

307 *The Downing Street Years* by Margaret Thatcher, pg. 42.

308 *Sir Robert Borden* by Martin Thornton, pg. xi.

309 *A Short History of Canada* by Desmond Morton, pg. 196.

310 *WSJ Central Edition* ISSN 1092-0935, editorial, pg. A16, 10/6/20 "An Illinois Tax Crossroads."

311 *WSJ Central Edition* ISSN 1092-0935, pg. A11, 10/17/20 "The Alternative to a Bailout for Fiscally Mismanaged States" by Jonathan Williams and Dave Trabert.

312 *A Concise History of Australia* by Stuart Macintyre, pg. 246.

313 *WSJ Central Edition* ISSN 1092-0935, editorial, pg. A18, 5/13/20 "'Faithless Electors at the Supreme Court."

314 *WSJ Central Edition* ISSN 1092-0935, pg. A15, 11/2/19 "Like Trump, Justin Trudeau 'Lost the Popular Vote'" by Jason Willick.

315 *WSJ Central Edition* ISSN 1092-0935, pg. A3, 1/18-19/20 "Justices to Consider Electoral College" by Brent Kendall and Jess Bravin.

316 *Reunion and Reaction: The Compromise of 1877 and the End of Reconstruction* by C. Vann Woodward, Oxford University Press, pg. 7

317 *WSJ Central Edition* ISSN 1092-0935, editorial, pg. A14, 1/27/21 "The Law That Fuels the Capitol Riot."

318 *WSJ Central Edition* ISSN 1092-0935, pg. A11B, 11/6/20 "Judges' Suit Calls Forced Retirement Age Discrimination" Joseph De Avila.

319 *Federalism and the Constitution of Canada* by David E. Smith, pg. 120.

320 *The Original Meaning of the Fourteenth Amendment: Its Letter and Spirit* by Randy E. Barnett and Evan D. Bernick,

Belknap Press, November, 2021, pg. 13.

[321] *The Original Meaning of the Fourteenth Amendment: Its Letter and Spirit* by Randy E. Barnett and Evan D. Bernick, Belknap Press, November, 2021, pg. 22.

[322] *WSJ*, "Climate Policy by Judicial Decree," editorial, June 21, 2021, pg. A16.

[323] *WSJ*, "Will Biden 'Sue and Settle' at the Border?", Nov. 10, 2021, by Peter J Wallison, page A17.

[324] *WSJ*, "Will Biden 'Sue and Settle' at the Border?", Nov. 10, 2021, by Peter J Wallison, page A17.

[325] https://www.fda.gov/about-fda/changes-science-law-and-regulatory-authorities/part-ii-1938-fooddrug-cosmeticact#:~:text=FDR%20signed%20the%20Food%2C%20Drug,adequate%20directions%20for%20safe%20use.

[326] *WSJ Central Edition* ISSN 1092-0935, editorial, pg. A16, 12/26-27/20 "Liberation Day for French Dressing."

[327] *WSJ Central Edition* ISSN 1092-0935, editorial, pg. A16, 12/26-27/20 "Liberation Day for French Dressing."

[328] https://www.fbi.gov/services/information-management/foipa/privacy-impact-assessments/firs-iafis

[329] *WSJ Central Edition* ISSN 1092-0935, pg. A17, 2/17/21 "An Unconstitutional Voting 'Reform'" David B. Rivkin Jr. and Jason Snead.

[330] *WSJ*, "New York City Mayoral Race," by Katie Honan, July 6, 2021, A1, A12.

[331] *WSJ Central Edition* ISSN 1092-0935, "Now Who's Contesting Elections?" 12/4/2020 pg. A14.

[332] *WSJ*, Opinion, "Manchin's Voter-ID Deception," by John Fund, June 21, 2021, A16.

[333] *WSJ*, "Two States Find Ballot Mischief," Editorial Board, Oct. 13, 2021, pg. A16.

[334] *WSJ*, Opinion, "Manchin's Voter-ID Deception," by John Fund, June 22, 2021, A16

[335] *WSJ*, Opinion, "Manchin's Voter-ID Deception," by John Fund, June 22, 2021, A16

[336] *WSJ*, Editorial, "About Those 300 Stolen Ballots...", January 6, 2022, A16.

337 *WSJ,* Editorial, "More Than 27,000 Mail Ballots Rejected", Associated Press, March 11, 2022, A6.

338 *Quartz,* "The Three things that Make British Elections so Different from American Ones," by Jenny Anderson, November 7, 2019. https://qz.com/1743234/the-three-main-differencesbetween-us-and-uk-elections/

339 *Foreign Affairs,* July/August, 2021, "A Measure Short of War", by Jill Kastner and Williams C. Wohlforth, pg. 120-121.

340 PMC, "Adolescent Maturity and the Brain: The Promise and Pitfalls of Neuroscience Research in Adolescent Health Policy," by Sara B. Johnson, PH.D et al. June 27, 2010 https://www.ncbi.nlm.nih.gov/pmc/articles/PMC2892678/

341 *To Rescue the Republic: Ulysses S. Grant, the Fragile Union, and the Crisis of 1876* by Bret Baier and Catherine Whitney, Custom House Books, 2021, pg. 66.

342 *Time Magazine,* "New York City Voters Just Adopted Ranks Choice Voting in Elections: Here's How it Works," by Anna Purna Kambhampaty, Nov. 6, 2016 https://time.com/5718941/ranked-choice-voting/

343 https://www.ncsl.org/research/elections-and-campaigns/ranked-choice-voting636934215.aspx

344 *A Concise History of Australia* by Stuart Macintyre, pg. 221.

345 *A Concise History of Australia* by Stuart Macintyre, pg. 290.

346 *The Federalist Papers,* "Publius" by James Madison essay #10

347 *The Australian Constitution as it is Actually Writte*n by Graham L Patterson, pages 181.

348 *Foreign Affairs,* Mar/Apr 2020, "Learning to Live With Despots", by Stephen Krasner, pg. 50.

349 *Foreign Affairs,* March/April 2020, "Learning to Live With Despots", by Stephen Krasner, pg. 50.

350 *The Federalist Papers* by Alexander Hamilton, John Jay and James Madison, pg. 226.

351 *A Concise History of Australia* by Stuart Macintyre, pg. 212.

352 *A Concise History of Australia* by Stuart Macintyre, pg. 245.

353 *The Rise of Theodore Roosevelt,* by Edmond Morris, pg. 518.

354 *Federalism and the Constitution of Canada* by David E. Smith, pg. 139.

[355] *WSJ Central Edition* ISSN 1092-0935, pg. A13, 11/7-8/20 "How Florida Became America's Vote-Counting Model" by Governor George W. Bush.

[356] *The Original Meaning of the Fourteenth Amendment: Its Letter and Spirit* by Randy E. Barnett and Evan D. Bernick, Belknap Press, November, 2021, pg 181.

[357] *WSJ Central Edition* ISSN 1092-0935, page A14, 2/14/20 "The American Dream is Real for My Family" by Nathan Nguyen.

[358] Center for Retirement Research at Boston College, "How Big a Burden are State and Local OPEB Benefits," by Alicia H. Munnell and Jean-Pierre Aubry, No. 45, March, 2016, pg.1

[359] *The Downing Street Years* by Margaret Thatcher, pg. 779.

[360] *The Downing Street Years* by Margaret Thatcher, pg. 646.

[361] *WSJ Central Edition* ISSN 1092-0935, editorial, pg. A12 12/1/19 "Mayor Pete's Senior Vote Plan."

[362] *WSJ Central Edition* ISSN 1092-0935, editorial, pg. A14, 6/4/20 "Unrigging the Poverty Trap."

[363] *The Original Meaning of the Fourteenth Amendment: Its Letter and Spirit* by Randy E. Barnett and Evan D. Bernick, Belknap Press, November, 2021, pg. 358.

[364] *Arguing with Socialist,* by Glenn Beck, pg. 43-45.

[365] https://www.philanthropyroundtable.org/almanac/article/fixing-problems-viaphilanthropy-vs.-government

[366] *WSJ,* "California won't Let BofA Out of Jobless Contract, by Ben Eisen and Christine Mai-Duc, Oct. 21, 2021, B2.

[367] *WSJ Central Edition* ISSN 1092-0935, page A17, 1/25/21 "Who Gets to Make the Rules? Washington My Finally Get It Right" by Todd Gaziano and Angela C. Erickson.

[368] *WSJ Central Edition* ISSN 1092-0935, page A8, 2/27/20 "Canada Warns Freight-Rail Delays Could Last Many Weeks," by Paul Vieira.

[369] AP News "Via Rail lays off 1,000 employees amid Canada rail protests," 2/19/2020, https://apnews.com/article/ebc43deddc2372bbef6b6bbb0f34f001

[370] *How to Hide an Empire: a History of the Greater United States* by Daniel Immerwahr, pg. 7.

[371] *How to Hide an Empire: a History of the Greater United States* by Daniel Immerwahr, page 86.

[372] *How to Hide an Empire: a History of the Greater United States* by Daniel Immerwahr, page 87.

[373] *How to Hide an Empire: a History of the Greater United States* by Daniel Immerwahr, page 86.

[374] *How to Hide an Empire: a History of the Greater United States* by Daniel Immerwahr, page 392.

[375] *America's Constitution* by Akhill Reed Amar page 430.

[376] *How the States Got Their Shapes* by Mark Stein, page 78.

[377] *WSJ Central Edition* ISSN 1092-0935, page A19, 7/13/20 "Native American Sovereignty Is No Liberal Triumph" by M. Todd Henderson.

[378] *WSJ Central Edition* ISSN 1092-0935, editorial, pg. A12, 7/11-12/20 "The Tempting of Neil Gorsuch."

[379] *Federalism and the Constitution of Canada* by David E. Smith, page 8.

[380] *WSJ, Central Edition,* "Scarce Credit Hinders Homeownership of Tribal Land, by Ben Eisen, 8/29/2021.

[381] *Federalism and the Constitution of Canada* by David E. Smith, pg. 124.

[382] *The Washington Post,* "Puerto Ricans Voted to become the 51st U.S. State—again by Abdiel Santiago, 11/13/2020.

[383] *WSJ Central Edition* ISSN 1092-0935, page A10, 12/1/20 "Scottish Leader Seeks Independence Vote" by Associated Pres.

[384] Rahbek-Clemmensen, Jon (August 28, 2019. "Let's (Not) Make a Deal: Geopolitics and Greenland". War on the Rocks. Retrieved September 1, 2019

[385] *WSJ Central Edition* ISSN 1092-0935, page A15, 7/16/19 "Trump Eyes U.S. Buying Greenland" by Vivian Salama, Rebecca Ballhaus, Andrew Restuccia and Michael Bender.

[386] *Neither Liberal Nor Conservative Be* by Larry R. Bradley, pg. 86.

[387] *The First Amendment Encyclopedia for Public Access* complied by John Siegenthaler, Middle Tennessee State University, https://mtsunews.com/first-amendment-

encyclopedia-online/

[388] *Thomas Jefferson An Intimate History* by Fawn M. Brodie, pg. 268.

[389] *To Rescue the Republic: Ulysses S. Grant, the Fragile Union and the Crisis of 1876,* by Bret Baier, Catherine Whitney, Custom House, 12/12/2021, pg. 262.

[390] *The History of Iceland* by Gunnar Karlsson, page 306.

[391] *The Last Lion* by William Manchester, page 689.

[392] *A Short History of Canada* by Desmond Morton, page 377.

[393] *Foreign Affairs*, September/October 2019, "Bad News", by Jacob Weisberg, page 204.

[394] *The Rise of Theodore Roosevelt,* by Edmond Morris, page 600.

[395] *Theodore Rex,* by Edmond Morris, page 437.

[396] *WSJ*, "Union Raises Pay-Gap Issues at New York Times," Business, May 12, 2016, by Lukas I Alpert

[397] *WSJ*, "Employers Need to Address Caregiving Crisis, Study Finds, Economy, January 16, 2019, by David Harrison

[398] "What If We Treated Guns Like Cars? Then We Might be able to Enact Truly Common Sense Gun Laws" by Trevor Burrus *Forbes Magazine* 10/06/2017

[399] *WSJ*, "Another Judge Evicts the CDC," WSJ Editorial Board, May 7, 2021, pg. A14.

[400] *America's Constitution* by Akhil Reed Amar, pg. 327 and 329.

[401] *LA Times* "How Canada is not Like the United States: Home Mortgage," https://www.latimes.com/business/hiltzik/la-xpm-2014-jan-16-la-fi-mh-canada-20140116-story.html

[402] *Inc.* "Things All Humans Want at Work" (and in Life) by Ryan Jenkins, Jan 21, 2020 https://www.inc.com/ryan-jenkins/3-things-all-humans-want-at-work-and-life.html

[403] *WSJ Central Edition* ISSN 1092-0935, editorial pg. A14, "Nevada Embraces Public Unions".

[404] *WSJ Central Edition* ISSN 1092-0935, page A15, 11/19/19 "'Halfway' With Warren Is To Far" by Amity Shlaes.

[405] *Just Watch Me: The Life of Pierre Elliott Trudeau* by John English, page 40.

[406] *Killing Reagan* by Bill O'Reilly and Martin Dugard, pg. 197.

[407] *Killing Reagan* by Bill O'Reilly and Martin Dugard, pg. 198.

[408] *Dutch,* by Edmond Morris, pg. 443.

[409] *WSJ Central Edition* ISSN 1092-0935, page A19, 12/9/19 "Trapped by the Teamsters" an editorial.

[410] *Capitalism VS. Freedom: The Toll Road to Serfdom,* by Rob Larson, Zero Books, 2018, pg. 26.

[411] *Grasping Power: Rethinking the Active Ingredient in Leadership, Education, Parenting, Global Survival, Forgiveness, Restraint, Identity,* by Schuyler Totman, Resource Publications, 2021, pg. 5.

[412] *WSJ,* "This New York Union is Taking 35% Pay Cuts for More Word," by Will Parker, 11/20/2020 pg. A9B.

[413] *New York Times.* Source is cdlife.com 8/16/20

[414] *The Downing Street Years* by Margaret Thatcher, pg. 345.

[415] *The Downing Street Years* by Margaret Thatcher, pg. 353.

[416] *The Downing Street Years* by Margaret Thatcher, pg. 364

[417] *The Downing Street Years* by Margaret Thatcher, pg. 272.

[418] *Theodore Rex* by Edmond Morris, pg. 195.

[419] *A Concise History of Australia* by Stuart Macintyre, page 126.

[420] *The Last Lion* by William Manchester, page 6787

[421] *The Last Lion* by William Manchester, page 796.

[422] *Entrepreneur Magazine,* "The True Failure Rate of Small Business," by Timothy Carter, 1/3/2021, https://www.entrepreneur.com/article/361350

[423] *The Downing Street Years* by Margaret Thatcher, Harper Collins, 10/1/1993, pg. 6

[424] *WSJ Central Edition* ISSN 1092-0935, page A2 "Move to Privatize Fannie, Freddie Falters" by Andrew Ackerman, 1/14/21.

[425] *WSJ,* "Justices Upend Plan for Fannie, Freddie," by Andrew Ackerman and Brent Kendall, June 24, 2021, pg. A1

[426] *WSJ Central Edition* ISSN 1092-0935, page A17, 10/14/20 "When Democrats Were Deregulators" by Ian Jefferies.

[427] *WSJ,* editorial, "Amtrack's $66 Billion Ticket," 8/7/21, pg. 14.

[428] *The Last Lion* by William Manchester, page 863.

[429] *Monthly Labor Review,* "Productivity in Aircraft Manufacturing," by Alexander Kronemer and J. Henneberger, June 1993.

[430] *The French Revolution* by Ian Davidson, pg. 37.

[431] *Thomas Jefferson An Intimate History* by Fawn M. Brodie, pg. 25.

[432] https://en.wikipedia.org/wiki/Prostitution_in_the_United_States#:_:text=Currently%2C%20Nevada %20 is%20the%20only,in%20the%20Nevada%20Revised%20 Statutes.&text=The%20other%20counties%20 theoretically%20allow,currently%20have%20no%20 active%20brothels.

[433] *WSJ Central Edition* ISSN 1092-0935, page A15, 1/14/21 "A Dose of Dissent" by Carl L. Hart.

[434] *WSJ Central Edition* ISSN 1092-0935, pg. A3, 11/25/20 "After Oregon Eases Drug Laws, a Race To Treat Addicts" by Donald Morrison.

[435] *WSJ* "Annual Drug Overdose Deaths Top 100,000, Setting Record," by Jon Kamp and Julie Weemau, 11/18/2021, pgs. A1 and A9.

[436] *WSJ Central Edition* ISSN 1092-0935, pg. A17, 11/19/20 "Legal Drugs Are Fashionable—and Treacherous for Children" by Noami Schaefer Riley and John Walters.

[437] *WSJ Central Edition* ISSN 1092-0935, pg. A16, 2/12/21 "Golden State Parachute."

[438] *The Great Reset* by Glen Beck and Justin Haskins, pg. 267.

Index

Bibliography

Bollyky, Thomas J. and Brown, Chad P. "The Tragedy of Vaccine Nationalism." *Foreign Affairs* September/October 2020: 99.

Brands, H. W., *The First American: The Life and Times of Benjamin Franklin.* New York: Anchor, 2002.

Cleveland, Hannah. "The Positive Effects of Education," *Borgen Magazine.* Aug. 2014, https://www.borgenmagazine.com/positive-effects-education/

Dezember, Ryan "Oil Takes Historic Dive Below $0," *Wall Street Journal* Central Edition, April 21, 2020: A1.

Immerwahr, Daniel. *How to Hide an Empire: a History of the Greater United States.* New York: Farrar, Straus and Giroux, 2019.

Macintyre, Stuart. *A Concise History of Australia.* Cambridge University Press, 2000.

Morris, Edmond. *Theodore Rex: The Rise of Theodore Roosevelt.* New York: Random House, 2010. New York: Random House, 2010.Morton, Desmond.

A Shorty History of Canada. Toronto: McClelland & Stewart, 2001.

Paterson, Graham L. *The Australian Constitution as it is Actually Written.* Singapore: Strategic Book Publishing & Rights Co. LLC, 2015.

Editorial board, "Economist vs. Common Sense," *Wall Street Journal* Central Edition, Aug. 3, 2020: A16

ACKNOWLEDGEMENTS

To MY MOM AND DAD who first taught me that I could do anything I wanted to do in life if I just worked hard and never gave up. With only one exception, they always supported me in everything I did and I can't begin to tell you of the impact it has had on my life. I started a lawn mowing business with my brother in my early teens, and my mom was there to push us when we needed to be pushed. As a child, when our family drove from Pittsburg, Kansas, to Tribune, Kansas, to see our mother's family, I was tasked with the job of asking my dad questions—to help keep him awake while he was driving in the dark and everyone else was asleep. It taught me to look at things and wonder, then ask questions. It was a great life skill that I learned. I was never alone in my journey through life, even after getting married. My parents were always there if I needed them. They taught me the importance of "family" and always being there for anyone in the family who needs help.

To MY WIFE of 46 years, Eleonore, for being there throughout our marriage in support of my career and the many different cities it took us, our family, starting our business, and this book. I couldn't have made it this far without her. Eleonore said "yes" when I wanted to start our business when she could have easily said "no." She could have said "no" to writing the book, but instead supported me in my endeavor. In life you need to surround yourself with people who keep telling you, "yes you can," and Eleonore has been there for me.

To MY DAUGHTER Andrea for stepping up and taking over the day-to-day operation of our business so that I would have the freedom to enjoy life a little more and write this book. Without Andrea I'm sure I would have died in my sixties from exhaustion from running our business and worrying about the business night and day. She took the load off my shoulders at just the right time and continues to successfully run our company.

To my editor, Mindy Reed, who took my huge mess of digital text, cut about a third out, and helped put it into some recognizable form that others could read, and make sense of what I was trying to say. She had the patience and perseverance I needed to get started.

Special thanks go to Larry Bradley who lives in the same subdivision. It is amazing what happens in life when you just stop to talk to someone else and listen. Larry wrote the book *Neither Liberal Nor Conservative Be* and is a huge proponent of Ranked Choice Voting. Larry took the time to read an early version of my book and provided much needed comments throughout the process. He has mentored me on several relevant issues in getting my book to the finish line.

Other people who read early versions were: Tracy and Debbie Hall, Gary Inselman, Stefan Magnusson, Sheryl Max, Ann and Howard Pate, Ellis Smith, Susie Schaeberle, Steve Welch, Andrea Worley, Mandy Zweimiller, and my lovely wife Eleonore. Thanks to all, but especially Ann, Ellis, Eleonore, Howard, Larry, Sheryl, and Susie—their especially keen eyes and skills saw things no one else did.

To Andrew Roberts, the British historian, whom I reached out to after he appeared in an article in 2020 for the *Wall Street Journal* about English-speaking people coming together for a brighter future. The couple of times I sent emails to him with questions, he graciously responded and tried to help the best he could. It gave me encouragement early on that I was working on a worthwhile cause.

To Australian author Graham Paterson who wrote *The Australian Constitution as it is Actually Written* and one of the first books I read in doing my research for this book. Graham and I also traded several emails giving me early encouragement of my endeavors.

About the Author

Jim, and his wife of 46 years, are residents of Dallas, Texas.

Jim has a BS in Business Administration from Kansas State University and an MBA from Drury College. He is also a veteran of the US Army. In Jim's career he has launched several products in the banking and utility industries. Jim started his current company in 1998 and later brought his daughter into the business. She currently runs the day-to-day operations.

Ameristralia is Jim's first book.

Contact Jim at https://ameristralia.org